Language Acquisition

A Lingui tic Int

Helen Goodluck

BLACKWELL
Oxford UK & Cambridge USA

Helen Goodluck is hereby identified as author of this work in accordance with section 77 of the Copyright, Designs and Patents Act 1988.

First published 1991
Reprinted with corrections 1992
Reprinted 1993, 1995, 1996 (twice), 1998, 2001
Transferred to digital print 2003

Blackwell Publishers Ltd
108 Cowley Road, Oxford OX4 1JF, UK

Blackwell Publishers Inc.
350 Main Street, Malden, Massachusetts 02148, USA

British Library Cataloguing in Publication Data
A CIP catalogue record for this book is available from the British Library.

Library of Congress Cataloging-in-Publication Data
Goodluck, Helen
Language acquisition: a linguistic introduction/Helen Goodluck
p.   cm.
Includes bibliographical reference and index.
ISBN 0–631–17386–2 (pbk)
1. Language acquisition   2. Generative grammar.   I. Title.
PII8.G59   1991   90–24628
401'.93—dc20   CIP

Typeset in 10 on 13 pt Sabon
By Mathematical Composition Setters Ltd, Salisbury, Wilts

Printed and bound in Great Britain by
Marston Lindsay Ross International Ltd,
Oxfordshire

Contents

Contents

Preface and Acknowledgements

This book is intended as a text in language acquisition for use in linguistics departments and courses in cognitive science. I have used various versions of the manuscript over the past few years as the basic text in an undergraduate introduction to language acquisition, and as background reading in graduate-level courses. The book is subtitled 'a linguistic introduction' because it focuses on the acquisition of aspects of linguistic knowledge that are of central interest to theoretical linguists: phonology, morphology, syntax and semantics. The prerequisites for the undergraduate course in which I use this book are a one-term course in syntax and a one-term course in phonology. A background of this kind will certainly make the book easier for the reader and will make him or her more capable of reading critically. However, I have tried to include enough basic detail to make the book usable for those without that background. Undergraduate students from psychology and computer science have sometimes taken the course for which I use the book as a text without the prerequisites and with great success. Introductory and semi-introductory texts that may be useful to the reader without a background are, for syntax, Cook (1988), Radford (1988a), Van Riemsdijk and Williams (1986) and Sells (1985); for phonology, Halle and Clements (1983) and Goldsmith (1990); and for morphology, Jensen (1990). Kempson (1977) and Fodor (1977) are clearly written elementary semantics texts. They do not deal with recent developments in semantic theory, but the background they provide covers most of the semantics-related topics in this text.

Language acquisition, broadly defined, covers far more than the topics in this book. Little or no attention is paid here to the role of language in the child's development of other skills: social skills, reasoning skills, mathematical skills, etc. None the less, the book may be useful to specialists in such fields who want to get a sense of what the child has achieved at the level of core areas of linguistic knowledge at a given point. That said, it has to be added that it is scarcely possible to write a comprehensive sketch of the childhood development of knowledge in core areas of language structure. In the following chapters the reader is introduced to the 'logical problem of language acquisition', the 'projection problem', the 'no negative evidence problem', etc. To these we might add the 'yawning gap' problem: namely, that there is in general a large disparity between the level of detail provided by linguistic theory in the description of adult languages and that provided in language acquisition studies of the development of that adult knowledge. So it is easy in teaching a class or writing a text on language acquisition to find oneself stopped short when it comes to saying how the facts of this or that linguistic analysis relate to children's linguistic behaviour; the detailed, theoretically well-informed studies of language development very often are just not there. There is no way around this problem (apart from giving up) other than to work harder at using the insights of linguistic theory to model and study the development of language. Many recent studies have done just this with considerable success, and it is such studies that I have placed some special emphasis on in the text.

I have been writing this book at an average speed of one chapter per year for about as many years as there are chapters: so some chapters will seem more in tune with this or that (once or still) hot topic in the particular area(s) dealt with in the chapter than others. Chapters 2 and 3 are of about 1984–5 vintage, with some revision in both; chapter 7 was written in 1987; chapter 5 was written in 1990; and the remainder were written – and often substantially rewritten – on and off between 1983 and 1990. It is easy to see new and potentially interesting directions in each area; for example, the last couple of years have seen quite a spate of new discussion, pertinent to the topics in chapter 7, of the interaction of pragmatic and discourse knowledge with early stages of syntactic processing. However, my impression is that there are no new results so basic that they do away with or solve the problems and questions discussed in that chapter or, indeed, any other.

I have been helped by comments from students in classes in which I used the manuscript text, as well as comments from colleagues who read longer and shorter stretches of the manuscript at various stages – Patrick Griffiths, Paul Hirschbühler, Ann Laubstein, Geoff Leech, Doug Pulleyblank and Peter Schreiber – and those of a reviewer from Basil Blackwell. Janet Fodor, Tom Roeper and Larry Solan provided a great deal of help by way of encouragement and realism. And numerous others provided stimulation and information. I am grateful to Philip Carpenter and his co-workers at Basil Blackwell for their help, including their kind but persistent reminders about deadlines.

H. G.

1 Introduction: Linguistics and Language Acquisition

Linguistics is concerned with discovering and defining the form and structure of human languages. All normal human children learn the language (or languages) that they hear around them. The study of language acquisition is the study of how and when children get a command of the thing linguistics sets out to define.

1.1 Knowledge of Language: Competence and Performance

An adult's knowledge of the rules of his native language is largely unconscious knowledge. A speaker of English who has never taken a linguistics course will have no trouble saying that both (1a) and (1b) are grammatical and mean the same thing, and that (2b) is not a grammatical paraphrase of (2a):

(1a)   Tony threw out the chair
(1b)   Tony threw the chair out
(2a)   Tony walked out the door
(2b)   *Tony walked the door out[1]

A speaker of English can make this judgement even if he has never thought about these types of sentences before; but without formal instruction it is very unlikely that the same speaker will be able to give an accurate account of why it is he finds (2b) ungrammatical.[2]

A native speaker's unconscious, implicit knowledge of rules that underlie his judgements of grammaticality and meaning is called the speaker's *competence*. A speaker's competence is distinguished from a speaker's *performance*, a term used to refer to actual events of language production and comprehension. The judgements that define a speaker's competence result from the speaker's introspection about whether a phrase or sentence is grammatical in the language, what the sentence or phrase means, etc. A speaker's performance is a matter of how the speaker uses language in non-reflective speech and understanding. The study of linguistic performance involves the study of the mechanisms for speech production and comprehension; these mechanisms are in part independent of the speaker's knowledge of rules of grammar (the speaker's linguistic competence). The distinction between grammatical competence and performance is essentially the distinction drawn by Chomsky (1965, p. 4, and elsewhere). The need for the distinction is clearly illustrated by the fact that we sometimes make performance errors. Sentence (3) is an example of an actual speech error. The speaker intended to say 'You can't figure out what that is,' but has misplaced 'out', presumably through a slip-up involving the rule that allows (1b) as an alternate form of (1a):

(3)   *You can't figure what that out is (Garrett 1980, p. 188)

Yet the speaker who made this error would certainly judge (3) as ungrammatical. (The error in (3) violates a rule that prevents a word such as 'out' moving to a position *inside* an object phrase – the phrase 'what that is' in the example.)

1.2   Types of Linguistic Knowledge

A speaker's linguistic competence covers several distinct areas of grammatical knowledge. Rules of *syntax* determine the organization of words into phrases and sentences and will account for phenomena such as the different grouping of words in (1a) and (2a) and the alternation between (1a) and (1b). Rules of *semantics* express the range of permissible meanings for words, phrases and sentences. Rules of *morphology* (word formation) will account for the formation of new words by combining words together – as in 'rat-catcher' – and by adding and combining sub-units of words (morphemes). For example, the '-er' ending, as in 'catcher', forms nouns that express agenthood from existing verbs. Morphological rules also express 'agreement' between elements in the sentence: an '-s' ending on the verb corresponds to the difference between singular and plural subjects: 'the boy dances; the boys dance.' Rules of *phonology* express regularities about the pronunciation of words and phrases.

1.3   The Projection Problem

A child is exposed to spoken speech. On the basis of the phrases and sentences the child hears she somehow abstracts unconscious knowledge of the grammar of her first language. Children do not receive overt instruction in the rules of their language. The task of getting from a necessarily limited range of input (speech the child hears) to implicit knowledge of the complete adult grammar has been called the *projection problem* (Peters 1972) or the *logical problem of language acquisition* (Hornstein and Lightfoot 1981; Baker and McCarthy 1981).

1.4   Universal Grammar

Among linguists and many psychologists it is more or less the received opinion that a solution to the projection problem must involve a substantial innate component of linguistic knowledge. Linguists believe that the gap between the evidence available to the child (the speech she hears) and the linguistic system the child ultimately constructs (her competence grammar) is so great that language acquisition can only be accounted for if we assume that children work with knowledge of principles of grammar. The linguistic system involves rules too abstract and complex to be learnt without the aid of innate knowledge about the nature of the system. The general idea is that the child is equipped with a set of blueprints that define and limit what a human language can be like. This innate knowledge goes under the name of *universal grammar*. Knowledge of universal grammar will help the child both by providing a set of candidate analyses for the speech she hears and by steering her away from any number of possible rule systems that are compatible with the input but simply not found in human languages.

   The role of universal grammar in language acquisition was influentially laid out and discussed by Chomsky (1965, ch. 1). There Chomsky sketched the distinction between *formal* universals and *substantive* universals. Substantive universals are the 'building blocks' of linguistic rules – the vocabulary in which linguistic rules must be stated. An example is the set of articulatory and/or acoustic specifications that characterize speech sounds (see chapter 2). Formal universals are restrictions on the types of operations linguistic rules perform and on the way in which linguistic rules interact. For example, syntactic rules generally pay attention to the hierarchical structure of phrases

rather than the simple linear and numerical order of words. Thus the alternation in (1a)/(1b) is one in which a word such as 'out' can occur either to
the left or the right of an object phrase – a rule that was violated in (3). This
alternation cannot be described by reference to simple linear order of words;
a rule such as '"Out" can occur directly after the verb ['threw' in the example]
or two words to the right' would work for (1a) and (1b), but fail when it came
to sentences such as 'He threw out the new chair' ('*He threw the new out
chair') and innumerable other cases.

Chomsky (1965) located his view of language development in the
philosophical tradition of rationalism associated with Descartes and other
philosophers of the seventeenth century. Chomsky's view of the nature of universal grammar and its role in language learning stands in opposition to views
of learning that rely on only very general mechanisms for learning, with the
presumption of little or no innate knowledge of particulars of linguistic
systems. In particular, it is in opposition to empiricist views of acquisition,
associated with Hume and with present-day philosophers such as W. O.
Quine. It is also in opposition, to a greater or lesser degree, to the ideas of
twentieth-century psychologists such as B. F. Skinner and Jean Piaget. These
philosophers and psychologists differ from Chomsky either by denying any
innate mechanisms other than very general ones of data-sorting and generalization or by crediting the child with more detailed innate mechanisms only
when these are common to language and other cognitive domains.

The basic concept of universal grammar and its role in language acquisition
as Chomsky sketched it in 1965 has not changed. But there has been a change
of emphasis in recent linguistic research towards the exact characterization of
variation in linguistic systems. An important part of the theory of formal universals is the specification of distinctions that define a quite small number of
language types and subtypes. Chomsky's 1981 book *Lectures on Government
and Binding* elaborates the notion of universal grammar as specifying *parameters* along which languages may vary. In some areas of grammar,
universal grammar will allow a limited range of options from which languages
can 'pick'. An elementary example is basic word order. Languages either have
relatively free word order or choose one of a small number of basic word
orders for the order of subject, verb and object. Linguistic theory must
characterize these different orders and the consequences the choice of a
particular order has for other rules in the language. (This example is explored
in more detail in chapter 4.) In this perspective, part of the child's task is to
work out which particular parameter settings are correct for her language.

1.5 Outline

The next four chapters deal with the acquisition of phonology, morphology, syntax and semantics. The idea that children's grammatical development is guided by innate knowledge of principles of universal grammar is assumed to be correct, but is not critical to the points made in those chapters. Linguistic analyses are sketched as a framework for evaluating what children know (and do not know) about the grammar of the language they are learning. Each chapter is more or less independent and they need not be read in their order of appearance. The sixth chapter takes up more general questions about the nature of innate knowledge and learning mechanisms. The last chapter deals with development in performance mechanisms.

Notes

1   The convention in linguistics is to use an asterisk (*) to mark ungrammatical sentences.
2   The rule is based on sentence structure. In (1a) the word 'out' and the words 'the chair' do not form a phrase (structural unit) and their order can be permuted (1b); in (2a) 'out the door' is a phrase and the order of words cannot be permuted within that phrase (2b is ungrammatical).

Further Reading

Read Chomsky (1965, ch. 1) for discussion of the distinction between competence and performance and the philosophical background to Chomsky's ideas on innateness. Chomsky (1986a) is a more recent exposition of those ideas and recent developments in grammatical theory. Bracken (1983, especially ch. 1) provides some interesting and very readable commentary on the history of ideas pertinent to innateness and language learning. Williams (1987) gives a clear summary of the implications for language learning of the shift in emphasis towards language variation and parameters in universal grammar. (Williams's paper is also suggested reading for chapter 6.)

2 Phonological Acquisition

Phonology concerns the regularities and rules governing pronunciation of words, phrases and sentences. This chapter concerns the development of phonological knowledge. Evidence from very early perception of sound units and spontaneous babbling of speech sounds provides support for the view that early perception and production must be characterized in terms of distinctions that have a prominent place in adult phonological systems. Later phonological development is not well understood, but none the less reveals on occasion striking abilities to abstract rules from the data, within the bounds of conformity to the general dictates of phonological theory.

2.1 Speech Sounds

Words can be analysed as a sequence of perceptually discrete units – for example the word 'cat' can be analysed as a sequence of three distinct segments. This section describes some of the major properties of sound segments, properties essential to understanding how segments function in phonology. The description is based on sound segments found in English; language variation is taken up later.

2.1.1 How Sounds are Made

The vast majority of speech sounds, and all English sounds, involve pushing air out from the lungs and through the mouth (or nose and mouth). The quality of the sound will depend on the shape of the resonance chambers (the mouth, pharynx and nose; see figure 2.1) and on whether or not the airstream is obstructed.

The most basic distinction is between vocalic and consonantal sounds. In the articulation of vowels, the airstream is interfered with only at the glottis (see figure 2.1); two bands of ligament and elastic tissue, called the vocal cords, obstruct the larynx and the airstream must force its way between them when a vowel sound is articulated, causing them to vibrate. But there is no

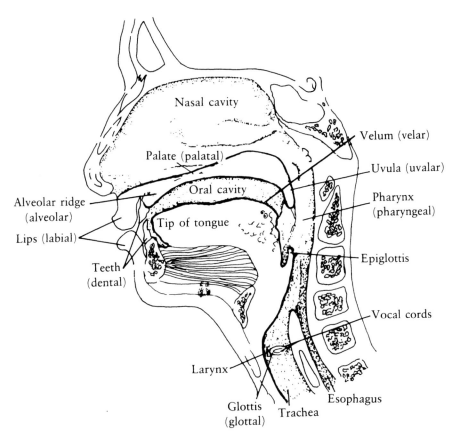

Figure 2.1 The human vocal tract
Language Files, second edition, Ohio State University

further obstruction as air passes out through the mouth. By contrast, for most consonants, there may or may not be obstruction at the glottis, but there will be some obstruction of the air passage through the mouth or pharynx.

Vowel sounds The quality of an individual vowel sound depends on the position of the body of the tongue – whether it is projected towards the front of the mouth or bunched towards the back, and whether it is held relatively high or relatively low. English has a series of front vowels and a series of back vowels. Table 2.1 lists the main English vowels and gives examples of English words in which they occur. (The phonetic symbols in table 2.1 and below are those of the International Phonetic Alphabet; they provide a 'one sound, one symbol' system that eliminates the inconsistencies of English spelling, where in many cases the same letter is used for different sounds and different letters

Table 2.1 English vowels

Tongue height	Tongue projection		
	Front	*Central*	*Back*
High	[i] beet		[u] boot
	[ɪ] bɪt		[ʊ] foot
Mid	[e] bate	[ə] banana	[o] boat
	[ɛ] bet		[ɔ] bought
		[ʌ] but	
Low	[æ] bat		[ɑ] bar

ᵃ The examples given are based on standard southern British pronunciation. Details and variants of pronunciation in different varieties of English should not affect the points that follow.
ᵇ The vowels [e], [o] are in fact diphthongs: combinations of a vowel with a glide sound (see the following section for a brief description of glides); so too are [i] and [u] though the glide is brief.
ᶜ The symbol [a] represents a more central version of [ɑ] and occurs as the first element in the diphthong in, for example, the word 'pie'. It is often used to represent [ɑ].

are used for the same sound.) The reader can check that the tongue height positions, etc. are as they are given in table 2.1 by saying these words and comparing the position of her tongue for the different sounds. The mid-vowel [ə] (the first and third vowel in the word 'banana') is used in the normal pronunciation of many vowels when they do not bear stress. All the back vowels in English (except [ɑ]) are pronounced with lip-rounding, and the front vowels without lip-rounding. This type of asymmetry is normal in languages, although front round vowels are not uncommon.

Consonants The quality of a consonant sound will depend on the type of obstruction and the place at which the obstruction takes place. *Stop* sounds involve very brief complete blockage of air; *fricative* sounds involve a loose occlusion rather than an absolute blockage. In English, stops are formed by closing the two lips together ([p], [b]) or by touching the tongue to the roof of the mouth at the alveolar ridge ([t], [d]) or the velum ([k], [g]). In English, fricatives are formed by loose contact between the upper teeth and lower lip ([f], [v]), between the tongue and upper teeth (the initial sounds in 'thin' and 'then', [θ] and [ð]), between the tongue and alveolar ridge ([s], [z]), and between the tongue and a position slightly to the back of the alveolar ridge (palato-alveolar fricatives, such as the first sound in 'sure' [ʃ] and the medial sound in 'measure' [ʒ]).

All of the above examples of stops and fricatives come in pairs – [t]/[d], [s]/[z], etc. The difference between the sounds in each pair is not a matter of place of obstruction in the vocal tract or degree of obstruction, but of whether or not the passage of air is additionally interfered with at the glottis. If the vocal cords are close enough together to be set in motion, as they are in the articulation of vowels, then as the air moves through the narrow gap between the cords, they will vibrate and the sound will be *voiced*. If the vocal cords are spread apart, allowing air to pass without obstruction at the glottis, the sound will be *voiceless*. In the pairs of stops and fricatives given above, the first member is voiceless and the second voiced; thus [t] is a voiceless alveolar stop and [d] is its voiced equivalent.

In *nasal* consonants there is free passage of air through the nose. For all the sounds described above, the soft part of the back region of the roof of the mouth (the velum) is raised up, so that the entrance to the nasal cavity is blocked and air cannot escape through the nose. If the velum is lowered, then air can pass through the nose and the result is a nasal sound. Each of the stops in English has a nasal variant: [n], the first segment of 'night', is the result of a stop articulation at the alveolar ridge plus free passage of air through the nose; [m], the initial sound in 'might', and [ŋ], the last segment in 'tang' (written 'ng'), are nasals resulting from labial and velar stop articulations, respectively. These nasals are all voiced, as is usually (though not invariably) the case in languages of the world.

Other types of consonantal sounds include *affricates*, where there is complete closure followed by a gradual, fricative release. English has the palato-alveolar affricates exemplified by the first sounds in 'church' ([tʃ], written 'ch') and 'judge' ([dʒ]). There are also *liquid* sounds such as English [l] and [r], formed with semi-free passage of air and somewhat similar acoustically to vowels. *Glide* sounds are also more similar to vowels than other consonants; like vowels they are made without obstruction in the vocal tract. The glides [j] and [w] such as the initial sounds in English 'you' and 'witch' are formed by raising the tongue towards the front and back of the mouth respectively and moving rapidly to or from the position of the following or preceding vowel: hence the term *glide*. The back glide [w] is lip-rounded.

Table 2.2 groups the English consonantal sounds described above by place of articulation and manner of obstruction.

2.1.2 Phonetic Features

A sound segment can be represented as a cluster of properties – a set of plus

Table 2.2 English consonants: place and manner of articulation[a,b]

Manner	Labial	Labio-dental	Interdental	Alveolar	Palato-Alveolar	Palatal	Velar
Stop	p, b			t, d			k, g
Fricative		f, v	θ, ð	s, z	ʃ, ʒ		
Nasal							
Stop	m			n			ŋ
Affricate					tʃ, ʤ		
				l			
Liquid				r			
Glide	w					j	

[a] The voiceless member of voiceless–voiced pairs is listed first in the table.
[b] Equivalent symbols commonly used in North American transcription are: š = ʃ; ž = ʒ; č = ʧ; ǰ = ʤ; y = j.

or minus specifications for *features* that refer to the articulatory or acoustic quality of the sound segment, or its 'function' in a syllable.

The basic distinction between consonant and vowel sounds is represented in terms of the feature [± consonantal]. If we add a second feature [± syllabic], reflecting roughly how central in a syllable an element is, we can make a three-way distinction between vowels, consonants, and glides, as shown in (1).

(1)   *vowels*   *consonants*   *glides*

$$\begin{bmatrix} -\text{consonantal} \\ +\text{syllabic} \end{bmatrix} \begin{bmatrix} +\text{consonantal} \\ -\text{syllabic} \end{bmatrix} \begin{bmatrix} -\text{consonantal} \\ -\text{syllabic} \end{bmatrix}$$

Individual segments will be specified for values of additional features, sufficient to characterize each sound uniquely. The full set of features needed to pick out each separate sound in the repertoire of English sounds need not be listed here (and the exact membership of the set is a matter of debate). The features in (2) will be sufficient with respect to the discussion in the following sections:

(2)   *for vowel sounds*
        [±high]   high vowels are [+high]; mid- and low vowels are
                         [−high];

| [±low] | low vowels are [+low]; mid- and high vowels are [−low]; |
| [±back] | back and central vowels are [+back]; front vowels are [−back]. |

for consonantal sounds

[±continuant]	stops are [−continuant]; fricatives are [+continuant];
[±anterior]	labial and alveolar sounds (pronounced in the front of the mouth) are [+anterior]; palato-alveolar, palatal and velar sounds are [−anterior];
[±coronal]	alveolar and palatal sounds are [+coronal] (produced with obstruction by the blade/tip of the tongue) and labial and velar sounds are [−coronal];
[±voice]	[+voice] sounds are produced with vibration of the vocal cords, as described above;
[±nasal]	[+nasal] sounds are produced with passage of air through the nasal cavity, as described above.

In terms of these features, the word 'cat' can be represented as a sequence of segments, each segment characterized by a set of feature specifications that distinguishes that sound from other sounds used in English:

(3)   k   æ   t

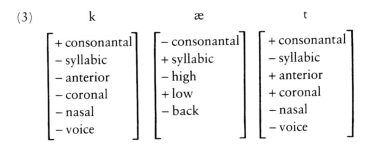

$$
\begin{bmatrix}
+\text{consonantal} \\
-\text{syllabic} \\
-\text{anterior} \\
-\text{coronal} \\
-\text{nasal} \\
-\text{voice}
\end{bmatrix}
\begin{bmatrix}
-\text{consonantal} \\
+\text{syllabic} \\
-\text{high} \\
+\text{low} \\
-\text{back}
\end{bmatrix}
\begin{bmatrix}
+\text{consonantal} \\
-\text{syllabic} \\
+\text{anterior} \\
+\text{coronal} \\
-\text{nasal} \\
-\text{voice}
\end{bmatrix}
$$

2.2 Phonetics, Phonology and Language Variation

Phonetics is concerned with the characterization of speech sounds − how they are produced and perceived and what their acoustic properties are; phonology is concerned with how sounds are used to distinguish meaning and with the rules governing the distribution of sounds and the properties of segments and strings of segments in languages.

Those phonetic properties of words that cannot be predicted by rule must be entered in the lexicon (dictionary) of a language; a representation such as that given above for the word 'cat' must be part of the dictionary entry of that word. Phonetic features that are specified in the dictionary entries for a particular language include only the *distinctive features* of the language – features that do service to distinguish between different words or morphemes. For example, *voice* is one of the distinctive features in English; if we change the feature specification for voicing in the last segment in 'cat', a different sound segment results, and the difference in sound corresponds to a difference in meaning ('cad' does not mean the same thing as 'cat'):

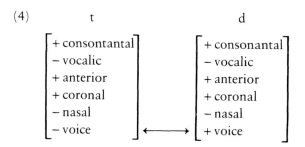

(4)   t   d

$$\begin{bmatrix} + \text{ consontantal} \\ - \text{ vocalic} \\ + \text{ anterior} \\ + \text{ coronal} \\ - \text{ nasal} \\ - \text{ voice} \end{bmatrix} \longleftrightarrow \begin{bmatrix} + \text{ consonantal} \\ - \text{ vocalic} \\ + \text{ anterior} \\ + \text{ coronal} \\ - \text{ nasal} \\ + \text{ voice} \end{bmatrix}$$

Other, predictable aspects of pronunciation will not be included in the dictionary representation, but are provided for by phonological rule. Thus there is a difference in the pronunciation of voiceless stops in English in initial position and after a consonant. Initial stops in English are *aspirated* – pronounced with a puff of air on the release of the stop; stops occurring in non-initial position (after the sound [s]) are unaspirated. This rule-governed difference in pronunciation of, for example, [k] in 'cat' versus [k] in 'scatter' or 'skittle' can be accounted for by a phonological rule that adds the feature [+ aspirate] in the appropriate environment. The occurrence of aspiration is predictable and non-distinctive in English: if a word such as 'cat' is pronounced without aspiration on the initial [k], then we still perceive the speaker's utterance as an utterance of the word 'cat', although with deviant articulation.

In sum, the sound segments that compose words as they are uttered in a language can be represented in terms of phonetic features, some of which will be part of the word's dictionary entry and others of which will be specified by phonological rule.

Languages vary with respect to the use to which they put phonetic features. Some features and feature combinations may not be used in a language. Thus English has no velar fricatives, although velar fricatives are not uncommon in languages. (The voiceless velar fricative does occur in dialects of English, as in Scots pronunciation of the last segment in 'loch'.) Features may also be distinctive in one language and non-distinctive in another. The feature [±aspirate] is an example; although in English the occurrence of aspiration is non-distinctive and predictable by rule, in other languages aspiration is used distinctively and the difference between, for example, [k] and [kʰ] (aspirate [k]) can signal a difference in the meaning of words (Thai and Sesotho, a language spoken in southern Africa, are examples of languages that use aspiration distinctively.) Finally, languages may differ with respect to the exact articulatory and acoustic values that are assigned to plus and minus values of phonetic features, a fact that is related in part to choice of which features are distinctive. In the next section we will show examples of this type of variation and infants' handling of the pertinent contrasts.

2.3 Categorical Perception in Adults and Infants

Phonetic feature specifications as we have considered them thus far are binary – plus or minus. There is evidence that the human speech-perception device imposes precisely such a type of yes/no distinction, dividing up speech sounds into categories that reflect a qualitatively arbitrary distinction as to where the boundary between one type of sound and another is drawn.

The acoustic cues for speech sounds are complex and may vary according to the position of the sound in the syllable and the nature of the sounds adjacent to it. Here we will consider only the perception of the voiceless–voiced distinction in syllable-initial position; this contrast offers some of the clearest examples of the phenomenon of categorical speech perception.

Perception of voicing is dependent on the timing relation between the release of the stop closure and the onset of voicing.[1] Experiments using synthetic speech stimuli have shown that for English speakers a stop sound in a stop-plus-vowel sequence will be perceived as voiced if voicing begins within about 30 milliseconds of the release of the stop closure; if the voicing begins more than 30 milliseconds after the release of the stop closure, the stop will be perceived as voiceless (see Lisker and Abrahamson 1970). The change in perception is quite abrupt. A difference of 10 milliseconds of voice onset time (VOT) in the critical 30 millisecond VOT region will produce a dramatic change in the perception of sounds as voiced or voiceless; a change of similar magnitude on either side of the critical region will not produce such a change in voicing perception. Perception of voicing is thus *categorical*: we divide speech events up into discrete categories, such as voiced and voiceless, based on a sharply defined point along the relevant acoustic parameter.

Eimas et al. (1971) performed a clever experiment, demonstrating that infants of one to four months are sensitive to the boundary that governs adult perception of voicing in English. Infants can be motivated to suck on a pacifier by an auditory feedback; when the infant sucks with sufficient force, he hears a sound. Typically, when an infant catches on to the relation between sucking and feedback, there is an initial period in which sucking rate increases. Following this, rate of sucking declines, presumably because the child becomes habituated. In Eimas et al.'s study, the pattern of increased sucking rate followed by decline was established for each subject with one stimulus type. When the sucking rate for the first stimulus type had declined by 20 per cent or more for two minutes compared with the minute preceding, a second stimulus was then presented for four minutes. Increase in the sucking rate at the point of changeover can be interpreted as evidence that the infants perceived the difference in the stimuli.

The stimuli in Eimas et al.'s study were synthetically produced syllables consisting of a labial stop plus a low back vowel. Six different stimuli were produced by varying the VOT. Voicing began 20 milliseconds before the stop release, at the stop release, and 20, 40, 60 and 80 milliseconds after the stop release. For English-speaking adults, stimuli with a VOT of up to and including 20 milliseconds after the release will be perceived as [b]; stimuli with a VOT of 40 milliseconds or greater will be perceived as [p]. There were two experimental groups of infants; the first group received stimuli with a VOT of 20 milliseconds after the stop release, followed by stimuli with a VOT of 40 milliseconds after the stop release. The two sets of stimuli for this group thus straddled the boundary for adult perception of [p] versus [b]. The second experimental group received two sets of stimuli that did not straddle the adult boundary – either stimuli with a VOT of 20 milliseconds preceding the release and stimuli with simultaneous voicing and release (both [b] to the adult ear) or stimuli with VOTs of 60 and 80 milliseconds after the release (both [p] to adults). A third, control, subject group heard the same stimulus throughout (different children hearing each of the six different stimuli used for the experimental groups).

Figure 2.2 displays the mean change in response rate for the two-minute intervals before and after the change in stimuli (or the point at which the change would have occurred, for the control group). The figure plainly shows that a change in stimuli that crossed the adult boundary for [b] vs. [p] produced a marked increase in sucking rate; a change that did not cross the adult boundary produced no such increase (the small rise for one-month-olds was non-significant). The control group showed no increase, but a continued decline in sucking rate, as would be expected for the continued presentation of the same stimulus.

Eimas et al.'s study involved infants whose exposure to their native

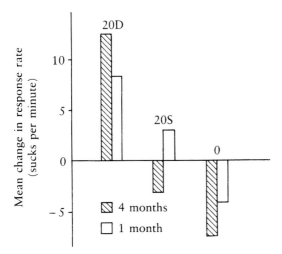

Figure 2.2   Mean change in response rate as a function of experimental treatments
20D = subjects who received stimuli differing by 20 msecs VOT across [p]–[b] boundary;
20S = subjects who received stimuli differing by 20 msecs where the difference did not cross the
[p]–[b] boundary; 0 = control subjects who received the same stimulus throughout
Adapted from Eimas et al. 1971, figure 3

language was minimal and who had not yet begun to produce speech-like
sounds. Thus, soon after birth we discriminate between sounds in a way that
reflects the type of distinction employed in adult phonological systems and
encoded in linguistic representations by means of binary (plus/minus)
phonetic features.

Many studies have followed on Eimas et al.'s initial findings, using a variety
of experimental techniques (see Eimas 1985 for an overview). Categorical discrimination of sounds has been shown in animals (chinchillas) as well as
human infants (Kuhl and Miller 1975), suggesting that the mapping between
linguistic distinctions and phonetic values may draw on physiological properties of the auditory system that are not unique to humans. Sensitivity to features other than voicing has been investigated, with varying degrees of success
(see Jusczyk 1981). Others have tackled the difficult and important question
of the relation between the infant's ability to discriminate and language
variation in use of particular features and their phonetic values.

Not all languages draw the boundary for perception of voicing at the same
point that English does: some languages (for example, Thai) have a boundary
at a point preceding the stop release. Thus the same stimulus will be perceived
categorized as voiced or unvoiced by adult speakers, depending on the
language they have learned (see figure 2.3). Such facts clearly illustrate the
abstract nature of our mappings between phonetic feature values and the

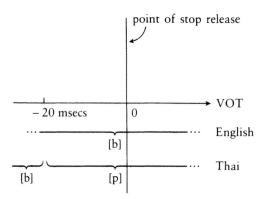

Figure 2.3

speech stimulus. A sound that is categorized as voiced in English will be categorized as voiceless in Thai, if the VOT is sufficiently close to the stop release. Moreover, the switch-point that signals the voiced–voiceless contrast in English signals a different switch-point in Thai. Thai is a language that uses aspiration distinctively, producing three-way contrasts among stop sounds – for example, [b], [p] and [pʰ]. Late VOT coincides with aspiration, and is a sufficient cue for perception of sounds as aspirated by speakers of Thai. At roughly the same VOT that signals the switch from voiced to voiceless sounds for English speakers, the switch from voiceless to voiceless aspirate will be made by Thai speakers (see figure 2.4). Our phonological abilities thus include not merely the capacity to use different acoustic values as the locus for the switch from plus to minus values of the same feature, but also the capacity to use the same acoustic value as the switch-point for different features (a VOT of 30 milliseconds following the stop release signals the switch from plus to minus voice for English and from minus to plus aspiration for voiceless sounds in Thai).

It is generally agreed that there are typical switch-points for plus and minus feature values. One is at around the English voicing boundary of 30 milliseconds following the stop; another is somewhere in the region 20–50 milliseconds preceding the stop release (the precise value being a matter of dispute: see Lisker and Abrahamson 1970; Eimas 1975). Other VOTs may be the locus of feature switches, but are arguably atypical. Spanish uses such an atypical value for the voiced–voiceless distinction, in the region between 20 milliseconds before and 20 milliseconds after the stop release.

Plainly, infants who display categorical perception cannot be credited with knowledge of the labels that adult speakers in different languages assign to different phonetic values. An appealing developmental hypothesis is that the

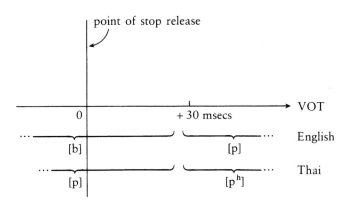

point of stop release

0   + 30 msecs   → VOT

[b]   [p]   English

[p]   [pʰ]   Thai

Figure 2.4

young infant is equipped with the perceptual apparatus to categorize according to a range of potential switch-points for feature values and learns the labels associated with particular points as he pieces together the phonological system of his language. When a particular potential switch-point for a feature is not used in a language, that point will no longer be a locus for categorical discrimination of sounds, and stimuli on either side of the boundary will come to be perceived as identical.

A separate, but related, developmental hypothesis concerns the claim that some potential switch-points for feature values are typical and used in many languages, while others are less frequently used. Developmentally, we might expect infants to be initially sensitive to typical boundaries and only later develop categorical perception for features whose values straddle less frequently used boundaries, such as the Spanish voicing boundary.

Thus there are two plausible developmental hypotheses: (1) children will show categorical perception for a range of distinctions, some of which will fade as the child acquires knowledge of language-particular facts; and (2) the earliest distinctions will involve typical switch-points, the perception of the less usual boundaries developing later. In general, early perceptual abilities will be refined and altered by experience with a particular language, and the appropriate phonological labels added into the perceptual categories the child retains and/or develops.

There is some support for this general picture. Lasky et al. (1975) found that four- to six-month-old infants in a Spanish-speaking environment discriminated between stimuli that had VOTs of 60 milliseconds and 20 milliseconds before the release of the stop closure and between stimuli with VOTs of 20 milliseconds and 60 milliseconds after the release. The same infants did *not* discriminate between stimuli at 20 milliseconds preceding the release and

20 milliseconds following the release. These infants picked up on the two differences that crossed boundaries used to demarcate speech-sound categories in many languages, but they were not sensitive to a difference of equal magnitude that less typically contains a boundary, and which in fact crossed the boundary used for voicing in the language they were to acquire (Spanish). Some studies of speech production have produced results that also support the idea that some boundary points are more basic than others; Gandour et al. (1986) found that three- and five-year-old children learning Thai more cleanly distinguished between voiceless aspirate and voiceless unaspirate stops, with a VOT boundary of approximately + 30 milliseconds, than they did between voiceless unaspirate and voiced stops, for which there was considerable overlap in VOT values. This overlap was not found in Gandour et al.'s test for adults, who sharply distinguished between voiceless unaspirate and voiced stops, restricting voiceless unaspirates to a VOT range of approximately 0– + 20 milliseconds. Another perception study that supports the view that the child's early discrimination is relatively independent of experience is Streeter (1976), who found that infants in a Kikuyu language environment distinguished a boundary prior to the stop release for sounds for which voicing is not contrasted in Kikuyu.

But some results also argue that perception is very quickly tuned to the language-particular. Eilers et al. (1979) found that six- to eight-month-olds in a Spanish-speaking environment were sensitive to the Spanish boundary, whereas English-learning infants of the same age were not. Thus sensitivity to atypical boundaries may be triggered by language exposure before the child has any appreciable knowledge of the contrast, at the level of which features are distinctive in his language. The facts are not completely clear-cut at present, a number of experimental factors being confounded in the studies undertaken to date (see Jusczyk 1981 for discussion).

In sum, infant speech-perception studies constitute strong evidence for a particular kind of ability: the discrimination of speech segments according to phonetic values that are frequently employed in adult phonological systems. The development of language-particular perceptual boundaries and feature labels is not well understood.

2.4   Early Speech Sounds

Most children begin to produce recognizable words at some point in the second year (see chapter 4). Before that, children pass through a period in which speech-like sounds are produced, with no obvious link to words in the adult language. Playful production of isolated consonant and vowel-type sounds (typical of four- to six-month-olds) is replaced at around six months by reduplicative *babbling*. The child produces series of consonant–vowel (CV) syllables, in which the individual syllables in each babbled series are identical or very similar to one another. At around ten months, this type of babbling gives way to syllable sequences with more varied members (different consonants and/or vowels) and a wider range of syllable types – VC and CVC in addition to CV (see, for example, Stark 1980). The next stage is the production of recognizable words, which may be preceded for some children by a 'silent period' in which babbling ceases (see Vihman et al. 1985 for a recent study).

The properties of babbled and first word speech have been the subject of many studies. Locke (1983, ch. 1) gives an extensive survey. When we look at the types of speech sounds children produce in the babbling and first word stages, and compare these to the inventory of sounds in the language around the child, the general picture is as follows. Babbling may include sounds not used in the language to which the child is exposed (for example, a child exposed to English may babble the velar fricative [x], mentioned above). None the less, there are clear preferences for certain sounds in babbling; stops, nasals and [h] are frequent in babbling, no matter what language the child is exposed to (see Locke 1983, p. 10); fricatives and liquids are generally avoided. Of the stops, voiced stops are more frequent in babbling than voiceless stops. A common change between early and later babbling is a decrease in the use of back (velar) stops. First words tend to be composed of a narrow range of sounds, typically front voiceless stops, nasals and the vowel [ɑ]. (That is, the child's pronunciations tend to favour these sounds, although this may involve a distortion of the corresponding adult word.) As the child progresses with real-word speech, more sounds are added to his inventory, so that the range of sounds he produces more nearly matches that of the language he is learning. Use of speech sounds in babbling and early speech thus broadly fits an hour-glass pattern; sounds used in babbling (for example, velar stops) may drop out in early speech and then be reintroduced.

Jakobson (1968) focused on babbling and early speech in the context of the distribution of sounds in languages of the world. He proposed that there are regular relationships between the distribution of speech sounds cross-linguistically and the order in which different sounds are acquired. Front voiceless stops, nasals and the vowel [ɑ] are found in virtually all languages. Drawing on many observational studies of child language, Jakobson proposed that such extremely frequent sounds were the first to be acquired. Other sounds occur less frequently in languages of the world and the presence of these less frequent sounds can be used to predict the presence of more frequent sounds. So, for example, back (velar) stops are less frequent than front stops and the occurrence of back stops is a good predictor of the presence of front stops in the world's languages: a language may have front stops without back stops, but not vice versa. Similarly, fricatives as a class occur less frequently than stops (a language may have stops without having fricatives, but the reverse situation does not occur). These frequency facts mirror acquisition facts: front stops are mastered before back stops and stops are mastered before fricatives. Some sounds are rare in the sound inventory of languages; an example is the English vowel [æ], which is a sound that occurs with high frequency in English, but is rather rare in the world's languages. Jakobson observed that cross-linguistically rare sounds are generally acquired late.

It has become usual to refer to frequency facts for the distribution of sounds in terms of *markedness*. Markedness is a term used to refer to the extent to which a phenomenon is 'normal' in language systems. The most frequent sounds are referred to as maximally unmarked; sounds whose presence can be used to predict the presence of other sounds are marked, relative to the sounds of which they are predictors. Rare sounds can be referred to as the most marked sounds.

A general goal of linguistic theory is to try to find out whether frequency (markedness) observations can be accounted for in terms of principles of linguistic structure. Can Jakobson's markedness observations be recast in terms of a principled organization of sound systems? Is it the case that phonetic features are intrinsically related in such a way that some sounds logically have priority in languages of the world and also must be acquired before others in language development? At present, the evidence does not exist to support such a strong position. It is certainly possible to formalize frequency observations with respect to sound systems. If segments are characterized in terms of plus and minus specifications on features, markedness values for segments can be viewed as default, or normal, specifications for the values of a feature in combination with other feature values. So the default, unmarked specification for a vowel (a $\left[\begin{smallmatrix}-\text{consonantal}\\+\text{syllabic}\end{smallmatrix}\right]$ sound) would be $\left[\begin{smallmatrix}+\text{back}\\+\text{low}\end{smallmatrix}\right]$, the specification for the most common vowel, [ɑ]. Other specifications will have a 'cost', which may be expressed as an algorithm that translates particular combinations of features into numerical values (see Kean 1976/1980 for a system of that type). But there is nothing in the algorithm itself that mandates that the maximally unmarked vowel sound is $\left[\begin{smallmatrix}+\text{back}\\+\text{low}\end{smallmatrix}\right]$, and so forth. Markedness values established in such a way are essentially stipulative, encoding the distributional facts that happen to hold in human languages, child and adult.

Another question with respect to babbling and early speech is the influence of factors other than markedness values on the patterns observed. Two possible sources of influence other than markedness values are articulatory control and the speech sounds to which the child is actually exposed. Articulatory factors may well play a role. The predominance of voiced stops over voiceless stops in babbling is a counter-example to the claim that unmarked sounds predominate; voiceless stops are more frequent in languages of the world than their voiced counterparts, and emerge earlier than voiced stops in early, non-babbled, speech. The predominance of voiced stops in babbling may be a consequence of insufficient articulatory control for the production of voiceless sounds, to produce which the vocal cords must be held apart.

The influence of speech sounds the child hears is not clear, beyond the obvious fact that the child ultimately acquires those sounds to which he is exposed. An early hypothesis was that there was a shift during babbling towards the sounds of the language to which the child was exposed (Brown 1958). There now seems little to support this idea. Adults do not generally find it easier to identify the language background of older babblers than younger babblers (Locke 1983, pp. 13ff; but see also Vihman et al. 1985). Possibly the illusion of a shift towards sounds of the language the child is learning may be created by a shift towards use of unmarked sounds (as, for example, when velar stops come to be used less frequently in latter babbling), which are those most likely to be found in any language.

2.5 Feature Acquisition

Even if markedness values that express the preferences for some sounds in babbling and early speech have not to date been made to follow from intrinsic properties of the phonetic feature system, that does not mean that features are not useful and necessary in describing children's early production of sounds. A child may impose patterns on her babbling or early speech that are neatly characterized in terms of features. Gruber (1973) showed that in later babbling one child in an English-speaking environment preferred sequences in which syllables with alveolar consonants preceded sequences with labials or velars. Sequences such as that in (5)

(5) [də tə   mə   gə]

     alveolar   labial/velar

were preferred, and sequences such as that in (6)

(6) *[də mə   tə   gə]

were avoided. Alveolar sounds are produced with an obstruction by the tip or blade of the tongue at the alveolar ridge (the hard ridge directly behind the teeth); the feature [±coronal] distinguishes alveolars from labial and velar sounds, where the obstruction is more peripheral. Alveolars are [+coronal] and labials and velars are [−coronal]. The sequencing constraint imposed by the child Gruber studied can be described as a constraint that all [+coronal] sounds precede [−coronal] sounds. (Gruber expresses the generalization in terms of the feature [±grave], a feature motivated by the fact that labials and velars share some acoustic properties that distinguish them from alveolars; Jakobson et al. 1952.)

Sometimes a child broadens her repertoire of sounds in a way that fits exactly with the introduction of a new phonetic feature. For example, when a child begins to make use of the voiced/voiceless distinction in stops she may do so for all the stops she uses. (Note that although Eimas's study demonstrated that even infants can distinguish voiced from voiceless stops, it is some time before children can use this distinction in producing and understanding the language around them.) When a child begins to use voicing for stops, a three-way distinction [p, t, k] may become a six-way split [p–b, t–d, k–g], as we would expect if the feature [±voice] is suddenly introduced into the set of features she controls. Other children, however, introduce contrasts piecemeal – for example, voicing labial or alveolar but not velar stops. This type of case is not problematic for the notion that the child is learning to make use of feature contrasts (contrary to what is sometimes assumed; see, for example, discussion in Dale 1976). Adult languages also on occasion do not impose the full range of possible contrasts allowed by the features needed to characterize their inventory of sounds. For instance, in English we need the feature [±continuant] to distinguish stops from fricatives, but there is no velar fricative in English, so this feature is not fully utilized. Piecemeal addition of contrasts by children represents acquisition stages analogous to these adult systems. For adult systems, feature representations are amply motivated. Not only are features an important descriptive device in characterizing speech sounds, they also have a critical role in characterizing the systematic patterning of sounds both within and across languages – phonological systems. The next section deals with children's developing phonological system.

2.6 Child Phonologies

Phonological systems have traditionally been viewed as comprising rules for two types of phenomenon: segmental and suprasegmental. Segmental rules affect the presence of and precise phonetic feature values associated with individual consonant and vowel segments. Learning the segmental system of a language will involve working out which properties of the sound segments that make up words in the language are non-predictable and distinctive (used to distinguish words from one another) and which properties can be predicted by rule. Non-predictable properties will be entered in the lexical entry for the word; predictable properties will be spelled out by phonological rules that work on and change the basic lexical entry for the word. To take the example of aspiration given above, a child learning English must work out that the aspiration that he hears on the [k] in a word like [kæt] is predictable from the word-initial position of the [k], and so need not be part of the lexical entry for that word. Aspiration can be spelt out by phonological rule. A child learning Thai will have to come to the opposite conclusion. In Thai aspiration is not predictable, does distinguish between the meanings of words, and must be entered as a feature in the lexical entries for Thai words.

Suprasegmental rules concern properties of pronunciation that typically affect constituents larger than the segment, particularly stress, intonation and tone. More details of these phenomena are given below.

We will assume a model of grammar of the following form. Rules of phonology operate on a structural, syntactic representation of the sentence. The lexicon specifies unpredictable aspects of pronunciation (the fact that the

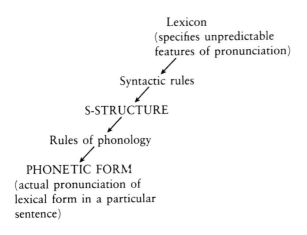

Lexicon
(specifies unpredictable
features of pronunciation)

Syntactic rules

S-STRUCTURE

Rules of phonology

PHONETIC FORM
(actual pronunciation of
lexical form in a particular
sentence)

Figure 2.5

word 'cat' comprises three segments, the first of which is a voiceless velar stop, etc.), and rules of syntax will provide a specification of the syntactic environment in which a word occurs, which may affect pronunciation in several ways. In terms of the model of grammar we will use in later chapters, rules of phonology apply to the S-structure of the sentence: this is approximately a representation in which the linear string of words in a sentence is organized in an abstract, hierarchical structure that represents some, but not all, of the logical and referential relationships between words and phrases in the sentence (see chapter 4). The output of phonological rules will be a representation called phonetic form (see figure 2.5).

2.6.1 Segmental Rules

Some rules of segmental phonology appear to be very quickly incorporated into a child's pronunciation: for example, aspiration of initial voiceless stops in English seems to be rapidly mastered. But children's pronunciations are far from error-free. Children may make frequent and systematic errors *vis-à-vis* the adult target words.

Many recurrent error types in child speech show a pattern corresponding to phonological rules in languages of the world. For example, children not uncommonly de-voice segments in final position, pronouncing 'bag' as 'bak' [bæk]; such a devoicing rule is found in many languages (for example, German), although it is not a rule of English segmental phonology. Or they may move the place of articulation forward for stops and other segments, pronouncing 'key' ([ki]) as 'tea' ([ti]), and so forth; again, processes of this kind are found in adult phonological rule systems. Children also frequently simplify consonant clusters, deleting consonants or introducing a vowel to break up the cluster. Table 2.3 gives a list of frequent types of child mispronunciations, with examples.

What is the status of children's mispronunciations? There are at least three separate possibilities. Child mispronunciations could reflect (1) incorrect lexical representations on the child's part, with a non-adult lexical entry for the word in question; (2) non-adult phonological rules operating to distort adult-like lexical representations; or (3) non-systematic errors of articulation.

It is not always clear which of these three possibilities is the correct way to look at a given child error, but it is evident that in many instances the child does have in his head something like the correct adult form, even when he does not pronounce the word correctly (consistent with (2) and (3)).

Table 2.3 Some typical child pronunciation errors in the second and third years

	Examples			
	Adult word	Child pronunciation	Age (yrs; mths)	Source
Substitution processes (replacement of a sound by another sound)				
Stopping (a fricative is replaced by a stop)	see	ti:	2; 9	Smith (1973)
Fronting (the place of articulation is fronted, with velar and palatal consonants being replaced by alveolars)	shoe goat	zu dut	2; 0 2; 0	Velten (1943) Velten (1943)
Gliding ([w] or [j] is sub-stituted for a liquid)	leg ready	jek wedi	2; 1 2; 1			
Assimilation processes (a sound becomes more similar to an adjacent sound)				
Voicing (consonants tend to be voiced pre-ceding a vowel and devoiced at the end of a syllable)	paper pig	be:bə bik	2; 3 1; 5	Smith (1973)	
Consonant harmony (Consonants tend to assimilate in words with the structure $C_1VC_2(X)$)	duck tickle tub	gʌk gigu bʌb	1; 7 2; 2 (no age given)		Smith (1973) Menn (1975)
Progressive vowel assimilation (an unstressed vowel will assimi-late to a preceding vowel)	bacon flower	bú:du fá:wa	2; 0 2; 0	Velten (1943) Velten (1943)

Table 2.3 (continued)

	Examples			
	Adult word	Child pronunciation	Age (yrs; mths)	Source
Syllable structure processes				
Cluster reduction	play	pe	1; 11	I
(a consonant	train	ten	1; 11	I
cluster is reduced	dress	dɛs	1; 11	I
to a single conso-				
nant)				
Final consonant	bib	bi	1; 5	I
deletion	more	mʌ	1; 5	I
(a CVC syllable is				
reduced to CV)				
Unstressed syllable	banana	nǽna	1; 9	I
deletion	potato	dédo	1; 11	I
Reduplication				
(in a multi-syllabic	TV	didi	1; 9	I
word, the initial	water	wawa	1; 9	I
CV syllable is				
repeated)				

I = example from Ingram's own files
´ = stress mark; : = length mark
Source: This taxonomy is an abbreviated version of that given in Ingram (1986).

Moreover, there is evidence that some mispronunciations are the result of non-adult phonological rules (consistent with (2)), rules that sometimes attest to considerable powers of generalization and abstraction at the phonological level.

One clear type of evidence of adult-like lexical forms is the fact that children can recognize their own mispronunciations as deviant (adult: 'Did you say "wellow"?'; child: 'No, I said "wellow"'). Another kind of argument for adult-like lexical entries is the fact that a systematic account of child articulations can be given if the adult forms are also the child's representations, at an underlying level. Some examples of plausible child rules operating on adult-like underlying forms will illustrate this point and also the child's rule-forming capacity.

In a detailed study of the phonological development of one child, N. Smith (1973) takes the position that the adult form is always the form in the child's mental dictionary, and mispronunciations are a matter of realization rules (Smith's term) that convert the adult form to the child's pronunciation. (These output rules can be regarded as non-adult phonological rules that must be eliminated as the child moves towards adult phonology.)

Smith proposed that between the ages of approximately two years two months and two years four months the child was using the rules in (7), among others (the rule numbers are taken from Smith):

(7) Rule 1: If a nasal is followed by a voiceless consonant, the nasal is deleted.
     Rule 2: If a nasal is followed by a voiced consonant, the voiced consonant is deleted.
     Rule 3: A coronal stop is velarized before /(ə)l/.[2]
     Rule 4: An unstressed vowel is raised (made higher) and backed before /l/.
     Rule 6: /l/ is deleted at the end of a word.
     Rule 13: /h/ is deleted.
     Rule 21: An alveolar consonant is deleted after another consonant.
     Rule 25: All voiceless segments are voiced.

These rules can be used to account for the child's pronunciation of words such as 'empty' and 'handle'. The path from the adult form to the child pronunciation as given by Smith is as shown in (8), where the adult pronunciation is taken as the starting-point and the rules are applied as shown to change the adult form into the child pronunciation:

(8a)
Adult form: 'handle'   /hændəl/
Child rules:
              Rule 2   /hænəl/
              Rule 3   /hæŋəl/
              Rule 4   /hæŋul/
              Rule 6   /hæŋu/
              Rule 13   [æŋu]   = child
                                              pronunciation

(8b)

Adult form: 'empty'   /ɛmpti:/

Child rules:

	Rule 1	/ɛpti:/	
	Rule 21	/ɛpi:/	
	Rule 25	[ɛbi:]	= child
			pronunciation

The child's rules Smith proposes are quite general, applying to all or almost all the relevant forms in the child's vocabulary. Two related points can be made concerning Smith's analysis. First, for the analysis to work the child must be credited with some knowledge of the correct adult forms since the child's pronunciations are dependent on features of the adult form that are not present in the child's pronunciation. For example, Rule 3 states that a coronal stop becomes velar before /l/; that is, in adult words without a following /l/, /n/ will not be pronounced as /n/. Yet the /l/ is not present in the child's pronunciation of words such as 'handle', since Rule 6 deletes /l/ at the end of a word. The fact that Rule 3 includes a condition that is based on the adult form entails that the child has some knowledge of that form, which is not directly revealed in the child's pronunciations. Similarly, Rule 6 requires the /l/ as the condition for raising and backing the second vowel in 'handle'.

The second point is that the child's rules must apply in a particular order. For example, the child's Rule 3 (and Rule 4) must apply to the adult form before Rule 6, since Rule 6 deletes the element /l/ that is the condition for application of Rule 3 (and 4). The ordered application of phonological rules is a characteristic of rule application in theories of adult phonology; thus it appears that although the child adopts rules that are not part of the adult phonological system of his language, he applies those rules in a way consistent with the constraints on rule application in adult phonologies.

Smith's analysis therefore entails that the child has available something identical or similar to the adult form and applies his own rules to that form in an ordered way to arrive at his own pronunciation. These basic points are widely accepted in the literature on phonological acquisition, although the very strong position that Smith takes – that the child has in his head a representation that is *identical* to the adult's pronunciation – has been challenged. Braine (1976) pointed out that there is a plausible perceptual basis for some of the phenomena Smith captures with his realization rules. For example, Rules 1 (which deletes a nasal before a voiceless consonant) and 2 (which deletes a voiced consonant after a nasal) may alternatively be accounted for in terms of perceptual error. Vowels in English are lengthened before a voiced consonant. Acoustically, vowels carry cues for the perception of a following nasal, and the lengthening of the vowel as a consequence of a following voiced consonant may thus cause a nasal in a V–nasal–C sequence to be perceived, where it would not be perceived if the consonant were voiceless and the vowel not lengthened (see also Macken 1980).

In addition to questions concerning the role of a perceptual filter, there is continuing debate over whether the child has only one lexical representation for a word that undergoes a set of phonological rules or two lexical representations, one accessed in comprehension and one that forms the basis for production of words; this point is returned to briefly below (section 2.7).

It is important to note that children's non-adult pronunciations are not a response to absolute inability to produce certain sounds. It is frequently the case that where a sound is eliminated by a child rule, the same sound will be introduced by another rule in the child's phonology. A well-known example from Smith's (1973) study concerns the pronunciation of alveolars and velars. For a time, the child velarized alveolar stops before [l], pronouncing the word 'puddle' as 'puggle' ([pʌgəl]). At the same period, he changed non-final [z] to [d], pronouncing 'puzzle' as 'puddle' ([pʌdəl]). The mispronunciation of adult 'puddle' is then clearly not rooted in some motor deficit, since the child produces the adult form in his version of adult 'puzzle'. Stampe (1972, ch. 1) lists many examples that make the same point.

2.6.2 Suprasegmentals

Recent phonological theory has argued that phonological representations are multi-dimensional. Stress, intonation and (for languages that use pitch height distinctively) tone are all 'suprasegmental' phenomena, and all are characterized in recent phonological theory by representations that are distinct from the phonetic feature representations we have discussed so far. The specifications for these suprasegmental phenomena are connected to the string of consonantal and vowel segments by rule, creating a multi-dimensional representation.[3]

Stress Stress rules must account for the fact that a particular syllable or syllables in a word or phrase is/are perceived as more prominent than the rest. The acoustic basis for prominence is a complex matter, with several factors (intensity, length, pitch) contributing to what we perceive as prominence (Lehiste 1970). The discussion below is concerned with the rules for stressing words only, not phrases. The type of representation that is now widely used for the stress pattern of words is a representation in terms of a hierarchical tree structure in which the branches are labelled as strong or weak. The syllable of a word that has maximum stress will be the syllable that is hooked to a strong branch, or chain of strong (s) branches. For example, the stress

on the words 'usurp' and 'develop' can be represented in terms of stress trees
of the (simplified) form in (9):

(9)   usúrp   devélop

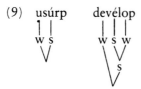

Tracing a path from the root of the tree up through a chain of one or more
s-nodes will lead to the syllable with primary stress, indicated by the stress
mark ' over the vowel. (The representations here are adapted from Hayes
1982, whose general approach to stress rules builds on Liberman and Prince
1977.)

Stress rules must construct the correct stress trees for a given language.
Stress rules for words offer a good example of parameters in the domain of
phonology. The rules for stressing words in a language tend to be 'anchored'
either to the right or the left of a word. There is thus an anchoring parameter
for which languages will choose a value. Some languages have rather simple
systems – for example, placing stress on the first or second vowel from the
left or right of the word's edge (see Hammond 1988 for a recent survey).
Other languages, including English, have a relatively complex system that
pays attention not merely to distance from the edge of the word, but also to
the nature of the material at the word's edge and the syntactic category (noun,
verb, etc.) of the word that is being stressed. The child's task in learning the
stress rules for words in his language will be to figure out the direction in
which stress is determined and the exact nature of the rules. Take the words
'usurp' and 'develop' given above. The stress pattern on those two words
taken alone is compatible with either of the following two hypotheses:

Hypothesis 1: English is a left-anchored language, with a general rule: stress
   the second syllable from the left edge of the word.
Hypothesis 2: English is a right-anchored language, in which stress is placed
   sometimes on the syllable immediately at the right edge and sometimes on
   the second syllable from the right edge.

The first hypothesis is clearly simpler, but it is incorrect. Hypothesis 2 is the
correct hypothesis for English, and the child will have to work this out, and
also to learn what the conditions are that determine when stress is placed on
the rightmost syllable of the word ('usurp') and when stress is placed further
back in the word ('develop'). Two factors affecting whether or not a word is
end-stressed in English or not are: (1) the 'weight' of the final syllable and (2)

the syntactic category of the word. The weight of a syllable depends on the number of consonants that follow the vowel and the quantity of the vowel (roughly, whether the vowel is long or short). The exact characterization of vowel length is a relatively complex matter.[4] It is sufficient here to note that length distinguishes between pairs of vowels in English, such as the long vowel [i] (the vowel in 'beet') and the short vowel [ɪ] (the vowel in 'bit'). In English, a syllable is heavy if it has a long vowel and/or has a final consonant.

Although the exact rules are complex, the broad effect of the weight of the word-final syllable in English is that a heavy syllable in final position is likely to prevent stress from moving towards the middle of the word. For adjectives and verbs, the weight of the final syllable is calculated ignoring the last consonant. Stress is placed on the last syllable of 'usurp' because the syllable has two consonants at the end, and is heavy even if the last consonant is ignored; similarly, stress goes on the last syllable of the adjective 'discreet' because the vowel in the last syllable is long, and a long vowel always means a heavy syllable. In a word such as 'develop', the vowel in the last syllable is short and followed by only one consonant, and stress can skip over the last syllable.

Syntactic category adds complication to the system. For nouns, there is a tendency for stress to be placed one syllable to the left of where it would be placed for verbs and adjectives. Thus we have nouns such as 'insect', with main stress on the first syllable despite the fact that the second syllable ends in two consonants. Although there is a good deal of complexity in the system, and it is recognized that the generalizations found are a matter of tendencies rather than absolute rules, the generalization that stress goes to the left in nouns as opposed to verbs is a real one, and shows up clearly in contrasts such as that in (10):

(10) convíct   cónvict
      (verb)   (noun)

How do children fare in learning the stress system of their language? It is notable that even in a language such as English, which has a complex stress system, children do not seem to make many errors with stress in their spontaneous speech. (Those errors that are made may be related to syllable structure; see Smith 1973 and Klein 1984.) Several studies support the idea that stress systems are quite easily mastered.

In computer simulation of stress acquisition, Dresher and Kaye (1986) have shown that various stress systems (left-anchored or right-anchored) can be 'learned' quite efficiently by a machine exposed to basic data (words in the language to be learned). The machine is equipped with prior knowledge of the factors that affect stress systems in the world's languages, such as anchoring direction and syllable weight, and formulates hypotheses based on this knowledge and the input data. This is the type of knowledge with which the child would be expected to tackle the language learning process, since these ingredients of stress systems are presumably part of universal grammar.

In experimental work, P. Smith et al. 1982 (summarizing results of Smith and Baker 1976 and Groat 1979) have argued that at least by age seven, children have grasped the elements of the English stress system – in particular, the effects of syllable weight and word class described above. Both child and adult subjects were asked to read aloud nonsense words, which were presented in contexts such as those in (11), which made the nonsense word unambiguously a noun or verb:

(11)   The *nuvit* was made in a factory (noun context)
       The man had to *nuvit* the tractor (verb context)

The child subjects were seven-year-old schoolchildren in Edinburgh, Scotland; the adult subjects were British university students. All of the test words had two syllables; they had either a single consonant in final position (as in the 'nuvit' example) above, or two consonants in final position (for example, 'rafust'). Length of vowels is not represented in a consistent way in English spelling, so whether the final vowel was interpreted as long or short was a matter of how the subject chose to pronounce the word. A word such as 'nuvit' could be pronounced with either a long or short final vowel. Table 2.4 shows the percentage first-syllable stress according to number of final consonants (one or two), quality of the final vowel (long or short) and category of the word (noun or verb). The table shows that children have essentially the

Table 2.4 First syllable stress (%)

Number of final consonants	Quality of final vowel	Example of nonsense word	Example of similar English word	Children Noun	Children Verb	Adults Noun	Adults Verb
1	Short	nʌvit (nuvit)	Edit	89	78	85	50
1	Long	nʌviːt (nuvit)	Discreet	65	38	71	18
2	Short	ræfʌst (rafust)	Distrust	87	56	50	25

[a] Smith et al. use the terms *tense* and *lax* for long and short.
[b] The transcriptions are as given by Smith et al. The vowel transcribed as [i] would appear to be the vowel we have designated with [ɪ].
Adapted and abbreviated from Smith et al. (1982), table 4.

same pattern of responses as adults. Both are more inclined to put stress on the first syllable if the word is a noun than if it is a verb; if it has a short final vowel rather than a long final vowel; and if there is one consonant at the end of the word rather than two (for children, the last holds only in the case of verbs). Thus the seven-year-olds in this study had extracted from the real words they had heard the essential elements of the rules of the stress system of their language. A recent study by Hochberg (1988) uses both experimental data and spontaneous speech to argue a similar point with respect to Spanish, using subjects as young as three years.

Intonation   Intonation and tone are two further phenomena for which phonological theory posits levels of representation separate from the string of consonant and vowel segments. Specifications of pitch height critical to the intonation patterns of a language such as English and for tone values in a language such as Chinese (see below) will be spelled out in terms of a sequence of pitch segments, linked to the string of vowel and consonant segments that make up a word or phrase by rule. In English, the normal intonation for a statement is a rise followed by a fall in pitch:

(12)   ╱   ╲ ╲ ╲
      John broke the balloon

This can be translated into a representation such as (13) where the pitch melody is (minimally) schematized as a sequence of H L (high; low) pitch segments, which can be linked to the consonant and vowel string by rule (Selkirk 1984, ch. 5 and references therein):

(13)

                    H L
                ╱ |
      John broke the balloon

The exact positioning of the pitch peak (H) may vary, but the general H-L contour will ordinarily be present in declarative sentences. Questions in English (and many other languages) have a different, L-H pattern, as shown in (14)–(15):

(14)   ── ── ╱   ╱
      Was the skunk black?

(15)   L   H
            | |
      Was the skunk black?

On this approach to intonation, the pitch melody is thus represented as a sequence of segments at a level separate from the sequence of consonant and vowel segments.

Studies of early child language show that children know the value of these basic intonation patterns early on. In early stages of development, children learning English frequently omit inversion of subject and verb ('The skunk was black?' – 'Was the skunk black?'), signalling a question with rising intonation only (see Klima and Bellugi 1973). Moreover, the speech of some children offers some support for a general approach to intonation in which the pitch melody is represented as an autonomous level, distinct from the sound-segment level. Peters (1977) studied the speech of one young child who appeared to have two distinct speech modes. At around one and a half years, this child produced on the one hand fairly intelligible one-word utterances and on the other hand longer utterances with low intelligibility. These latter utterances, Peters argues, preserve the intonation contour of the target utterance, omitting or severely distorting the segmental content. For example, the (initially unintelligible) utterance

(16)   [ˈá lər ri gʊ̀ mu nyai]

was pronounced with an adult-like intonation tune for the intended sentence, 'I like to read Good Moon Night' (Good Night Moon).

This kind of behaviour makes sense within the picture of intonation sketched above, where the intonation tune is separate from the segmental string. At one and a half or two years the child may have a quite solid command of vocabulary, syntax and prosody, but calling up those different features of his knowledge in a single utterance may be simply beyond his capacities. So he may plan a fully-fledged utterance, complete with syntax, words and appropriate intonation, but be able to execute only one part of that plan – either one or two individual words are carefully articulated or the overall intonation and a few features of the words are realized at the expense of intelligibility. The partial independence of intonation and the segmental (CV) representation of words can be explained in terms of the partitioning of the child's energy in speech production. (Peters 1977 presents a somewhat different account.)

Tone   In tone languages, pitch is used to distinguish words and morphemes and is thus a lexical property. As an example, Mandarin Chinese uses four distinctive tones: high-level, rising, falling and dipping. These terms reflect the pitch levels associated with each tone; high-level tone is a relatively high pitch, rising tone is a shift from a lower to a higher pitch level on a single vowel,

falling tone is a shift downwards in tone and dipping tone is a slight fall .
tone followed by a rise. The forms in (17) illustrate the way in which tone can
distinguish between otherwise identical words:

(17)	HIGH	bā	'eight'
	RISING	bá	'to pull'
	FALLING	bà	'a harrow'
	DIPPING	bǎ	grammatical marker for object

(The diacritics for the different tones are from the Pinyin romanization
system.) In addition, Mandarin has a 'neutral' tone, which occurs in
unstressed syllables and has different level tone values (mid, half-low, low),
depending on the tone of the preceding syllable. Tone languages differ with
respect to the level tones (high, mid, low) and contour tones (rising, falling,
ect.) they use, and the extent to which lexically assigned tones (tone values
that are part of the lexical entry of the word) are adjusted by phonological
rule.

A standard approach to tone systems in recent linguistic analysis is to treat
tone as a specification of pitch height in terms of pitch segments, just as in the
treatment of intonation in the preceding section; contour tones can be represented as the assignment of a string of two or more pitch height segments to
a single vowel. The Mandarin words in (17) can be represented as in (18):

(18)　bā　　bá　　　bà　　　bǎ

　　　|　　　/\　　　/\　　　/|\

　　　H　　L　H　　H　L　　M　L　H

　　　'eight'　'to pull'　'a harrow'　object marker

　　　(H = high pitch; L = low pitch; M = mid pitch)

Both general constraints and language-particular rules will govern the linking
relations between tone segments and vowels (see Goldsmith 1976 for an early
treatment).

Li and Thompson (1978) and Clumeck (1980) review studies on the acquisition of tone. Overall, studies of children acquiring a number of different tone
languages reveal little evidence of any special difficulty with tone-to-word
mappings, which generally seem to be mastered before the segmental system
is fully acquired. Demuth (1989a) uses data from children acquiring Sesotho
to argue that from an early stage (two years) children distinguish tone from
stress.

One particularly interesting finding concerns the acquisition of contour tones. Although there is some variation concerning which tones are mastered earlier than others, at least some children disfavour contour tones. For example, Li and Thompson (1977) report that one child learning Mandarin Chinese replaced contour tones with level tones of different heights, using a low tone for falling and dipping tones in adult forms and a mid or high tone for rising tones in adult forms (in the examples Li and Thompson cite). Within the type of tone system sketched above, this type of behaviour is easily characterized. One has simply to say that the child imposed a ban on many-to-one mappings between tone segments and vowels; he does so by systematically adjusting the adult representations above, stripping away the left of the adult tone segments in falling and rising tones and both peripheral segments in the dipping tone.

A system of representation with tone segments thus permits the child's behaviour to be perspicuously described. Difficulty with contour tones can be accounted for in terms of a plausible restriction – one-to-one mapping between levels. Moreover, systematic simplification of contour tones is another type of evidence that the child may have an adult-like representation for a form, even though his pronunciation deviates from the adult's pronunciation. We cannot explain why a child produces a low tone for a falling or dipping tone and a mid or high tone for a rising tone unless we credit the child with having perceived a difference between these contour tones. The child's treatment of the different tones can be described in terms of a systematic adjustment to the adult's representation of the word.

Syllable structure and sonority   Syllables have a hierarchical internal structure whose organization is sensitive to the feature composition of the component parts. Much linguistic and psycholinguistic evidence points to the syllable in English having a structure in which there are two primary units: an onset and a rhyme. The former comprises the initial consonant (or consonant cluster) and the latter comprises the vowel or other syllabic element, together with any syllable-final consonants. Thus a monosyllabic word such as 'drunk' has approximately the internal structure shown in (19):

(19)

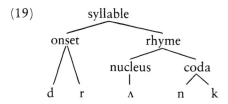

(See Cairns and Feinstein 1982 for one example of a more detailed account of the internal structure of syllables.)

Although there are language-specific variants, the ordering of elements in both the syllable as a whole and its internal units generally conforms to the dictates of a 'sonority hierarchy'. Sonority is the acoustic property we perceive as resonance. The less obstruction there is in the vocal tract, the more vowel-like or sonorant a consonant is. Stops are the least sonorant sounds, fricatives somewhat more sonorant, nasals and liquids more sonorant still. The normal case with respect to syllable organization is that segments on the periphery of the syllable are the least sonorant, with progressively more sonorant elements towards the nucleus of the syllable. The dictates of this hierarchy are followed in the example 'drunk' above, where the stop [d] precedes the liquid [r] in the onset, a vowel occupies the nucleus and the nasal [n] precedes the stop [k] in the coda. There are, however, exceptions to this general organizational pattern. For example, English permits words such as 'skunk', where the initial [sk] cluster contains a fricative followed by a stop, i.e. a sequence in which sonority decreases on the path to the nucleus.

Children's performance shows a sensitivity to different syllable types that reflects the relative frequency of the various syllable types in languages of the world and their internal organization. CV is the most common type of syllable in languages of the world (a fact that has been unified with the dictates of the sonority restrictions on syllable organization by Clements 1988; see Martohardjono 1989 for discussion with respect to language acquisition). Children initially eschew clusters of consonants; they babble primarily CV and then CV and CVC syllables, and in their first words frequently delete elements from consonant clusters or break up clusters with vowels to make syllables that conform to a CV pattern (see table 2.3 for examples). Experimental tests carried out with older children confirm sensitivity to hierarchical structures such as that above: Treiman (1985) found that children aged eight find it easier to perform a task that requires them to replace two sound segments in nonsense words when the replacement respects the onset–rhyme boundary of the stimulus item than when the onset–rhyme boundary is crossed by the replacement.

When the child begins to produce consonant clusters, there is evidence of sensitivity to the sonority hierarchy. For example, the child studied by Smith (1973) at a particular stage reduced initial triconsonantal clusters of the form [str] to two consonants. Of the three logically possible reductions – [st], [tr] and [sr] – he used only the last two. Thus a word such as 'straw' was pronounced 'traw' or 'sraw', but not 'staw'. The reduced forms uttered by the child were those that conformed to the sonority hierarchy restriction on syllable organization – in the syllables 'traw' and 'sraw' the ordering least-to-more sonorant is observed; the syllable 'staw' (not used by the child) violates that ordering. The effects of a general property of syllable structure rather than language-particular forms are clear in this example; in his cluster simplifications, the child used a cluster that does not occur in adult English (English has no words beginning with [sr]) and avoided a sequence ([st]) that is found in English (in words such as 'sting'), beginning with the offending [st] cluster.

2.7   Problems and Ideas

The thrust of all the above sections is that the child's phonological abilities reflect the units, levels of representation and (as far as is known) the constraints that characterize adult phonological systems. However, it is not always the case that the child's behaviour mirrors the general patterns of adult phonologies. One example that has been frequently discussed is consonant harmony – agreement of consonants for features such as nasality and manner of articulation. Such harmony processes are quite rare in adult languages, but quite common in child pronunciations (see table 2.3 for some examples). Why should this be?

An idea that has recurred in various forms is that consonant harmony reflects the child's utilization of levels of phonological structure (such as the syllable) that are not normally the 'home' of the phonetic features that characterize the harmony. (See Menn 1978, Iverson and Wheeler 1987 for pertinent discussion). Thus, for example, a child who pronounces 'dog' as [gag] and 'coat' as [kok] may be hypothesized to be associating the feature [–anterior] with the entire syllable (equivalent in these examples to the word), as shown in (20):

(20)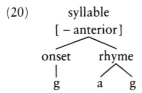

All of the segments to which the feature [–anterior] is potentially relevant will be so characterized. Iverson and Wheeler propose an analysis along these lines. This type of analysis is appealing to the extent that (1) it provides a means of characterizing a phenomenon in child pronunciation that is odd, *vis-à-vis* the characteristics of adult languages and (2) the explanation provided ties in with levels of representation necessary in adult phonologies. However, the idea is unsatisfactory to the extent that in a sense it does little more than re-state the problem by notating the syllable node with particular features.

Recent phonological theory has argued that many or all of the phonetic feature specifications for consonants and vowels should be represented in terms of hierarchical structures that constellate around a core of slots (linear positions for segments); see, for example, Clements and Keyser (1983); Pulleyblank (1989); Goldsmith (1990, ch. 6). Thus (on one version of this general family of theories) the segment [s] will have a partial representation along the lines of (21):

(21)   The segment *s* (Goldsmith, 1990, p. 281)

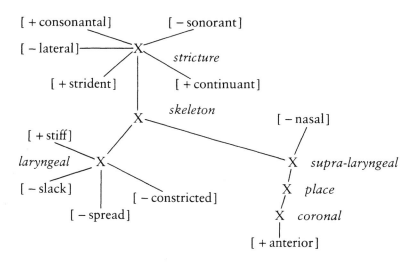

The central X labelled *skeleton* represents the positional slot for the consonant; the satellite Xs *stricture*, *supra-laryngeal* and *laryngeal* represent classes of phonetic features that are themselves organized in partial hierarchies. Thus there is a hierarchy of features under supra-laryngeal, in which, for example, the class node *place* is further differentiated in terms of features specifying points of articulation. Each of the nodes in this hierarchical organization occupies a position on a level of representation (a tier) that can be hooked up (subject to constraints common between segmental phonology and tone and intonation phenomena) to one or more positions on the skeleton. On the particular version of the theory illustrated in (21), the terminal points on the path are plus and minus feature specifications of the traditional kind.

The theoretical debate over the virtues of such systems of feature representation is only beginning to penetrate work on child language acquisition, but there are at least two areas where such representations may have some explanatory force, over and above more traditional representations of the structure of segments as bundles of plus and minus feature specifications. The first is the consonant harmony phenomenon just mentioned; the second is an account of Jakobson's observations concerning the order of emergence of sound segments.

With respect to consonant harmony, harmony processes in recent theory are in general accounted for in terms of the spreading of a specification on a particular tier to a sequence of slots on the skeleton. For example, harmony of consonants with respect to backness, as in the example in (20) (the pronunciation [gag] for 'dog'), can be represented as shown in (22):

(22)   Consonant slot Vowel slot Consonant slot

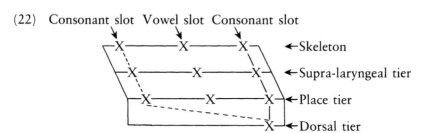

The harmony process will consist of the dorsal specification spreading from the final consonant to the first. (*Dorsal* is a feature distinguishing velars from front consonants in recent feature systems, in which [±anterior] is reserved for distinguishing between types of coronal consonants; the essential idea of harmony via feature spreading will be the same regardless of which features are involved in the spread.) An account of child consonant harmony processes along these lines is suggested in Spencer (1986).

Do such representations of child harmony processes offer any insight into why harmony is so common in child, but not adult, pronunciations? In Spencer's analysis spreading (and hence harmony) is made possible because the child has only partially-specified representations for the target word; these are the result of processes that in effect strip the adult representation of words, used by the child for recognition purposes, of some of their details (a similar suggestion is made by Menn 1978). Thus on this type of analysis the dorsal specification of the final consonant would be 'free' to spread on to the first consonant because the first (alveolar) consonant has been stripped of the specifications (for coronal and [+anterior] place) that distinguish it from velars, in the pared-down representation the child uses as a basis for his production of words. This type of account entails that the child has at least two representations for words: a recognition form, which is similar or identical to the adult representation, and a production form, in which segments have less than their adult representation and on which the spreading process operates. For the data he discusses, Spencer draws on recent ideas concerning the representation of unmarked segments in terms of underlying forms that are only partially specified for feature values (Archangeli 1984). Such underspecified forms potentially provide targets for the processes that produce the child's production forms from his more adult-like recognition forms. Whether the overall distribution and frequency of observed child harmony forms will lend itself to an analysis in terms of unmarked underlying forms is an important question for research.

With respect to the order of emergence of different segments, we noted above that an account of markedness values for more and less rare segments such as Kean's is stipulative, in so far as it relies on an arbitrary assignment of values to segments according to their observed distribution in the world's languages. The hierarchical organization of features central to recent conceptions of the segment at least offers the prospect that the order of emergence of sounds can be related to organizational properties of adult segments. (Broadly, the idea would be that major class distinctions should emerge before distinctions of sounds within classes; see Berwick 1985 for an attempt along these lines.)

2.8   Summary and Conclusions

Several different topics have been covered in this chapter. Speech segments are characterized in terms of specifications for phonetic feature values; some of these features will be distinctive in a language (necessarily specified in the dictionary entry of a word or morpheme), others will be 'unused' in a language and others still specifiable by phonological rule. The child must learn which features are used in her language and how – what the repertoire of speech segments in her language is and how they are distributed. Studies with very young infants argue that children are able to perceive certain phonetic distinctions that correspond to cut-off points for adult discrimination between minimally different sound segments. Other such cut-off points are less widely used in human languages and sensitivity to them may develop over time (possibly within the course of the first year). Children's spontaneous babbling and early intelligible speech show a distribution of speech sounds that can be matched in many ways to the gross frequencies with which speech sounds occur in adult languages – unmarked (cross-linguistically frequent) sounds predominate, while more marked (rarer) sounds are on the whole later acquired and less frequent in children's utterances.

Children's early speech characteristically shows several types of error and misarticulation. On occasion, the errors *vis-à-vis* the adult system show clear evidence of rules that are not part of the adult phonological system. Because such rules can only be coherently formulated in terms of the adult phonological forms (lexical entries), those forms must in some way be part of the child's knowledge. Many of children's mispronunciations and non-adult rules have parallels in adult phonological rules. Moreover, the child's rules must apply in order, and in that sense the child's system is adult-like.

Children appear to do rather well in their handling of stress, intonation tunes and (in languages that use pitch distinctively) tone. By seven years and plausibly much earlier, children learning English have a grasp of the component parts of a rather complex stress system. Children quickly pick up on intonation and may use intonation contours without fully spelling out the segmental properties of an utterance. Tone specifications in tone languages have been found to be mastered before segmental specifications; some evidence suggests that level tones may have priority over contour tones for some children, a fact that can be perspicuously described within current linguistic models of tone.

Syllable structure, like suprasegmental phenomena, requires reference to sequences of segments. As in the case of production of speech sounds in babbling and first words, children's performance with different types of syllable reflects markedness values. The most usual syllable type in languages (CV) is favoured and children's simplifications of consonant clusters show sensitivity to the normal ordering of consonant types in clusters (the sonority hierarchy).

Overall, the child quickly develops a system that reflects many of the levels of representation in the adult phonological system and many of the details of the rules of the adult system, although the child may temporarily form non-adult rules and may temporarily favour pronunciations that do not parallel common processes in adult phonological systems (in particular, consonant harmony).

Notes

1   As mentioned above, the cues for speech perception are complex and voicing perception is no exception. Perception of voicing may be manipulated in relation to the acoustic structure of adjacent vowels. Vowel sounds are characterized by bands of intense energy in the speech spectrum (formants). In stop-plus-vowel sequences, voicing perception is dependent on the onset of the first (lowest) formant relative to the second and third formants – a relatively early onset signalling voicing and a later onset, after the second and third formants, signalling voicelessness.

2   It is the convention in phonology to use slashes to enclose pre-final forms and square brackets to enclose phonetic output.

3   In recent phonological theory, the multi-dimensional character of phonological representations extends to the feature representation of consonant
and vowel segments, as sketched below.

4   In particular, it is of issue how quality correlates with and contributes to
the characterization of vowels as long or short. The phonetic feature
tense/lax (characterized, for example, in terms of greater or lesser constric-
tion of the tongue root or tongue body) frequently correlates with length,
tense vowels being longer. A vowel is also long if it is diphthongal.

Further Reading

Jakobson's (1968) monograph is short and very readable and its ideas are
largely not outdated. Locke (1983, ch. 1) provides a detailed critique of some
of Jakobson's claims and a clear summary of a great deal of research on early
phonological development.

Questions and Exercises

1.   Back stops [k, g] are common in early babbling. Discuss this fact with
respect to markedness and order of acquisition.

2.   The pronunciation of certain forms by two brothers aged four and five
(Applegate 1961) deviated systematically from the pronunciation of their
parents; the parents spoke the (American English) dialect of their community. Study the following child forms, and propose two rules to account
for the way in which the children's pronunciation differed from the adults'
pronunciation. Do not concern yourself with the pronunciation of vowels;
concentrate on rules for the pronunciation of consonants. How must the
rules be ordered? (ʔ is a glottal stop, heard, for example, in Cockney British
English pronunciation of the [t] in words such as 'bottle'; [ɨ] is a centralized [i]; [y] is
a palatal glide, [j]).

adult word	child pronunciation
walks	wɑkt
talks	tɑkt
talked	tɑkɨʔ
toot	tuwʔ
suit	tuwt
kick	kɪʔ
pet	pɛt

bit	bɪt
tag	tæg
died	daɣ?
does	dad
takes	teɣkt

(This problem is adapted from Halle and Clements 1983, p. 117.)

3. What do you think about drawing general conclusions about children's phonological abilities on the basis of cases such as the one in the problem (3) above, where the children behaved in a way that was special — not typical of other children's development?

4. Hochberg (1988) used an imitation task to test children's knowledge of stress rules in Spanish. She asked children to imitate non-existent words that either conformed to the regular rules of Spanish stress or violated them. The basic finding was that children made more errors in imitating non-sense words with non-regular stress than nonsense words with regular stress. Find some English-speaking children and try out her task using materials such as those in the Smith et al. (1982) experiment described in the text. That is, ask children to repeat sentences with nonsense words in noun and verb contexts, with stress either on the last syllable of the word or further back. For example:

noun context: The $\left\{ \begin{array}{l} [\text{ræfʌst}] \\ [\text{ræfʌst}] \end{array} \right\}$ was made in the factory

verb context: The man had to $\left\{ \begin{array}{l} [\text{ræfʌst}] \\ [\text{ræfʌst}] \end{array} \right\}$ the tractor

Vary the weight of the final syllable of the nonsense words both in terms of number of syllables and length of the vowel.

3 Morphological Development and Innovation

One of the adages of language acquisition studies is that acquisition is a creative process. Yet the thrust of the studies summarized in the last chapter would seem to be that the opposite is true. Some of the results reviewed there suggest that constraints found in adult phonologies also place bounds on the possible analyses a child can make with respect to the words and sentences she hears. We will see in chapters 4 and 5 a similarly close correspondence between child and adult systems in many areas of syntactic development. Overall, language development can be seen as a highly constrained process, with quite strict limits on the types of rules that a child can formulate.

Where, then, is the creativity? A plausible answer is that the examples most frequently cited as evidence of creativity are innovative word forms. Morphological rules in the adult grammar account for the formation of new words (innovations in the vocabulary) and for the outer shape of existing words in particular contexts ('one dog' but 'two dogs', with the plural '-s' occurring after 'two'). Novel forms created by children strike the ear as such and give evidence for the child actively using the rules in her grammar to produce word forms not in the adult vocabulary; we will see several different types of example below. None the less, the child's innovations appear to adhere to constraints or morphological rules that govern the adult grammar. Thus we will see that the child's 'creativity' with respect to word formation in fact offers quite firm evidence that child grammars are constrained by principles that also govern adult word formation rules.

3.1 Types of Morphological Rules

Morphological rules are traditionally divided into two types: *derivational* and *inflectional*. The distinction between derivational and inflectional rules has been drawn in various ways (see Anderson 1982). For convenience, we can think of the term derivational as referring to rules for forming new words, including processes for forming new words by adding affixes or by joining words together to form a compound word. For example, in English we can derive a noun from a verb by adding the affix '-er', which carries an agentive meaning:

(1)   to shave (verb); shave + er → shaver (thing or person who
                                                 shaves)

We can also form compounds with '-er' agentive nouns by joining another noun with the '-er' noun, in which case the first element of the compound is understood as the thing that undergoes the action expressed by the second element of the compound:

(2)   man (noun) + hater (-er agentive noun) → man-hater (one who hates
                                                              men)

Compounding is another example of derivational morphology.

Rules of inflectional morphology can be thought of as rules that do not create new words; they regulate the form of the word according to the syntactic context in which it occurs. Thus, in English we have a rule that requires a plural noun to have the affix '-s', and the past tense of a verb to have the affix '-ed':

(3a)   One dog (singular) – two dogs (plural)
(3b)   I walk (present) – he walked (past)

The different characters of derivational and inflectional rules (the coining of new words versus the spelling out of the correct form of an existing word in a particular context) gives each of them a rather different status. Derivational rules are rules that speakers of a language use on occasion to form new words; the word that is formed in a particular instance may either be a 'one-off' coinage, which never enters the permanent vocabulary (lexicon), or it may became a word in the permanent vocabulary of the speaker who coins it, and potentially also of others in his speech community. Inflectional rules are rules that must be used to produce the required agreement in any sentence in the language, acting on existing words to produce their correct form in a particular environment. Their use is obligatory in a way that use of derivational rules such as the '-er' agentive noun rule and the compounding rule described above is not. However, despite this difference it is clear that we make grammaticality judgements with respect to the product of derivational rules that are just as strong as those we make with respect to inflectional rules. For example, speakers of English will agree that the compound 'man-eater' means 'one who eats men' and not 'a man who eats (something)' and that the order of elements in the compound must be 'man' + 'eater' and not 'eater' + 'man'. '*Eater-man' is just as ungrammatical as '*I walk to town yesterday' (with failure to apply the inflectional rule for past tense).

3.2   A Morphological Model

Recent linguistic research has attempted to characterize the nature of morphological rules and the way in which they fit into a model of a speaker's competence – how they interact and relate to syntactic, semantic and phonological rules and knowledge (see, for example, Anderson 1982; Kiparsky 1983). The model sketched here derives from Kiparsky.

In Kiparsky's model, a number of different types of morphological rule apply in a specified order; that is, in forming a word, all rules of a given type must apply before rules of another type apply, according to the ordering stipulated in the model. These blocks of rules of particular types define levels in the model, which is referred to in general as the 'level-ordering' model of morphology. For our purposes, it will be sufficient to look at three types of morphological rule and their associated levels.

We have already had examples of two of the three types. The derivational rules of '-er' agentive noun formation ('shave' → 'shaver'; 'eat' → 'eater') and of noun + noun compounding ('man' + 'eater' → 'man-eater') share a number of properties. They apply productively (we can coin new words at will using the rules), and the results are semantically fairly predictable (we interpret the '-er' agentive affix in a consistent way, and regularly interpret the first element in a compound such as 'man-eater' as the logical object of the action denoted by the second element). The '-ed' past tense rule and the '-s' plural rule share these properties (productivity and semantic predictability) with '-er' agentive and noun + noun compounding rule, but differ from those rules in being inflectional rather than derivational – relying for their operation on the immediate syntactic environment in which the word undergoing the rule is embedded. In Kiparsky's model, such inflectional rules are a separate rule type.

To these two morphological rule types – corresponding to derivational and inflectional rules as we have considered them so far – we must add a third. This type will cover both derivational and inflectional rules when the rules are less productive or regular than the rules we have looked at so far. In this class are rules such as that for forming nouns from verbs by adding the affix '-ion' to a verb ('populate' + 'ion' → 'population') and various irregular rules such as the plural rules producing the forms 'oxen' and 'mice' (rather than 'oxs' and 'mouses') as the plurals of 'ox' and 'mouse', respectively. Another irregular rule is the past tense rule producing 'went' rather than 'goed' as the past form of 'go'. Derivational rules in this category are frequently semantically unpredictable or only semi-predictable (the meaning of 'population' is not in any straightforward way a product of 'populate' + 'ion'). Rules in this category frequently have phonological effects on the basic form (e.g. the addition of '-ion' causes a change in the pronunciation of the final sound in 'populate').

In Kiparsky's model, the three types of morphological rule are ordered as in figure 3.1. Kiparsky's model makes a number of correct predictions about word formation in English. First, it predicts that affixes added to a basic word by a regular inflectional rule will occur outside affixes added by derivational rules: regular inflectional rules are third-level rules in the model above, and such rules apply after derivational rules at levels 1 or 2. Thus if a level 3 inflectional rule says 'add affix "x"' to the end of a word, it will add that affix to the output of derivational rules such as '-er' agentive noun formation and compounding. This prediction is correct; the plural of 'eater' is 'eater-s' not '*eat-s-er', and the plural of 'man-eater' is 'man-eaters' not '*man-eat-s-er'.

Second, it predicts that while the output of regular inflectional rules cannot be used as the input to derivational rules, the output of irregular inflectional rules (such as the rules for irregular plural) can be so used. This also is a correct prediction. In forming compounds, we cannot use the plural form of a regular noun as an element in the compound. Thus the compound is 'rat-catcher' and not '*rats-catcher' even though we mean by the compound 'rat-catcher' a person who catches rats in general, not a person who aims to catch

Level 1 Rules– *Properties* –(a) Derivational: unproductive; semantically
                    unpredictable
                (b) Inflectional: irregular
                (c) Phonological effects on the base form in many cases
       Examples– + 'ion' noun formation ('population')
                irregular plurals ('mouse', 'mice')
                irregular past ('go', 'went')'

Level 2 Rules– *Properties*–Derivational; productive; semantically predictable
              Examples– 'er' agentive noun formation ('eater'); compounding

Level 3 Rules– *Properties*–Inflectional; regular
            Examples– '-s' plural
                  '-ed' past

Figure 3.1 The Level-Ordering Model (Based on Kiparsky 1983. In Kiparsky's model, phonological rules apply after each level of morphological rules in a manner not indicated in this figure.)

pounding rule is a level 2 rule, and so can take as its input the output of level 1 rules, which include specifications for irregular inflections. Accordingly, if we want to form a compound to denote a person or thing whose function it is to catch mice, we can say either 'mouse-catcher' or 'mice-catcher'. The irregular plural form 'mice' will be available via a rule of level 1 as the input to compounding at level 2. It is not obligatory to use the irregular plural form rather than the singular form of the word, but it is permitted according to the organization of the model. This fits our intuition that either 'mouse-catcher' or 'mice-catcher' is grammatical, although the singular form of the compound perhaps sounds more natural (possibly due to the obligatoriness of the singular form for compounds formed with regular plurals).

3.3   Children's Knowledge of Level Ordering

Kiparsky's model is a model of the organization of morphological rules that potentially regulates morphological processes in human language in general. That is, Kiparsky's model is a hypothesis about the structure of universal grammar. Other languages may make greater or less use of rule types at particular levels, and may distinguish a different number of levels, but the rules of every language should fit within the pattern of an ordered series of rule types, in which the more idiosyncratic rules of the language are contained in the first level or levels. The constraints imposed by the model are putatively part of universal grammar, and so may be expected, on the approach to acquisition pursued in previous chapters, to govern children's rules of word formation.

Gordon (1985b) tested three- to five-year-old children's ability to produce compounds of the 'rat-catcher' type. Other studies indicate that the '-er' agentive rule and compound formation are within the abilities of three-year-olds (Clark and Hecht 1982); Gordon's study tested knowledge of the restrictions on those rules imposed by the level-ordering model. In his experiment, the child was shown sets of objects corresponding to both regular and irregular plural nouns – for example, a string of beads (regular: 'bead'; 'beads') and some teeth (irregular: 'tooth'; 'teeth'). Knowledge (or lack of knowledge) of these irregular forms was established for each child. The child's task was to tell the experimenter if she thought a puppet, Cookie-Monster, would like to eat the set of objects before him. Then the experimenter asked the child: 'What do you call someone who eats X?' (using in the position X the plural form that the child had previously supplied).

The children's responses to questions of the form 'What do you call someone who eats X?' gave strong support to the claim that children's word formation processes are sensitive to the constraints of the level-ordering hypothesis. First, in almost every case (161 out of 164 instances) children used the singular form in producing compounds with regular plurals: thus they produced forms such as 'bead-eater' but not forms such as '*beads-eater'. Second, those subjects who demonstrated that they knew the correct plural form for irregular words also freely used that irregular form in forming compounds: thirty-six out of forty compounds involving irregular words by children who knew the irregular plural were of the form 'teeth-eater' (as opposed to 'tooth-eater'). Those subjects who did not command the irregular plurals also performed in a way consistent with knowledge of the level-ordering constraints.

As Gordon argues, it is very implausible that the children's behaviour can be put down to rules that the child works out on the basis of the speech around her. As noted above, although either the singular or the plural of irregulars is allowed as the first element of a compound in the adult grammar ('mouse-eater' or 'mice-eater'), the singular sounds somewhat more natural. Gordon inspected compound forms in a corpus of written English (Kučera and Francis 1967) and found that singular forms were used as the first element of compounds in almost all instances of compounds formed with irregular nouns in that corpus (151 out of 153 instances). So, although the grammar allows irregular plurals to occur inside compounds, this is not an option that is taken with any frequency in the adult language. A child who was forming rules based on the forms for which she has evidence in the speech around her would seem likely, then, to conclude that irregular plurals, like regular plurals, are *not* permitted inside compounds. Yet the children in Gordon's experiment strongly preferred to use irregular plurals inside compounds, although they avoided using regular plurals in the same situation. The fact that children preferred irregular plurals in compounds (in contrast to the adult preference for the singular form of irregulars in compounds) can be put down to the experimental situation. In the pre-tests of the experiment and in the questions used to elicit compounds ('What do you call someone who eats X?') the child heard plural forms which may have biased her towards use of the plural option for irregular nouns in producing compounds. But, as Gordon argues, that potential biasing factor was present in the questions that elicited regular as well as irregular plurals. Yet children consistently reduced the regular plurals to the singular form in producing compounds, in the teeth of potential bias towards plural forms. In other words, they were biased by the form of the test towards use of plurals in compounds only in that circumstance where the level-ordering model permits plurals to be used.

Both the overall pattern of results and the children's differential sensitivity to bias towards plurals in the experimental set-up argue that young children are following the constraints of the level-ordering model. The fact that the adult language offers them little or no clue to the relevant constraints (at least in written language, singulars predominate inside compounds in the adult language, even for irregular forms) makes it implausible that the child has induced these rules on the basis of the speech forms she has heard. Gordon proposes that the constraints are part of an innate programme for language learning. Once the child has learned what the regular rules for pluralization and so forth in her language are, and has also learned which items are exceptional, the constraints imposed by the general form of the model will automatically apply when the child produces novel words through operations such as compounding.

3.4   Rule Use and Innovation

Gordon's study elicited novel compounds from children in an experimental situation. Children's spontaneous utterances are also a rich source of evidence concerning children's knowledge of morphological rules; non-adult word forms testify to the child's rule-forming capacity and her implicit knowledge of various types of morphological operation.

The most familiar examples of children's innovative use of morphological rules are cases where the child has extended a regular inflectional rule to forms that are exceptional in the adult grammar. A three-stage sequence of development is often found. First the child uses the irregular adult form; then she regularizes it with the morphological rule that covers the majority of cases in the adult language; and then she reverts to correct use of the irregular form. Thus the child may first correctly use 'went' as the past tense of 'go' and then – as she gains control of the regular '-ed' past tense inflection – extend that regular inflection to the irregular form, producing 'goed' in place of 'went'. After a period of this type of incorrect use of regularized forms, she arrives at a system incorporating both regular forms ('walk'; 'walked') and irregular forms ('go'; 'went'). Such over-use of regular rules is clear indication that the child has abstracted a rule from the speech forms around her.

Derivational rules are also used innovatively. Clark (1982) studied children's production of *denominal verbs* – verbs formed by using a noun as a verb, such as 'to garden' or 'to table' (a decision). She shows that children innovate such forms with a variety of meanings, most frequently instrument and locatum (in locatum verbs, the noun that is used as a verb denotes an entity that is being placed somewhere). Some examples from English-speaking children are given in table 3.1 (similar innovations are made by French- and

Table 3.1 Examples of instrument and locatum denominal verbs

Age of child (yrs; mths)	
	Instrument
2; 4	'You have to scale it first' (wanting to have some cheese weighed)
2; 7	'I broomed her' (having hit his baby sister with a broom)
3; 2	'Is it all needled?' (asking if the pants his mother is mending are ready)
	Locatum
2; 3	'Mummy trousers me' (talking about getting dressed)
3; 11	'I'm crackering my soup' (putting crackers in her soup)
5; 0	'Will you chocolate my milk?'

German-speaking children). While such denominal verbs are quite richly documented in children's spontaneous utterances, *deverbal nouns* (for example, 'the shave' meaning 'lather') are observed much less frequently, matching the observation of grammarians that the process of forming nouns from verbs has always been much less frequent in English than the process of forming verbs from nouns (Marchand 1969, cited by Clark 1982, p. 418). Kiparsky (1983) argues that the prevalence of denominal verbs can be made to follow from the level-ordering model; level 1 rules will include the rule for forming deverbal nouns and level 2 rules will include the rule for forming denominal verbs. This is in keeping with the general claim that level 1 rules are generally not productive, while level 2 rules are. Kiparsky gives several additional arguments to support the classification of the deverbal noun rule as level 1 and the denominal verb rule as level 2. For example, since compounding rules are level 2 operations, it is correctly predicted that compound nouns formed at level 2 can be used as verbs via the denominal verb rule (for example, 'to wallpaper' 'to snowball') but deverbal nouns cannot be formed from compound verbs (we do not have nouns of the form 'an air-condition' or 'a stage-manage'). While sensitivity to such restrictions among children has yet to be tested, the fact that denominal verbs are frequent in children's innovations and deverbal nouns are rare can be taken as further evidence that children's morphological innovations obey the constraints of the level-ordering model.

Sometimes children's morphological innovations exploit devices that are quite marginal, in terms of their use in the particular adult language the child is learning. Some examples collected by Melissa Bowerman illustrate this (see

Table 3.2 Innovative causatives

Age of child (yrs; mths)	
4; 3	'It always sweats me (=makes me sweat)
5; 3	'This is aching my legs' (=makes my legs ache)
5; 8	'Enough to wish me one of those beds' (=to make me wish for)
6; 0+	'Do you want to see us disappear our heads?' (=make our heads disappear)

Bowerman 1982). She found that at a certain stage her daughters innovated causative forms of verbs – using verbs with the intended meaning that the subject of the verb caused the object to undergo the action denoted by the verb. Some examples are given in table 3.2. These examples are striking because they show children experimenting with a morphological device widely used in languages of the world, but confined in modern English to a relatively small number of alternations (for example, 'the door opened' (non-causative) vs. 'he opened the door' (causative)). In terms of a level-ordering model, such examples suggest that what a child must learn is not merely the particular morphological forms of his language (e.g. that the past tense ending in English is '-ed' and that the suffix '-er' is a suffix for agentive nouns), but in some cases also the level at which a rule operates. In some languages, causative formation may be a level 2 rule, and hence productive; in others, such as English, causative formation may be a level 1 rule, rarely used for forming new words in the language. For a period the child learning English may assign the causative operation level 2 status, resulting in frequent and innovative use of verbs with a causative meaning.

3.5 Problems and Unknowns

Recent studies in the theory and acquisition of morphology raise many questions that are only beginning to be explored.

First, the causative examples collected by Bowerman suggest that acquiring the morphological system for a particular language may involve learning which rules belong to which levels – or perhaps, more specifically, which are non-productive lexical rules (level 1 rules) and which are productive rules (level 2 or 3 rules). How and why a child may misconstrue a non-productive rule as a productive one is unknown.

Another area in which language-particular facts may take some time to learn concerns the details of rules governing the internal structure of words. Although children in Gordon's experiment knew the meaning of agentive '-er' and in general produced adult-like compounds, an experiment by Clark et al. (1986) shows young children (particularly three- and four-year-olds) quite frequently producing compounds of the form 'giver-present' rather than 'present-giver'. In Clark et al.'s experiment, children were shown pictures and questioned in a way designed to elicit compounds (for example: 'This is a picture of a boy who gives presents. What would you call him? A boy who gives presents is a _____?'). Compounds of the form V-er + N ('giver-present') are ungrammatical in adult English; the first element of a N + N compound in English may not be an '-er' noun. One possible explanation for the error of putting the '-er' word first is the following. Words can be thought of as having head–modifier structure, just as sequences of words at the level of syntactic structure do (see, for example, Selkirk 1982). As outlined in the next chapter, English is a language in which the head of a phrase (roughly, the main, obligatory, element in the phrase) generally precedes modifying material. Thus verbs precede their objects ('give presents') and most of the material modifying a noun follows the noun ('presents wrapped in paper', etc.; adjectives are an exception, since they precede the noun). By contrast, at the word level, English imposes the reverse order, with the head following the modifying material, as in 'present-giver'. One explanation of early errors with compounds of the 'giver-present' type is that at an early stage children impose the same (head–complement/modifier) order on compounds that they impose on the structure of phrases. (Clark et al. give a similar explanation, which they phrase in terms of basic verb–object word order in sentences.)

One other important question now being explored is how much children know about the relationship between phrasal syntax and morphological rules. Individual words, particularly verbs, frequently restrict the nature of their modifying material. So a verb like 'catch' takes an object ('he catches rats') but verb like 'sleep' does not have an object ('*he sleeps rats'). These restrictions are known to affect morphological operations. So we have 'rat-catcher' (cf. 'to catch rats') but not '*rat-sleeper', parallel to the ungrammaticality of '*he sleeps rats' (see Roeper and Siegel 1978; Lieber 1983). The evidence to date concerning children's knowledge of morphological restrictions related to syntactic structures sometimes suggests that the child has a sophisticated knowledge, including knowledge of restrictions that are not well understood at present (for discussion and data see Bowerman 1982; Roeper 1981; Randall 1982). For example, there is a constraint against the co-occurrence of many prefixes with a particle (an intransitive preposition), as illustrated in (4):

(4a)   He folded up the blanket
(4b)   He heated up the soup
(4c)   *He unfolded up the blanket
(4d)   *He reheated up the soup

If 'un-' or 're-' is prefixed to a verb, the particle 'up' may not occur. The source of this constraint is a matter of debate in linguistic analysis (see discussion in Roeper 1981 and Smith 1981), but children appear to know that these prefixes preclude a particle. Roeper (1981) reports an experiment by L. Seraydarian, in which five-year-old children added the particle 'up' when completing sentences with the verb 'heat', but did not add the particle when completing sentences with 'reheat'. Similarly, two children studied by Bowerman (1982) created new words with the prefix 'un-', which is used in adult words such as 'uncover' and 'unfold' to mean reversal of the action of the base verb. Some of the children's innovations – such as 'he . . . unburied her' – involved understanding of the adult (reversative) meaning of the prefix, while others involved an emphatic use of 'un-', without reversative meaning. An example of the latter sort is 'then unpress it out' meaning 'press it out'. In the examples that Bowerman gives, 'un-' is used with particle verbs such as 'press out' only with emphatic force, not with reversative meaning, consistent with knowledge of the fact that reversative 'un-' prefixation in the adult language does not apply to verbs when a particle is present.

3.6   A Cross-Linguistic Perspective

Some recent studies of the acquisition of languages with rich systems of morphology have given an important perspective on results obtained in English. The system of inflectional morphology in English is quite impoverished. For verbs, past vs. present is marked ('I walked'; 'I walk'), as are person and number of the third person singular present ('I/you/we/they walk' but 'he/she/it walks'); progressive and perfective aspects are marked by a combination of auxiliary verb and inflection ('John is walking'; 'John has walked'), as detailed in chapter 5. For nouns, singular and plural are distinguished by the presence of the plural inflectional morpheme ('a box'; 'two boxes') and the genitive is marked by the morpheme '-s' ('John's book'). Many other languages have far richer systems of inflectional morphology, marking with separate morphemes person and number throughout the verbal paradigm, and/or a variety of tense, modality and aspectual modulations of verb meaning, and/or a variety of semantic roles that nouns may have in the sentence. These functions are expressed in English by non-inflectional, syntactic mechanisms. Thus, for example, future tense may be expressed by an auxiliary verb ('will'), and some nominal roles such as location and instrument are expressed via prepositions such as 'on' and 'with', as in (5):

(5)   Sue will cut the meat on the table with a knife

A basic finding of Brown (1973) was that those inflections that do exist in English are not particularly early acquisitions. Brown studied three children's use of fourteen grammatical elements, including the morphemes mentioned above: third person present singular '-s' morpheme, the regular past tense morpheme '-ed', present progressive '-ing', the regular plural morpheme for nouns '-s', and the possessive marker '-s'. Brown found that there was a fairly regular order of development for mastery of the fourteen elements for the children he studied, although there was no necessity that this should be the case, since the elements were largely heterogeneous and mastery of one did not generally of necessity require mastery of another (for discussion see Brown 1973; de Villiers and de Villiers 1985). The age at which a particular element was mastered varied from child to child, but most pertinent to the point here is that regular inflections were not particularly early acquisitions. Table 3.3 gives the ages at which the regular inflections were mastered, with two other grammatical elements (the prepositions 'in' and 'on') included for comparison. As the table shows, although the most precocious of the children (Eve) had mastered all but one of the morphemes by age two, the other two children were slower: one (Sarah) was almost five years old before she mastered the regular past tense ending.

Table 3.3 Age of mastery of seven morphemes

Morpheme	Age of mastery (yrs; mths)		
	Adam	*Sarah*	*Eve*
Present progressive '-ing' ('John is walk*ing*')	2; 6	2; 10	1; 9
Preposition 'on'	2; 6	2; 10	1; 9
Preposition 'in'	2; 6	2; 10	1; 9
Plural marker ('two books')	2; 6	2; 3	1; 11
Possessive marker ('John*'s* book')	3; 2	2; 10	1; 11
Past regular '-ed' (John walk*ed*')	3; 6	4; 10	1; 11
Third person singular ('John walk*s*')	3; 6	4; 0	2; 3

The criterion for mastery was 90 per cent or greater use in contexts where the elements were obligatory. The ages listed in the table are the ages of each child as s/he entered the stage at which the element was mastered. A series of stages was defined by Brown in terms of the mean length of utterance (MLU) for each child. Brown argued that MLU is a better predictor of mastery of the elements than age.

These results with English, a language with an impoverished inflectional system, stand in contrast to results with several other languages that have much richer morphological systems. For example, Fortescue (1984/5) reports a study of a two-year-old child's acquisition of Greenlandic Eskimo. The study was a small one, based on just half an hour of recorded speech during which the child was playing with his mother, but the results are neither more nor less remarkable because of that. Eskimo has a great number of productive affixes: 'A typical word consists of a stem followed by from zero to at least eight derivational affixes then an obligatory inflectional ending . . . all bound together by complex morphophonemic patterns of morpheme attachment and falling under one potential intonational tone unit' (Fortescue 1984/5, pp. 101–2). During the half hour recorded the child produced forty separate inflectional endings as well as twenty-four derivational affixes (Fortescue reports there are 318 inflectional and over 400 derivational endings in Greenlandic). The child's longest single word utterances are given in table 3.4.

The differences between the structures of English and Greenlandic Eskimo make it difficult accurately to match up children learning the different languages as being at 'the same stage'; for example, it is not obvious that MLU

Table 3.4 Single-word utterances of Aqissaq, a two-year-old speaker of Greenlandic Eskimo

Utterance: Morpheme-by- morpheme gloss: Meaning:	tattuus-sinnaa-nngil-angut be crowded-can-not-1st person plural indicative 'We cannot be (so) crowded together (in it)'
Utterance: Gloss: Meaning:	nangia-ssa-nngil-anga be scared-future-not-1st person singular indicative 'I shan't be scared'
Utterance: Gloss: Meaning:	uppi-ti-le-qa-akkit fall-cause-begin-intensifier-1st/2nd singular indicative 'I'm going to make you fall!'
Utterance: Gloss: Meaning:	anartarfilerisu-u-pput sewage collector-be-3rd personal plural indicative 'they are the sewage collectors'

Adapted from Fortescue (1984/5) p. 108, table 2.

can be calculated in a satisfactorily parallel manner for the two languages (see Fortescue 1984/5 for relevant discussion). But none the less the two-year-old Greenlandic child gives the impression of having forged ahead in his mastery of inflectional affixes, whereas English-speaking children may take four or more years to master all of the relatively sparse inflections of English. It might of course be that this child was a precocious learner, like Eve in Brown's study. But the Greenlandic study is not an isolated case: fairly rapid and error-free mastery of inflection seems to be the rule in languages where the inflectional system is regular and rich (see, for example, Clancy 1986; Aksu-Koc and Slobin 1986: and Mills 1986 on aspects of the acquisition of inflection in Japanese, Turkish and German, respectively).

3.7   Summary and Conclusions

Children's innovative word forms are clear evidence that the child is more than a rote-learner. The child who says 'goed' in place of 'went' for the past tense of 'go' has clearly formed a rule and is applying it to make a word that he has never heard. A similar account can be given of children's spontaneous productions of denominal verbs ('I'm crackering it') and novel causatives ('It sweats me'). Both experimental evidence and the distribution of innovative forms in production argue that the rules the child applies are governed by principles of word formation that not only license some of the innovations for which we have evidence, but also block other conceivable rules. Children in Gordon's study created compound forms with irregular plurals as the first element ('teeth-eater'), but failed to produce compounds with regular plurals as the first element ('bead-eater' not '*beads-eater'). This distribution of responses will follow if children obey the constraints of a recent model of the organization of morphology, the level-ordering model of Kiparsky (1983); it cannot be accounted for in terms of the frequency with which children heard plurals in the experiment or the frequency of different plural types in compounds in the adult language. The level-ordering model can also account for the fact that children frequently produce denominal verbs, but rarely produce deverbal nouns.

Recent linguistic studies of morphology raise many questions and hypotheses that are only beginning to be looked at in child language studies. The causative examples collected by Bowerman (1982) suggest that children may in some cases make errors in assigning particular rules to levels in the level-ordering model. Errors such as 'giver-present' are consistent with the hypothesis that at an early stage the child may impose the head–modifier order of his language at the level of word structure. The extent of children's knowledge of the relationship between syntactic restrictions and restrictions on word formation is just beginning to be explored. Studies of the acquisition of languages which, unlike English, have a rich system of inflectional morphology indicate that the pace at which children master inflections in English is comparatively slow, a finding that is not well understood.

Questions and Exercises

1. Berko (1958) demonstrated children's command of several morphological endings with a nonsense word test. She showed children pictures and supplied nonsense words for objects and actions and then asked questions that required the child to put an ending on the nonsense word. For example, children were taught the word 'wug' as the word for (a picture of) an imaginary bird-like creature; then a second creature of the same kind was introduced. The child was questioned as follows: 'This is a wug. Now there are two of them. There are two _____?' The numeral two requires a plural noun, and a child who supplied the correct plural form ('wugs') clearly demonstrated that s/he had command of the regular plural rule in English. (Preschool children could do this test.) Try to think up a similar nonsense word test to elicit from children use of the following affixes:

'-er' agentive ('bake'; 'baker')
'-ly' manner adverbs ('happy'; 'happily')

Try your test out on some adults and/or children.

2. Table 3.2 contains examples of innovative causative forms. In what way is the last example different from the first three?

3. Dutch seems to be a language that has counter-examples to the claim that plurals cannot appear inside compounds (see Gordon 1985b). There are two different plural endings ('-en' and '-s'), whose use separates nouns into two different classes, for example, *tand-en* ('teeth') and *vleugel-s* ('wings'). The '-en' plural is the most frequent, although the '-s' plural also occurs with some frequency. The '-en' plural sometimes affects the pronunciation of the word to which it is added as, for example, in *schip*; *schepen* ('ship'; 'ships'). There are compounds in Dutch such as *tand-en borstel* ('tooth-plural-brush'). How can these facts be accounted for, consistently with the level-ordering model described in this chapter? What does this imply with respect to what children have to learn about the morphology of their language?

4.   Clark et al. (1986) found that children do produce ungrammatical compounds of the form 'hugger-man', meaning a man who hugs. These forms are doubly ungrammatical, since subjects may not occur inside '-er' compounds (as we noted in the text, 'man-eater' means something that eats men, not a man that eats). (Lieber 1983 gives a principled account of the exclusion of subjects from compounds.) Can you think of other compounds in English (not involving the '-er' ending) that might be a model for this error and so avoid the conclusion that children can include subjects in their compounds?

4   The Acquisition of Syntax

Syntactic acquisition is the area of child language acquisition that has been most studied from the perspective of linguistic theory. This is probably because it is syntactic facts that have been most frequently used, particularly by Chomsky and others, in establishing arguments for the position that our linguistic abilities are not derivable from other aspects of cognition and that linguistic constructs are innate (see chapter 6). This chapter summarizes some basic findings about the nature of syntactic systems, together with results from language acquisition studies. The broad descriptive framework used is the 'government and binding' theory of Chomsky (1981) and later works.

4.1   Syntactic Structures and Universal Grammar

4.1.1   Basic Syntax

Several concepts are basic to the description of syntactic systems. Words are assigned to syntactic categories (noun, verb, adjective, preposition and others to be mentioned below); words head or 'project' phrases – thus a noun heads a noun phrase, a verb heads a verb phrase, etc.; and these syntactic phrases organize the linear string of words that makes up a sentence into a hierarchical structure. Thus English sentences such as (1) and (2) will have the approximate structures shown in (3) and (4):

(1)   Sue left
(2)   The judge gave the verdict

(3)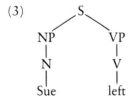

S = Sentence

N = Noun

V = Verb

NP = Noun phrase

VP = Verb phrase

(4)

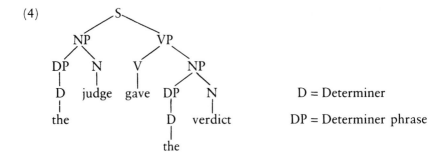

D = Determiner

DP = Determiner phrase

Sentences and phrases may be embedded one within another, producing structures of potentially infinite depth. For example, sentences can be stacked up inside a verb phrase, as illustrated in (5a–c) and (6):

(5a)   Sue said that Horace sighed
(5b)   Sue said that Hilda thought that Horace sighed
(5c)   Sue said that Hilda thought Alice said that . . . Horace sighed

(6)

C = Complementizer

Similarly, relative clauses follow the noun they modify in English, and again can be stacked up to build potentially infinite phrases:

(7a) Dogs that gnaw on bones
(7b) Dogs that gnaw on bones that fall from trucks
(7c) Dogs that gnaw on bones that fall from trucks that drive into towns that . . .

Languages differ in the nature of their basic syntax. Languages such as English, with a subject–verb–(object) order in simple sentences, are *right-branching* – the head of the phrase is generally on the left and modifying material is built up to the right, as illustrated by the structure in (6). Languages such as Japanese, with a subject–(object)–verb basic order for simple sentences, are *left-branching*, building up a modification structure to the left of the head. Thus a complement sentence is placed to the left of the verb it modifies in Japanese, and the pattern of embedding of nodes in the VP will be broadly the mirror image of that for English, as shown schematically in (8):

(8)
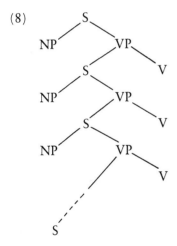

And in Japanese, relative clauses precede the noun they modify.

Languages such as English and Japanese are frequently called *configurational* languages, because they organize the linear string of words into hierarchical structures of some complexity. Other, so-called *non-configurational*, languages have 'flatter' structures, and permit almost free variation of order within sentence units. The Australian language Warlpiri is an example of a non-configurational language (see, for example, Hale 1983 for a description of some of the properties of Warlpiri). The division between configurational and non-configurational languages is not always clear-cut (it has been argued that Japanese has at least some non-configurational properties), and even non-configurational languages are held to build hierarchical structures at some level of abstraction. Nor is the organization of phrases perfectly regular in all languages – for example, in English adjectives precede the noun they modify, contrary to the general right-branching pattern of the language.[1] But the general division between configurational languages, with relatively rigid word orders and a characteristic type of hierarchical structure (left- or right-branching), and non-configurational languages with free word order is valid as a first approximation and represents a basic distinction for which the theory of syntax must account.

4.1.2   Levels of Representation

Almost all modern work in syntactic theory recognizes that sentence structures involve 'invisible' (or 'inaudible') parts: syntactic positions that are not fleshed out by words. Positing such invisible categories aids, *inter alia*, in the explanation of the way we understand some types of ambiguity and relations between non-adjacent elements. For example, the title of an article by the psycholinguist Richard Cromer,

(9)   Children are nice to understand

is ambiguous: it can mean either 'It is nice to understand children' or 'It is nice of children to be understanding'. This ambiguity can be represented if the rules of English syntax permit two different structures to be imposed on the string in (9). On the first reading given above there will be an empty object position of the embedded verb, to which the main clause subject 'children' is linked, as shown schematically in (10a), accounting for the fact that 'children' is understood as object of the embedded verb; on the second reading there is no empty object position and the main clause subject is linked to the empty subject position of the embedded sentence, as shown in (10b), accounting for the fact that 'children' is understood as subject of the verb 'understand':

(10a)   Children are nice [Ø to understand Ø]

(10b)   Children are nice [Ø to understand]

Several types of sentence, not merely ambiguous sentences, give rise to abstract, 'empty' categories. Some very common types of sentence have orders that deviate from the basic word order of the language. For example, in questions in English, the questioned element appears at the front of the sentence, and may correspond to a variety of types of phrase and positions in the sentence structure that follows. Positing invisible syntactic positions helps us to account for these relations. We can represent the fact that a question word such as 'what' in (11) is understood as object of the verb 'drink' by postulating an empty object position, to which the question word is linked:

(11a)   What will Frances drink?
(11b)   What will Frances drink [Ø]?

Similarly for an object placed in initial position for emphasis:

(12a)   Drano, he drank!
(12b)   Drano, he drank [Ø]!

In short, we can account for facts about our understanding of sentences with an order that deviates from the basic order of the language by reference to a more abstract structure in which that basic order is represented. Chomskyan generative grammar proposes an abstract level of representation, deep structure (or D-structure), in which the basic order of phrases is represented, as well as S-structure (or surface structure; see note 4), in which the actual linear order of phrases is observed and deep structure positions of phrases are represented by empty categories. The 'derivation' of a sentence involves changing D-structures into S-structures, by moving elements from their D-structure positions; the relationship between moved elements and their underlying position is represented by placing an identical index on the two. So the sentence (12a) will have a derivation roughly as given in (13):

(13)   D-structure

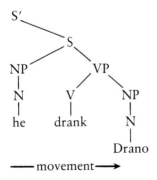

— movement —➔

S-structure

```
              S'
           /     \
        NPᵢ        S
         |       /   \
         N     NP     VP
         |      |    /  \
       Drano    N   V    NP
                |   |     |
                he drank  tᵢ        t = trace
```

In the S-structure in (13) the moved NP occupies a presentential slot, under the S′ node that also dominates complementizers such as 'that' in (5)–(6); an inaudible copy of the moved phrase (its *trace*) is left in the D-structure position of the moved phrase. Likewise, question formation involves moving a whole phrase to presentential position (the phrase may be only one word long, as in (11), or it may be more complex, as in, for example, 'Which roses with no thorns did Sue draw?'). Question formation will in fact involve a double movement, since an auxiliary verb such as 'will' in the example (11a) is inverted around the subject:

(14)   D-structure

```
            S'
            |
            S
          /  |  \
        NP   I   VP
         |   |   | \
         N  will V   NP        I = Inflection
         |      |    |
      Frances  drink N
                     |
                    what
```

⟶ movement ⟶

S-structure

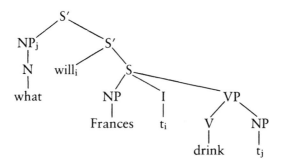

(The inflection node is a ~~syntactic position associated~~ with some morphological features (e.g. ~~tense~~) ~~and some auxiliary verbs~~, such as the modal 'will'; some of its prop~~erties are taken up in chapter 5~~).

In Chomsky's t~~heory of syntax a third level of syn~~tactic representation is proposed: this is lo~~gical form (or LF). Logical form rep~~resents aspects of the meaning of a sentenc~~e that depend on its syntactic struct~~re and which are not represented in D-struc~~ture or S-structure. LFs are created f~~rom S-structures by movement of elements a~~nd co-indexation of elements. Let u~~s first look at some examples of the latter.

Not all empty position~~s are created by m~~ovement (leaving a trace). For example, the empty subject ~~position in~~ some types of embedded sentences is represented by an abstract pr~~onom~~inal element (PRO). We have already seen a sentence with such an empty position – a more exact structure for the reading of (9) ('Children are nice to understand') in which 'children' is taken as logical object of 'understand' is one in which there is a PRO subject of the embedded verb; thus (10a) can be recast as follows:

(15)   Children$_i$ are nice [PRO to understand t$_i$]

with the subject PRO having no specified reference.[2] In other examples, PRO must refer to a specific NP inside the sentence. This will be the case for the alternative reading of (9), and for examples such as (16):

(16)   My aunt promised [PRO to leave]

where the subject PRO of 'leave' is interpreted as 'my aunt'. The interpretation of the subject PRO in (16) does not change, even if we embed the sentence (16) inside another sentence:

(17)   Lucinda said my aunt promised [PRO to leave]

although there is no logically necessary reason for that – grammar aside, (17) might well mean something like (18):

(18)   Lucinda said my aunt promised that she (Lucinda) could leave

but it does not. The reference of PRO will be determined by rules that place indexes on the NP to which it may refer. Thus 'my aunt' and PRO will receive the same index in (16). Similarly, co-indexation will be used to represent co-reference relations for overt pronouns, such as the definite pronoun 'him' in (19) and the reflexive pronoun 'himself' in (20):

(19)   Lucifer claimed that the angel deceived him
(20)   Lucifer claimed that the angel deceived himself

In (19), 'him' may refer to 'Lucifer', but not to 'the angel'; in (20) 'himself' must refer to 'the angel' and not to 'Lucifer'. These facts are dependent on syntactic structure (as we will see in section 4.4.1), and are accounted for by rules and principles that apply to S-structures to produce appropriately indexed LFs.

Movement, too, applies to S-structures. The trace left by movement is considered equivalent to a variable in an operator-variable relation. Thus the S-structure in (14) can be construed as comparable to a representation along the lines of (21), where 'for which' is intended as an English language representation of an interrogative operator corresponding to question words such as 'what' and 'x' is a variable corresponding to the S-structure trace of the NP.[3]

(21)

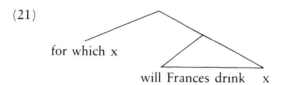

Movement as an operation between S-structure and LF has been argued to be necessary for the interpretation of some sentences containing question words that have not yet been moved at S-structure (as, for example, the word 'what' in 'Who ate what?') and sentences containing quantifier words such as 'all' and 'every'. For example, movement between S-structure and LF provides one way to account for the fact that a sentence such as 'Every leprechaun kissed a unicorn' has two meanings, corresponding to whether each leprechaun kissed the same unicorn, or not. There is only one S-structure for the sentence, but its ambiguity can be represented in terms of two logical forms, differing in whether the quantifier corresponding to 'every' or a quantifier corresponding to 'a' occupies the topmost position in the structure.

To summarize, three levels of syntactic representation are proposed for sentences: D-structure, S-structure and LF.[4] The relationship between them can be represented as in figure 4.1.

What is the nature of the lexicon, which is the repository of lexical items used to fill out D-structure trees? Much of the information in the lexicon of

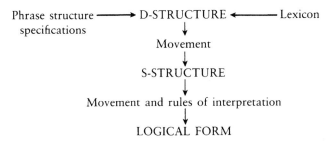

Figure 4.1

a generative grammar is the sort of information in an ordinary dictionary: an indication of the pronunciation of a word (as we saw in chapter 1, what is represented in the lexicon of a generative grammar will be aspects of pronunciation that are not predictable) and of its meaning (see chapter 5), together with information about the local syntactic environments into which a word can enter – its *subcategorizations*. Thus, for example, a transitive verb such as 'devour' subcategorizes for a direct object NP; an intransitive verb such as 'dive' does not:

(22a)　John devoured a banana
(22b)　*John devoured
(23a)　*John dived a banana
(23b)　John dived

Subcategorial restrictions limit the phrasal categories that can be sister to a node – thus a verb can in general impose subcategorial restrictions on the nodes that occur with it directly under the VP node, but not on the internal structure of those sister nodes; nor do subcategorial restrictions generally extend to the subject NP.

As well as subcategorial restrictions, the lexical entry for a word will specify the semantic or *thematic* roles associated with the phrases with which it combines, including the subject NP. Thus in (23b), the subject of 'dived' has the thematic role 'agent', but if we change 'dived' to 'died':

(24)　John died

the subject NP is no longer an agent, but rather the entity to whom the event of dying occurs, and thus has the thematic role of *experiencer* or *theme*. There is controversy about the exact set of thematic roles needed in grammatical descriptions, but the set is frequently taken to include *agent, patient, experiencer, theme* (thing acted upon or affected, perhaps subsuming patient and experiencer), *goal* (approximately, recipient or end-point with respect to physical or mental transfer of some entity) and *location*.

The role of notions such as 'subject' and 'object' in grammatical theory is highly controversial. However, it is widely thought that the grammatical relation subject (or 'external argument' in the terminology of Williams 1981) has some special status, and the thematic role assigned to the subject position is frequently marked as such in the lexical entry of verbs.

4.1.3   Universal Grammar: Principles and Parameters

The overall form of the syntactic component given in figure 4.1 is that found in Chomsky's work from the late 1970s onwards. In terms of the general organization of subcomponents, the organization of the grammar does not seem very different from that in Chomsky's 1965 book *Aspects of the Theory of Syntax*. In *Aspects* there was a level of deep structure, representing basic word order, which was transformed into surface structure, representing more or less the actual order of words in the sentence, and there was a set of interpretative rules that produced a level of semantic representation. One difference established early on between the *Aspects* model and later models was that in *Aspects* semantic interpretation is based on deep structure, whereas in later models it is based on surface structure as shown in figure 4.1 (see Newmeyer 1980 and Kempson 1977 for summaries of the debates surrounding this change). In this model, S-structure retains D-structure information thanks to traces and other null elements.

Another fundamental difference between sixties-style syntax and current work is a change in emphasis from the formulation of individual rules of grammar to the formulation of general principles from which the properties of particular grammatical phenomena will follow. The most frequently given illustration of this is the fact that whereas in the earlier-style grammar there were a great many different transformational rules linking deep structures to surface structures (e.g. a specific rule of question formation, a rule for topicalizing phrases, a rule of auxiliary verb movement, various rules deleting elements, etc.), the difference between the D-structure and S-structure levels in current theory is reduced to the results of a single general operation: movement. What can move, and where to, are motivated and restricted by the dictates of principles of grammar.

The form and nature of these principles and the range of variation in their execution is a matter of the theory of universal grammar. Some principles will be absolute. For example, phrases may move to a position higher in the syntactic tree, but not to a position lower in the tree ('height' may be defined in terms of the c-command relation detailed in section 4.4 below). Other principles may take on a limited number of values, accounting for observed differences in human languages. For example, the theory of phrase structure must permit both head-first and head-final type languages and must allow also for free word order languages. These are the broad parameters of difference in phrase structure. This general approach to universal grammar is thus termed the 'principles and parameters' approach.

4.1.4   Modules of Government Binding Theory

'Government binding theory' is a general term used to refer to the theory of principles and parameters developed in Chomsky's 1981 book *Lectures on Government and Binding* and later work. Its general goal is to identify principles that constrain the levels of representation and their connections one to another. Syntactic theory on this view comprises several interacting modules, each of which constrains a particular type of grammatical entity and construct. Here I will simply list the major subtheories, with an indication of their functions and some examples of the way they interact. More details are supplied for some of the subtheories in the sections on acquisition below.

X-bar (X') theory   X' theory is the theory governing phrase structure configurations and hence controlling the level of D-structure. (X is to be construed as a variable ranging over the various syntactic categories, N, V, P, etc.) The term *bar* or *prime* (X') refers to layers of structure posited within a phrase, e.g.

$$N'' = NP$$
$$|$$
$$N' = \text{intermediate level}$$
$$|$$
$$N = \text{word level}$$

Since intermediate phrasal levels are generally not crucial in what follows, with one or two exceptions only the word and phrase levels are given.

Theta theory   Theta theory governs the assignment of thematic roles.

Case theory   NPs are assumed to require *case* – a marking by another element (verb, preposition or inflection) that may or may not be overtly realized as a morphological element of the phrase. In English overt marking occurs only in a limited number of cases – nouns in determiner position are distinguished from other nouns ('Claude bribes' but 'Claude's bribe'), and subject pronouns have a different form from pronouns in other positions ('She left' but 'find her address and mail her her book'). Case theory is concerned with the conditions on assignment of case.

Binding theory Binding theory deals with restrictions in co-reference of anaphoric elements, including definite and reflexive pronouns and the trace left by movement.

Bounding theory Bounding theory deals with structural restrictions on the operation of movement.

Control theory Control theory is the theory determining the referential possibilities for the empty (PRO) subject of clauses.

Each of the subtheories is a semi-autonomous module, with its own principles. However, the subtheories draw in many instances on the same concepts. For example, the notion 'height on the tree' (defined in section 4.4 below in terms of c-command) enters into principles of binding theory, bounding theory and control theory.[5]

   To get a sense of the interaction between modules and also the manner in which principles of the theory can force the application of operations, consider a passive sentence in English, such as

(25) Pies will be devoured by choirboys

This sentence is derived by movement of a direct object NP into a subject position that is empty in D-structure:

(26) D-structure

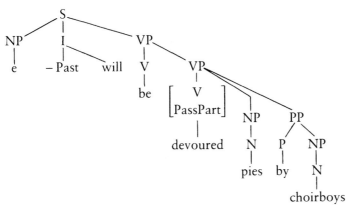

PassPart = passive participle
e = empty node, with no lexical material inserted in D-structure

———movement——→

S-structure

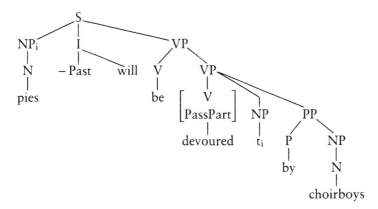

The general spirit of the theory is to account for as much as is possible of the relationship between D-structure and S-structure in terms of principles that extend beyond the derivation of this individual sentence or passive sentences in general. Thus, it is claimed, *inter alia*, that the trace left by movement in passives (as well as in questions) is mandated by a general principle, the projection principle:

> *The projection principle*: representations at each syntactic level are projected from the lexicon, preserving the subcategorial properties of lexical items.

'Devour' is obligatorily transitive and the projection principle requires that a trace be present in object position, even after movement. Moreover, the movement to subject position in the formation of a passive will follow from two separate requirements – that movement be to a position higher in the tree (precluding, for example, forming a passive by moving the object to a position inside a prepositional phrase) and a requirement of case theory, the case filter:

The case filter: every (phonetically realized) NP must be assigned case.

If a passive participle is not part of the inventory of elements that may assign case, movement to the subject position (where case is assigned by the element I (inflection)) will be needed for the D-structure object of 'devoured' to pass the case filter.

4.1.5 Government Binding Theory and the Acquisition of Syntax

A child's acquisition of the syntax of his native language should be, to put it grossly, a matter exactly as complex and as simple as the theory of government and binding itself. That is, he must find out which type of language he is learning (what the parameter values for his language in the various modules of the theory are), and in doing so he should be aided by the fact that such variation is limited and that general principles and concepts traverse the different modules, reducing the complexity of the system. A common-sense first guess at how syntax acquisition progresses might be to say that the child first must set the general configurational parameters of his language and then may take some time to sort out the details of the system within the separate modules. Although many of the studies of language acquisition mentioned in the following sections were not carried out in the context of government binding theory, we can use their results to piece together a picture of development largely compatible with this view of syntax development as 'basics first, details and interactions later'.

4.2 The Outer Course of Development

Before beginning a topic-oriented account of syntax development, it is worth summarizing some basics about the outer course of language development –

what kinds of utterances a child tends to produce at what ages. In the early 1970s, many detailed studies were carried out on children's early speech (for examples, see Brown 1973; papers in Ferguson and Slobin 1973; Bowerman 1973); these studies systematically recorded the language of one or more children and (together with older diary studies such as Grégoire 1937, 1947) provide a body of data concerning the emergence of grammar. Such studies revealed some striking regularities in development, with the same or very similar patterns being found for different children in different homes and environments. Although there are sometimes substantial differences in the age at which a child passes through a particular stage of development, the general pattern is the same in most respects from child to child, as demonstrated by Brown (1973). Moreover, there are general age guidelines that we can indicate. At around the turn of the first year, children began to produce one-word utterances – that is, single words that are for the most part recognizable words in the adult vocabulary. By twenty months the child has a vocabulary of about fifty words (Nelson 1973) and enters a 'two-word' stage, combining words together, although not always in sequences that are well formed in the adult language. Children's early multi-word utterances are frequently referred to as 'telegraphic speech' since children learning languages such as English tend to omit the sorts of words (determiners such as 'the' and 'a', auxiliary verbs, prepositions) that we leave out when we write a telegram. By the end of the third year, the child may be producing a range of complex sentence types (complements to verbs and relative clauses) and a four-year-old frequently gives the impression of being a fully fluent speaker of a language comparable to the adult language he is learning, if not identical to it. The reader can get some sense of the kinds of utterances and sentence types found in early child speech by studying table 4.1, which gives data from the early multi-word speech of one child, and table 4.2, which shows a typical order of emergence of a number of sentence types, based on several studies.

4.3 Early Syntax

Determining the exact nature of the child's earliest syntactic system is an extraordinarily difficult task and we will go back to debates surrounding the earliest stages in the final section of this chapter. Here it is sufficient to observe that there is evidence that fairly early on – certainly by the third year – children do have a system that conforms in basic ways to the syntactic patterns of the language being learnt. Evidence for this view comes from two areas of grammar: phrase structure configurations and subjectless sentences.

4.3.1 Early Phrase Structure

When do children catch on to which of the basic language types they are learning: configurational or non-configurational and, within configurational

Table 4.1 Early multi-word speech

Pivotal constructions

all broke	no bed	more car[d]	other bib	airplane by[f]
all buttoned	no down[a]	more cereal	other bread	siren by
all clean	no fix	more cookie	other milk	
all done	no home	more fish	other pants	mail come
all dressed	no mama[b]	more high[e]	other part	mama come
all dry	no more	more hot	other piece	
all fix	no pee	more juice	other pocket	clock on there
all gone	no plug	more read	other shirt	up on there
all messy	no water	more sing	other shoe	hot in there
all through	no wet[c]	more toast		milk in there
		more walk		light up there
all wet			boot off	fall down there
	see baby		light off	kitty down there
	see pretty	hi Calico	pants off	more down there
I see	see train	hi mama	shirt off	sit down there
I shut		hi papa	shoe off	cover down there
I sit			water off	other cover down there

Other utterances

airplane all gone	byebye back	what's that	look at this
Calico all gone	byebye Calico	what's this	outside more
Calico all done[g]	byebye car	mail man	pants change
salt all shut	byebye papa	mail car	dry pants
all done milk	calico byebye	our car	off bib
all done now	papa byebye	our door	down there
all gone juice		papa away	up on there some more
all gone outside[h]			
all gone pacifier			

Andrew's word combinations, first five months (from Braine 1963). First five months = first five months after combinations of two or more words were used.

[a] 'Don't put me down'
[b] 'I don't want to go to mama'
[c] 'I'm not wet'
[d] 'Drive around some more'
[e] 'There's more up there'
[f] 'A plane is flying past'
[g] Said after the death of Calico the cat
[h] Said when the door is shut: 'The outside is all gone'

Table 4.2 Emergence of sentence types

Approximate age	Type of speech	QUESTIONS	CO-ORDINATION	EMBEDDING
18–20 months	One word utterances			
20–24 months	Telegraphic speech	Yes–no questions signalled by intonation only: Fraser water? See hole? No eat? Wh-questions with the form wh-word–NP or wh-word–NP–V. Question words limited generally to 'what' and 'where' and wh-questions involve only a narrow range of verbs: What(s) that? What cowboy doing? Where Anna pencil? Where kitty? Where horse go?		
Third year		'Why' and 'why not' questions; 'what' questions with a wider range of verbs: Why you smiling? Why not he eat? What the dollie have? Yes–no questions with some auxiliary verbs and some inversion of the subject and auxiliary: Will you help me? Can I have a piece of paper? Can't it be a bigger truck? Wh-questions with some auxiliaries but frequently without inversion of the subject and auxiliary: Why kitty can't stand up? Which way they should go?	Co-ordination by juxtaposition: You lookit that book; I lookit this book. Co-ordination with *and*: He was stuck and I got him out	V–V sentences, often with 'wanna' (want to), 'hafta' (have to) and 'gotta' (got to) as the first verb: I hafta peepee. Infinitival complements with the infinitive marker 'to': I want to go. Embedded wh-complements: I know when to go. Subordinate clauses introduced by 'if', 'so', 'cos', 'when': I want this doll because she's big. Some types of relative clauses: .... ones Mommy got .... ball that I got. Tensed complements to verbs: I {guess / think} she's sick

Based primarily on Limber (1973); Klima and Bellugi (1973).

languages, left-branching or right-branching? Little empirical work has been done on the acquisition of non-configurational languages (see Bavin and Shopin 1985 for one study of children past the earliest stages and Pinker 1984 for some discussion of how early acquisition of non-configurational syntax might be expected to progress). However, data on the acquisition of configurational languages suggest that the basic distinction in branching structure is quickly incorporated into the child's grammatical system.

Children's telegraphic speech is frequently characterized by what have been called 'pivot–open' patterns. Children tend to place certain words in either initial or final position in the utterance. Braine (1963) called these words 'pivots'. Other words ('open' class words) have a freer distribution and can occur in either initial or final position in combination with a pivot or another open word. The examples of child speech in table 4.1 provide some good examples of such 'pivot–open' speech. The words 'all', 'no', 'more' and 'other' tend to occur in initial position and the words 'off' and 'there' tend to occur in final position; these words can be characterized as pivots. Words such as 'papa' and 'Calico', by contrast, occur in either initial or final position and can be characterized as open words. Although the use of individual words as 'pivot' or 'open' words is not completely invariable (see Bowerman 1973 for one discussion), the overall distribution of facts observed by Braine and others does point to certain words having priority in utterance-final or utterance-initial position; thus from a very early age children's utterances are governed by a system that goes beyond simple concatenation of words. Moreover, it is possible to interpret pivot–open speech in terms of first explorations with phrase structure schemata. Above we saw that the phrase structure component of the grammar offers a basic example of parameterization: configurational languages may be head-initial or head-final. Pivots can be viewed as occupying the position at the head of a phrase, with pivot-initial and pivot-final utterances then corresponding to realizations of each of the two basic patterns for configurational languages:

Right-branching   Left-branching

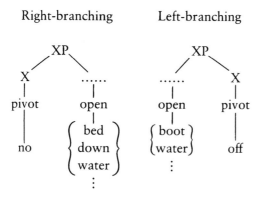

On this view, 'pivot' and 'open' can be seen as under-specified syntactic categories corresponding to the head and modifier positions in adult phrase structure schemata, rather than (as the original work of Braine implied) as part of a system quite unrelated to the rules and structures of adult languages. Moreover, the distribution of pivots and opens suggests that the child's system becomes very quickly tuned to the particular language type he is acquiring: in Braine's study, and also Bloom's study (1970) of other English-speaking children, initial pivots were more frequent than final pivots, as one would expect if pivots represent a head position, and the child has already tuned in to the fact that English is right-branching.

For slightly more advanced children, there is experimental evidence that the child's grammar conforms to the structural pattern basic to her language. In studies of children learning English (Lust 1977), children aged two to three did better at repeating sentences such as (27):

(27)   The teddy bear walks and sleeps

than they did at repeating sentences such as (28):

(28)   The kittens and dogs hide

Sentences of type (27) have a surface structure in which the right-hand side of the tree consists of a relatively 'heavy' phrase, the conjunction 'walks and sleeps'. By contrast, sentences such as (28), with a conjoined noun phrase as subject, have a structure in which the left-hand side of the tree is complex. Thus the general configurational pattern for (27) is right-branching, with expanded material to the right, whereas the general pattern for (28) is left-branching, with expanded material to the left:

Pattern for (27)   Pattern for (28)

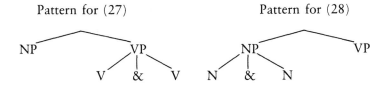

The fact that young English-speaking children do better at repeating sentences of type (27) than sentences of type (28) suggests that they are attuned to the configurational patterns most typical of their language. This conclusion is confirmed by the fact that the opposite order of difficulty was found for young Japanese-speaking children (Lust and Wakayama 1979). For Japanese

children, sentences equivalent to (27), such as (29), were harder to repeat than
sentences such as (30), which is parallel to (28):

(29) *Inu-wa hoeru-shi kamitsuku*
      dog topic bark and/also bite
      'Dogs bark and also bite'
(30) *Sumire-to tanpopo-ga saku*
      violet and dandelion subject bloom
      'Violets and dandelions bloom'

This contrast in performance for the two sentence types argues that children
rapidly become attuned to the phrase structure patterns of the particular
language they are learning (see also Tager-Flusberg et al. 1982; Lust and
Chien 1984; Clahsen and Muysken 1986).

4.3.2   Subjectless Sentences

Sensitivity to the parameter settings of the particular language to which the
child is exposed has also been argued for in recent analyses of a phenomenon
common in early child speech: subjectless sentences. Many studies have
observed that in early child speech sentences are produced both with and
without subjects. The following examples from the speech of a child under
two (from Bloom 1970, quoted in Hyams 1986) illustrate the phenomenon:

(31) throw away   Mommy throw it away
      make a house   'chine make noise
      helping mommy   Lois coming

One of the areas of cross-linguistic difference in adult grammars that has been
quite intensively studied in recent theoretical syntax is the permissibility of
subjectless sentences. Languages differ in whether they permit sentences with
no overt subject in main clauses. English is a language that does not permit
such sentences, Italian is a language that does. Thus in English only the first
of the pair of sentences in (32) is permitted, whereas in Italian both versions
of (33) are permitted:

(32a) I am going to the cinema
(32b) *Am going to the cinema

(33a) *Io vado al cinema*
       I go to the movies
(33b) *Vado al cinema*   (examples from Hyams 1986)

The presence of an overt pronominal subject is thus optional in 'pro-drop' languages such as Italian. The existence of null subjects in simple sentences is part of a cluster of a number of grammatical phenomena which define different families of languages. For example, languages which permit null subjects tend to be those which have a rich set of inflectional endings on the verb: intuitively, this permits information concerning the nature of the subject (whether it is first person, second person or third person, etc.) to be retrieved, although the situation cross-linguistically is in fact more complex than that (see Jaeggli and Safir 1989). And the presence of null subjects has been argued to correlate with other subtle grammatical phenomena for which no such intuitively appealing link exists (see Rizzi 1982 and chapter 6 below).

The fact that young children learning English omit subjects raises the possibility that they temporarily entertain a grammatical system that is more like that of Italian than that of English: that is, it is conceivable that children learning English begin with a grammar in which subjectless sentences are grammatical. That in fact was the proposal of Hyams (1986). This proposal is of great potential interest for a theory of language acquisition, since it in effect claims that at a very early stage the grammatical system of the child is an incorrect one *vis-à-vis* a basic property of the language to which he is exposed.

It seems likely that the basic claim made by Hyams is not correct and that at the stages of speech that Hyams analysed the child learning English already has some awareness that subjects are required in his language, in contrast to Italian-speaking children, who show some awareness of the possibility of omitting subjects. Valian (1989) presents two types of evidence in favour of this view. First, she shows that there is no clear statistical relationship in the speech samples of the English-speaking children between use of subjects and other grammatical features that cluster with the phenomenon of null subjects. For example, modal verbs (such as 'will' in 'I will go') in languages such as English have been argued in some grammatical accounts to have properties that mandate the use of a subject, but Valian found no statistical relation between children's use of modals and use of subjects which could be separated out from general effects of increased age and sentence length. Second, a comparison between young English-speaking children and young Italian-speaking children showed that the former use subjects more frequently than the latter. Thus, although young English-speaking children make the error of leaving out subjects, it is also the case that their speech reflects some knowledge of the fact that subjects must be present. Their omission of subjects may be a matter of problems in executing that knowledge (Valian 1989; Bloom 1989; see also Lillo-Martin 1986 for evidence contrary to the idea that subjectless sentences represent a general first stage in language acquisition).

To summarize, two frequently observed phenomena in the early speech of children, pivot–open type utterances and subjectless sentences, are consistent with the idea that children very quickly develop a syntactic system that reflects the patterns of the adult language. In the terminology of parameter setting, children early on set the head-position parameter for phrase structure and the pro-drop parameter that separates English-type languages from Italian-type languages.

4.4   Syntax in the Pre-School Years

This section deals with the syntactic knowledge of children aged approximately two and a half to six or seven years. Once the basics of the language system are in place (whether the language is left- or right-branching, pro-drop, etc.) it makes sense to ask about the development of operations and principles whose application depends on the basic structures. We will look at knowledge and development in three of the modules of grammar listed in the first section: binding theory, bounding theory and control.

4.4.1   Children's Knowledge of the Binding Theory

As we saw in section 4.1, the binding theory is concerned with the referential possibilities for various types of pronouns. The principles of the binding theory operate on S-structure and constrain the co-indexing of elements in logical form. Some of the strongest and most interesting results in recent child language acquisition research have concerned children's knowledge of these principles.

The binding theory can be given in a simplified form in terms of three principles:

The binding theory
Principle A: An anaphor must be bound in its local domain
Principle B: A pronominal must be free in its local domain
Principle C: An R-expression must be free

The crucial terms to understand are: *anaphor*; *pronominal*; *R-expression*; *bound* (and *free*); and *domain*.

An *anaphor* is a pronoun of the type of reflexives such as 'himself' in English, for which there must always be a co-referential NP in the sentence. A *pronominal* is a pronoun of the type of definite pronouns such as 'he' or 'him' in English, which may or may not refer to an NP in the same sentence (i.e. it may refer to an entity – mentioned or unmentioned – in the discourse environment). *R-expression* is an abbreviation for 'referring-expression' and for our purposes it will mean a noun phrase such as 'John', 'the boy', 'the government', 'a girl I know', etc. An element is *bound* when it is co-indexed to another element that is at the same height or higher in the syntactic structure. If something is not bound, it is *free*. *Height* can be formally defined in terms of the relation *c-command* (short for 'constituent-command'). The following definition of c-command derives from Reinhart (1976):

C-command
Node A c-commands node B if and only if the first branching node above A dominates B and neither A nor B dominates the other.

In the schematic tree below, node Q c-commands nodes R, S and T; node R c-commands node Q, node S c-commands T and T c-commands S. In other words, a node c-commands all its sister nodes and all the nodes dominated by its sisters:

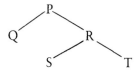

Finally, *domain* refers to the structural 'space' in which the principles operate, and for our present purposes we can take the domain of an element (anaphor or pronominal) to be the S node most immediately above that element.

We will look at some facts that are accounted for by the binding principles and then at children's sensitivity to relevant distinctions in the adult grammar, taking first principle C (which does not require reference to the notion of domain) and then principles A and B.

Principle C Principle C is the principle that accounts for facts such as those illustrated by (34a–b):

(34a)   He said that John would leave before noon
(34b)   John said that he would leave before noon

In (34a), the pronoun 'he' and the noun 'John' may not be co-referential, but they may be co-referential in (34b). The basic generalization is that a pronoun and a full noun phrase cannot co-refer when the pronoun is in a structurally dominant position with respect to the noun phrase. The structure for (34a) is given in (35):

(35)

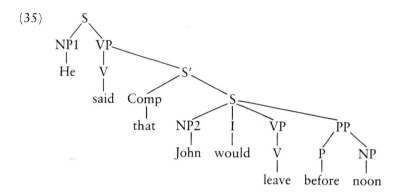

It is easy to see that the top NP (NP1) is in a structurally superior position to the lower subject (NP2). 'Structural superiority' can be defined in terms of c-command: NP1 c-commands NP2. Principle C accounts for the ungram-maticality of (34a), on the interpretation where 'he' and 'John' are co-referential, in the following way: NP2 ('John') is an R-expression; if it is co-indexed with an NP that c-commands it (NP1), it is bound. But principle C requires that an R-expression be free (not bound) and so under principle C co-indexation of NP2 to NP1 in (35) is barred, and 'he' and 'John' may not be taken to be co-referential. If the positions of the pronoun and the referring expression are reversed, as in (34b), co-indexation can take place with no violation of the principle: the lower NP (NP2) is then a pronoun, not an R-expression, and can be bound to the higher NP (NP1).

Several studies have shown children to be sensitive to reference facts accounted for under principle C (Lust et al. 1980; Solan 1978, 1983; Crain and McKee 1985; McDaniel and McKee to appear). The earliest of these used an experimental task invented by C. Chomsky (1969) in which children act out their understanding of sentences using dolls and other props. One or more dolls not mentioned in the sentence are made available to the child, and the child can use these if s/he wishes to act out an interpretation in which a pronoun refers to an entity not mentioned in the sentence. Several studies have found that when the pronoun precedes the NP to which it could potentially refer, children have a strong tendency to take the option of making a definite pronoun refer to an entity outside the sentence. But, crucially with respect to knowledge of the structural restrictions on reference imposed by principle C, children take the option of making a pronoun refer *inside* the sentence most frequently when sentence-internal reference is permitted under principle C.

Thus in Lust et al.'s study, which tested pre-school and young school-age children, there was an average of 14 per cent of sentence-internal responses (reference between the pronoun 'he' and the other NP in the sentence) for sentences such as (36), where principle C blocks co-reference, compared with 23 per cent of such responses for sentences such as (37), where principle C permits co-reference:

(36)   He turned around when Snuffles found the penny
(37)   When he closed the box, Cookie-Monster lay down

If we look at the structures for these sentences, we can see that the lower proportion of sentence-internal co-reference responses (14 per cent) is for the sentence type in which co-reference involves linking an R-expression to a c-commanding pronoun:

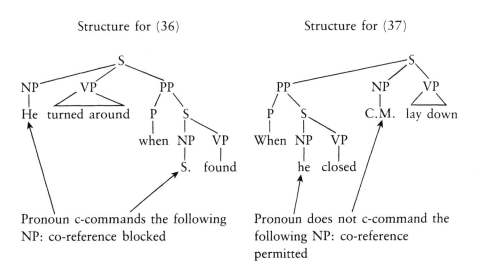

Structure for (36)   Structure for (37)

Pronoun c-commands the following   Pronoun does not c-command the
NP: co-reference blocked   following NP: co-reference
                                      permitted

Solan's studies provide evidence that children are paying attention to c-command and not to some alternative structural restriction. For example, the results with sentences of the types (36) and (37) above could be accounted for if children blocked co-reference when the first S node (as opposed to the first branching node) above the pronoun also dominated the noun phrase to which the pronoun is to be made co-referential. Solan's results argue that such alternatives are inadequate to account for the behaviour of five- to seven year-olds, the youngest age he tested (see Solan 1978, 1983 and exercise 3 at the end of this chapter). Crain and McKee's 1985 study, using a different task to the acting-out task used by Solan and Lust, confirms sensitivity to co-reference restrictions imposed by principle C among children as young as three years.

Principles A and B   Principles A and B of the binding theory account for the difference in distribution of NPs to which definite pronouns and reflexives may refer. We saw above that in sentences such as (19) and (20), repeated here as (38a–b),

(38a)   Lucifer claimed that the angel deceived him
(38b)   Lucifer claimed that the angel deceived himself

the reflexive pronoun is constrained to refer to the subject of the lower clause ('angel'), whereas the non-reflexive pronoun may not refer to that NP. If the definite pronoun refers to an entity inside the sentence, it must refer to the higher subject ('Lucifer'). Principle A of the binding theory requires that a reflexive be bound in its domain and principle B precludes binding a definite pronoun in its domain. Taking the S node immediately above the pronominal element to define the domain of the element, we can see from the structure for (38a–b) that the principles will produce the right results for the co-reference facts.

(39)

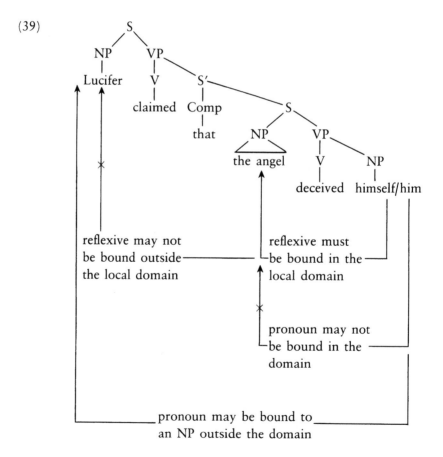

There are now numerous studies, using a number of different tasks, that have looked at children's knowledge of facts accounted for by principles A and B of the binding theory. In general, these studies show sensitivity to the requirements of principle A and more variable performance with principle B. Taking sensitivity to principle A first, there is good evidence that children are attuned to both the binding and the domain restrictions imposed by the principle. Solan (1983) showed that children aged five years reliably pick the lower subject for referent of a reflexive pronoun in sentences such as (38b). Others have manipulated the internal structure of the subject of the sentence in which the reflexive is found, demonstrating that children pick as a referent for a reflexive only a c-commanding NP, as the requirement that the reflexive be bound mandates (c-command is essential to the definition of binding). When children are presented with sentences such as (40a) and (b), they will make 'the friend' referent of the reflexive pronoun, not the other NP within the S-domain ('Dave'). As the structures for (40a–b) show, the only NP node that c-commands the reflexive pronoun is the circled NP node, the subject NP. The entity picked out by the circled NP is 'the friend', not 'Dave'.

(40a) The friend of Dave washed himself
(40b) Dave's friend washed himself

Structure for (40a)   Structure for (40b)

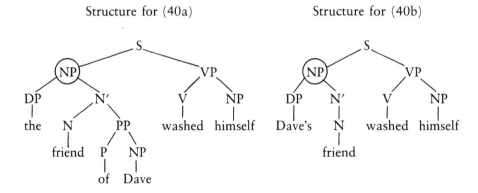

Studies that show sensitivity to c-command in selecting a referent within the local domain for an anaphoric pronoun are Deutsch and Koster (1982); Jakubowicz (1984); Deutsch et al. (1986) and Wexler and Chien (1985). The children in Jakubowicz's study were as young as three years.

Turning to principle B, it is clearly the case that children distinguish between definite pronouns and anaphors, picking a referent outside the local domain more frequently for the former than the latter. But it is also the case that in many studies the error rate for definite pronoun reference is higher than for reflexives. Children tend to make the mistake of binding a definite pronoun to an NP in the same local domain. (See the studies cited in the last paragraph; also Solan 1987; Stevenson and Pickering 1987.) The source of the difficulty children have in this respect with definite pronouns is a matter of controversy; but there is a growing consensus in the literature that the errors that occur are due not to lack of knowledge of principle B, but to difficulty in applying the principle in the course of sentence comprehension (see, for example, Solan 1987; Stevenson and Pickering 1987; Grimshaw and Rosen 1990; Goodluck 1990).

In sum, experimental studies of children's knowledge of the binding theory argue that pre-school children have a fairly firm grasp on the principles of the theory, although some errors are made in definite pronoun reference. Since the principles of the binding theory are formulated in terms of hierarchical syntactic structures, children's success with the binding theory argues that they are imposing an adult-like structure on the sentences they hear (and, presumably, on those they produce also). The binding theory is subject to a degree of parametric variation, in particular with respect to the definition of 'domain' for the application of principle A (see Wexler and Manzini 1987). Cross-linguistic study of the development of knowledge of the binding theory is now getting underway (Lee 1987; Jakubowicz and Olson 1988; Hyams and Sigurjonsdottir 1990; Solan 1987; McKee 1989; and see also chapter 6 below).

4.4.2 Bounding Theory and the Development of Movement

In section 4.1 we saw that movement is an operation that applies to the D-structure of English sentences to move a phrase to a presentential position or to subject position. How and when children begin to use the movement operation is a topic of considerable complexity and interest.

Wh-movement Taking first movement to presentential position, it is easy to see that the formation of English questions and other sentence types is structurally restricted. The moved phrase may not refer to a number of structural positions in the sentence, including positions inside a relative clause (41), the complement to a noun (42), an adverb clause such as the temporal clause in (43), the subject of a sentence (44), or an indirect question (45):

(41) *What did Fred see a dog that was eating?
      (cf. Fred saw a dog that was eating something)
(42) *What did Fred make the claim that a dog was eating?
      (cf. Fred made the claim that a dog was eating something)
(43) *What did Hugh drink whiskey before reading?
      (cf. Hugh drank whiskey before reading something)

(44) *Who did the poem about annoy Ted?
    (cf. The poem about someone annoyed Ted)
(45) *What did she wonder who ate?
    (cf. She wondered who ate something)

(The D-structure position of the question word in these ungrammatical questions corresponds to the position of the word 'something' or 'someone' in the declarative sentences provided for comparison.)

There are some core observations for which grammatical theory must account. First, the constraints exemplified by (41)–(45) are constraints on movement *per se* (the position of the empty element, trace, left by movement). The relation between a definite pronoun and its antecedent, for example, is not similarly constrained. This can be seen clearly in contrasts such as that in (46):

(46a) *Bones$_i$, I know a dog that loves t$_i$
(46b) Bones, I know a dog that loves them

(46a) shows that an NP cannot be topicalized out of a relative clause, but an NP in presentential position can be linked to a definite pronoun inside a relative. Second, there is cross-linguistic variation in whether question formation is subject to structural constraints. There are two levels to this variation. First, there is a gross division between language types. Right-branching configurational languages such as English tend to obey structural constraints on question formation and other constructions; left-branching configurational languages such as Japanese allow questioning into positions to which a question word may not refer in English. This division of language types confirms the claim that the constraints are constraints on movement, since left-branching languages tend not to form questions by dislocation of a questioned word or phrase from D-structure position, but rather to mark the questioned element *in situ*. Thus obedience to structural constraints is a litmus test for whether a language has movement 'in the syntax', as an operation between D-structure and S-structure. English-type languages do use movement in the syntax, Japanese-type languages do not. (It is argued that all languages use movement as an operation between S-structure and logical form.)

The second level of cross-linguistic variation concerns differences among languages that do use movement in the syntax. Some structural positions are stronger 'islands' (positions from which extraction is blocked) than others. Thus questioning from within a subject or an adverbial clause is generally eschewed, while questioning from within a relative clause or an indirect question is permitted in some languages that otherwise obey constraints. For

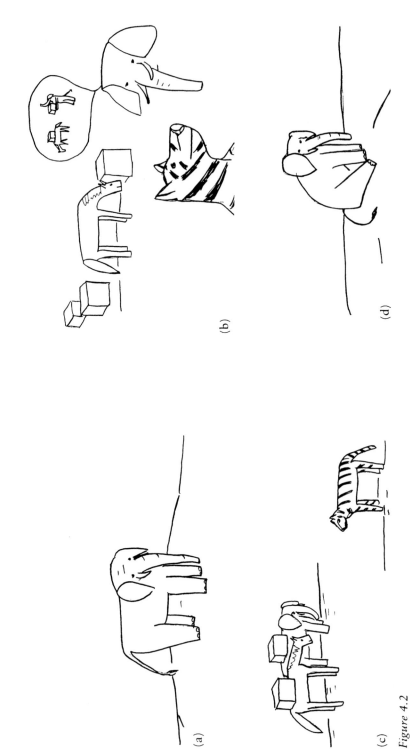

(a)

(b)

(c)

(d)

Figure 4.2
a The elephant liked to work. *b* She asked the tiger: 'Shall I help the horse carry those boxes?'
c The tiger said 'Yes!', so the elephant helped the horse. *d* The elephant was tired at the end of it all.
Question: Who did the elephant ask before helping?

example, Swedish, a language very similar in its broad characteristics to English, permits under some circumstances questioning from within relatives and indirect questions, although other structural conditions are obeyed. The strength of islands is known to vary with a number of factors, including whether the clause from which an element is moved is tensed or untensed and the length (specificity) of the phrase that is moved.

I will not give detailed linguistic accounts of these facts, but simply consider at a superficial level their significance in terms of language acquisition and what is known about when constraints are acquired.[6] Clearly, the addition of a movement operation 'in the syntax' will be a vital step in the acquisition of some languages. Since movement is characterized by constraints, we can use obedience to constraints as a diagnostic of whether children's grammars use movement. Indeed, we must use that as a test, rather than simply, for example, looking at whether the child places question words or focused elements in sentence-initial position, since, as mentioned above, we know from the facts of some adult languages that do use movement that in some cases constraints appear to be violated. Thus ungrammatical English sentences such as (46a) contrast with grammatical Swedish sentences such as (47):

(47)   *Ett ben ser jag en hund som äter*
       A bone, see I a dog that is eating

(example from Allwood 1982, p. 29)

A common approach to examples such as (47) is to assume that the focused element is present in sentence-initial position in D-structure and is linked to a lexically empty position by a rule similar to that for linking pronouns to full NPs in English – that is, to assimilate examples such as (47) to examples such as (46b) in some manner. Such examples demonstrate that the child's discovery that his language uses movement as an operation will not necessarily tell him the exact range of constructions for which it is used.

The available evidence concerning the development of movement is quite limited, in terms of the range of constructions tested and the clarity of the data. One study that has produced relatively clear results is Goodluck et al. (1989) (see also Goodluck et al. to appear), who tested children's knowledge of the constraint exemplified by (43). Children were read short (four- or five-sentence) stories, accompanied by a sequence of four pictures. While looking at the last picture, the child was asked a potentially ambiguous question – a question for which the story provided two possible answers. An example is given in (48); the pictures that accompanied the sentences are reproduced in figure 4.2a–d.

(48)   The elephant liked to work (figure 4.2a)
       She asked the tiger: 'Shall I help the horse carry those boxes?' (figure
          4.2b)
       The tiger said 'Yes!' so the elephant helped the horse (figure 4.2c)
       The elephant was tired at the end of it all (figure 4.2d)
       Question: Who did the elephant ask before helping?

There are two logically possible answers to the question in (48), depending
on whether the question word is construed as object of the main verb ('ask'),
for which the answer is 'the tiger', or as object of the verb in the temporal
clause ('helping'), for which the answer is 'the horse'. However, only the
former interpretation is possible under the constraint that blocks extraction
from within a temporal clause. Children aged three (the youngest age tested)
strongly preferred to interpret the question in examples such as (48) in a
manner consistent with the constraint – for that example, they strongly preferred to answer 'the tiger' rather than 'the horse'. Moreover, the children's
preference was truly a structural one, based on clause type. In answering
questions such as

(49)   Who did the elephant ask to help?

following a story that again provided two candidate answers, the children did
not avoid making the question word refer to the object position of the subordinate clause. (In (49), the embedded clause is a complement to 'ask', and
movement from this position is permitted in the adult grammar.)
   Other studies testing children's knowledge of the block on extraction from
within a relative clause (Otsu 1981; Crain and Fodor 1985a) and from within
an indirect question (de Villiers et al. 1990) have produced results that are less
clear-cut, although there is evidence of knowledge of these constraints at five
years and younger in some cases. Arguably, the difference in clarity in the
results of experiments to date reflects the relative 'strength' of the islands in
adult grammars. The block on extraction from an adverbial clause is a block
that appears to hold quite consistently across languages; the blocks on extraction from a relative clause or indirect question are rather more variable.
Another recent study of children's knowledge of movement is Lillo-Martin (to
appear), which presents evidence that children of three and over learning
American Sign Language are aware of the fact that that language imposes very
rigid restrictions on movement, excluding extraction from any embedded
clause.

NP-movement   The discussion of wh-movement in the last section illustrates
a typical problem in language acquisition studies: for a given sentence type,

what kind of analysis does the child impose on the word string? Linguistic theory shows us that very often the superficial form of a sentence is amenable to more than one abstract analysis – a given linear string of words may be formed by a movement operation, or not, and it is up to the researcher to work out which particular analysis the child is using. Exactly the same sort of situation arises in the case of passive sentences.

In the analysis of passives sketched in section 4.1, a passive sentence is formed by moving the object of the sentence to an empty subject position, leaving a trace:

(50a)   [e] were devoured the bananas (by Sue)
        The bananas$_i$ were devoured [t]$_i$ (by Sue)
(50b)   [e] were arrested the girls (by the police)
        The girls$_i$ were arrested [t]$_i$ (by the police)

Does the child form passives in this way, or does he impose a different analysis, perhaps forming and interpreting passives in a manner similar to that for predicate adjective sentences such as (51), where there is no movement of an object into subject position in the adult grammar?

(51a)   The bananas were yellow
(51b)   The girls were happy

This might seem at first an unlikely possibility, given that we saw above that quite an array of grammatical principles conspire to dictate the adult analysis of passive sentences, in the framework of government binding theory. However, the application of these general principles is dependent on language-particular facts – for example, the projection principle (which requires the subcategorizations of a verb to be preserved at all levels of representation) will not necessarily be violated by a non-movement (no object trace) analysis of (50a) if the child does not know that the verb 'devour' is obligatorily transitive in English. Moreover, a non-movement analysis of passives is a particularly plausible idea with respect to early passives for English-speaking children in view of the fact that there is good evidence that the adult grammar of English does have two types of passive, one of which is 'adjectival'. Adjectival passives are found with verbs that roughly denote states rather than actions and they display a number of adjective-like properties, including prefixation of the passive participle by 'un-', co-occurrence with 'very' and a tendency for the passive to sound awkward or even ungrammatical with an agentive 'by' phrase (see Wasow 1977 for an enumeration of the properties of adjectival passives).

Some examples of adjectival passives are given in (52):

(52a)   The island was (un)inhabited
        (cf. The island was (un)popular)
(52b)   His work is very respected
        (cf. His work is very tidy)
(52c)   ??The eggs were unbroken by Sue
        (cf. *The eggs were brown by the hen)

Although there is not complete agreement on the matter even in analyses within the framework of Chomsky (1981), it is frequently assumed that the two types of passive, adjectival and non-adjectival, will differ in that only the latter will be formed by movement of an object from its deep structure position.

The hypothesis that the child's early passives do not involve movement was put forward and defended in Borer and Wexler (1987). They point to several findings compatible with the view that children's early passives are adjectival, including the rarity of 'by' phrases in children's production of passives. Borer and Wexler's proposal runs into some difficulties, however. Maratsos (1985) and Pinker et al. (1987) both find that children generally do better in comprehension tests with passives involving action verbs (such as 'kick') than passives involving non-action verbs (such as 'see' or 'hear'), a result that goes against the grain of the adult semantic restriction on adjectival passives and forces Borer and Wexler to propose that the semantic restriction on adjectival passives is not available to the child. Another difficulty pointed out by Pinker et al. (1987) is that the absence of 'by' phrases in children's speech may be an artefact of the circumstances in which the speech was produced. The idea that children's competence with passives may be deficient is also undermined in a general way by the fact that studies of languages other than English show that very young children may have a strong command of sentence types that are equivalent to passives (see Pye and Poz 1988 for a study of Quiche Mayan) and/or with the formal characteristics of movement passives (see Demuth 1989b for a study of Sesotho).

In general, none of the studies published to date produces a convincing argument for young English-speaking children's use or non-use of movement as a formal operation linking deep and surface structure in the formation of passive sentences, and this important question is thus even more open than the question of the acquisition of movement in wh-questions and other constructions.

To sum up this section on the acquisition of movement, movement is a central grammatical operation and the child who uses movement has introduced into his grammar a formal operation subject to its own particular constraints. There is some evidence that by three years children learning English form questions by movement; similar evidence for movement to subject position in passives is currently lacking. As mentioned above, movement is not necessarily used uniformly across constructions in the adult grammar and it is possible that movement as an operation is introduced in children's grammars at different times for different constructions. (See Weissenborn 1992; Labelle 1988; Goodluck and Behne 1992 for some pertinent data and discussion.)

4.4.3   *Children's Grammar of Control*

The grammar of sentences with 'missing' subjects is one of the thorniest topics in syntactic theory (see, among many others, Bresnan 1982; Manzini 1983; Williams 1980 for pertinent data and partially competing theories). As we saw in section 4.1, the missing subject of tenseless subordinate clauses in government binding theory is represented by an unpronounced element, PRO. Infinitival complements to verbs such as 'tell' and 'choose' (53a,b), tenseless temporal clauses (53c) and infinitival subject clauses (53d) are among the clause types that have a PRO subject in Chomsky's 1981 theory:

(53a)   Fred told Jane [PRO to leave]
(53b)   Fred chose Jane [PRO to dance]
(53c)   Fred kissed Jane [before PRO leaving]
(53d)   [PRO to kiss Jane] would be a crime

Control theory regulates the reference of PRO. Despite the complexity of the grammar of PRO, there are some generalizations that can provide a framework for evaluating children's knowledge. First, as mentioned in section 4.1, control may be either obligatory or optional. In the case of (53a–c), the PRO must be interpreted as referring to another NP inside the sentence. In the case of the complements in (53a–b), the controller (NP interpreted as referent of PRO) is the main clause object ('Jane' in the examples). In the case of (53c) with a temporal clause, the main clause subject ('Fred') is controller. For these clause types, PRO is obligatorily interpreted as co-referent with an NP inside the sentence. In contrast, the PRO in (53d) refers to some entity not mentioned in the sentence, although sentence-internal reference is possible (in 'To kiss Jane would please Bill', Bill may be the one who does the kissing). Control is optional for the sentence type in (53d). A number of properties have been proposed as characteristic of obligatory control constructions, one of which is whether or not there is a c-command relation between the PRO and the NP to which it refers. In (53a,b), where the subordinate clause is attached to the VP node, both the main clause subject and object c-command the PRO; in (53c), with a clause that attaches to the main clause S node, the subject c-commands the PRO; in the structure (53d), there is no NP inside the sentence that c-commands the PRO:

Structure for (53a,b)

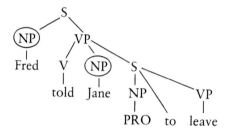

Structure for (53c)

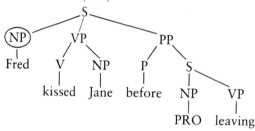

Structure for (53d)

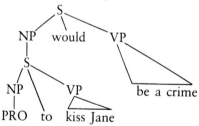

(NPs that c-command PRO are circled)

Second, control for complements in the VP, such as (53a,b), is semantically (thematically) determined. For such complements, it is the general consensus that control rules make reference to the thematic structure of the main clause, picking out one of the two c-commanding NPs as controller. In the examples in (53a,b) the controller is the NP ('Jane') with the thematic role of *theme* or *goal*; this is the general case for control of complements in the VP. The verb 'promise', which requires the subject of the main clause to be controller of the complement in the VP, is an exception to the general rule:

(54)   Fred promised Jane to leave

How do children handle PRO constructions? Comprehension experiments with children aged four and older show two consistent findings. First, children do well in their comprehension of the missing subject of complements in the verb phrase, such as (53a,b), correctly making the main clause object (the NP with the role theme or goal) the controller of the PRO (see exercise 5 at the end of the chapter for additional pertinent facts). Moreover, they overgeneralize this rule to the exceptional case of 'promise' (Chomsky 1969; Maratsos 1974a; Goodluck 1981). Second, children's performance is much more variable and non-adult-like in the case of temporal and other adverbial clauses, such as (53c), although children's treatment of adverbial clauses in any individual study is rarely random (Goodluck 1981, 1987; Hsu et al. 1985; Lust et al. 1986; Goodluck and Behne 1992).

Various proposals have been put forward to try to account for the successes and failures that children have in interpreting control constructions (Wexler 1989 provides a partial review and some original hypotheses). One recent account is that children have an adult-like grammar for complements to verbs such as 'tell' and 'choose', but initially treat temporal clauses as optional control constructions, permitting the missing subject to refer both inside and outside the sentence. This would account for the fact that children have been found on occasion to permit even a prepositional object, such as the passive 'by' phrase in (55), to be controller of the PRO in the temporal clause (Goodluck and Behne 1992), an interpretation that cannot easily be fitted with a c-command condition on obligatory control:

(55)   Jane was kissed by Fred before leaving

4.4.4   Summary

To summarize what we have said about syntactic knowledge in the pre-school years: children as young as three have a complex, structurally-based system which obeys many of the principles governing the adult grammar (notably, the principles of the binding theory and at least some of the structural restrictions on movement rules). Sensitivity to the restrictions imposed by such principles implies knowledge of the structures on which the principles operate. There are, however, many unknowns concerning the degree of match between the child and adult systems. For example, it is an open question at present whether children learning English use a movement operation to form passive sentences.

4.5   Syntactic Development after Age Six

Although we have seen many examples of sophisticated, adult-like knowledge of syntactic structures and principles on the part of pre-school children, this does not mean that language development is complete by age five or six. A number of studies suggest that the years between ages five and ten may be a period when the child gets to grips with exceptional and relatively infrequent constructions and constructions that involve accessing more than one type of grammatical knowledge.

Some examples of late development are relatively well documented; most involve cases where there are lexical restrictions on rules and constructions. It is generally between six and ten years that children sort out lexical exceptions such as the fact that 'promise' does not obey the general rule for control of the PRO subject of a complement clause. Where the lexical specifications involve not just an individual exception, but rather a mapping between fairly large classes of words and constructions, the learning process may go on even beyond ten years. The ambiguity of sentence (9), 'Children are nice to understand', hinges on the fact that the complement to the adjective 'nice' can have two different structures; other adjectives may take only one of the two possible structures. Thus 'eager' does not allow a trace in the object position of its complement, and 'easy' requires one:

(56)   Sue is eager [PRO to please]
(57)   Sue is easy [PRO to please t]

Pre-school children frequently treat 'easy'-type sentences as if they were 'eager'-type sentences. Even after the child begins to recognize that there is an object gap in the complement in the case of 'easy'-type adjectives, she may be ten or older before she reliably assigns the right structure to the right adjectives (see Cromer 1970, 1987). In a fairly simple-minded way we can say that these are complex constructions (involving not only a movement operation but lexical restrictions on its application) and that as such they are not mastered until into the school years.

One hypothesis for which there is some scattered evidence is that the years between five and ten are a period in which the child moves away from a reliance on thematic relations (agent, patient, etc.) in interpreting various constructions (Goodluck and Birch 1988). One example of children's initial reliance on thematic relations is found in their treatment of the subject of temporal clauses, which, as we saw above, appear not to be obligatorily controlled by the main clause subject in children's grammar. A child who treats the PRO subject of the embedded clause in both (53c) and (55) as referring to 'Fred' is plausibly relying on the thematic role *agent* to interpret PRO:

(53c)   Fred kissed Jane [before PRO leaving]
(55)   Jane was kissed by Fred [before PRO leaving]

This pattern of responses is not uncommon among pre-school children, and extends into the period between six and ten years (Goodluck and Behne in press).

In brief, there is some indication that the middle childhood years are a period in which the syntactic system continues to develop, with refinement of existing knowledge (such as the learning of lexical exceptions) and the introduction of some new structures and/or rules, perhaps also with changes in general strategies for interpretation that may straddle the boundary between sentence grammar and discourse grammar (see chapter 7).

The particular examples cited here are not necessarily an accurate example of middle-childhood developments. They are simply prominent among those that have come to light to date; middle childhood remains relatively under-studied with respect to syntactic development.

4.6   Syntactic Development: Some Popular Ideas Reconsidered

This section evaluates some ideas concerning the development of syntactic and semantic knowledge. Since the 1960s, the relative priority of syntactic structures and semantic knowledge has been hotly debated in the child language literature. We will consider two recurring ideas: that semantic representations have some kind of priority in development, and that syntactic rules and representations are relatively late to develop. Both are shown to have little support, in the forms they frequently take, although both may ultimately contain a core of truth.

4.6.1 'Semantics First'

In the late 1960s and early 1970s a debate began concerning the role of semantic and syntactic structures in very early speech. Three separate questions have been at issue: (1) whether a semantic analysis was needed as part of the grammar of very early speech; (2) whether there exists some special mapping relationship between semantic categories and syntactic categories in very early speech; and (3) whether all or some syntactic categories and structure can be dispensed with in analysing early speech.

There is no doubt that the answer to the first question is 'yes'. Many researchers – often reacting to what they regarded as an excessively narrow application of the formalism of transformational grammar to child language data – pointed out that early speech displayed regularities in the range of semantic relationships expressed. For example, early telegraphic speech has a predominance of words filling the semantic roles of agent, theme and location (see Bowerman 1973). A complete account of early speech must express those semantic roles and their distribution in some manner. The second and third questions are still being debated.

Clearly, the fact that in previous sections we have seen evidence that children aged three and even younger are sensitive to syntactically based principles of grammar argues that any asyntactic stage of development cannot last long. This point is reinforced by studies that have looked explicitly at the question of the existence of syntactic categories. Gordon (1985a) has argued that children are imposing syntactic categories on words by age two at the latest, contrary to claims such as those of Macnamara (1982), who proposed that 'children arrange their words in semantic, not syntactic categories'.

Gordon examined young children's command of the syntax of *mass* and *count* nouns in English. This noun class is one in which there is generally a close relation between a semantic (perceptual) property and syntactic class. Mass nouns such as 'water' and 'bread' generally denote substances that are not perceptually discrete ('blobby things') whereas count nouns such as 'chair' and 'book' generally denote objects that are perceptually discrete (objects that have defined perceptual boundaries and can be combined with other objects of the same type without losing their perceptual integrity). The two classes of nouns have separate syntactic behaviours, including the fact that in normal usage mass nouns cannot pluralize or occur with a numeral ('*waters'; '*two waters'), whereas count nouns can ('chairs'; 'two chairs'). There are also exceptions to the correlation between semantic/perceptual properties and syntactic behaviour: the word 'fruit' denotes a perceptually discrete class of objects, but is a mass noun in English ('*two fruits'). Such cases demonstrate that the mass–count distinction is a formal distinction within the class of nouns and cannot be reduced to a distinction in the semantic properties of nouns, although it is plainly related to such properties. Gordon reasoned that if children have word categories that are not syntactic, but are rather based on semantic and perceptual classes, then we would expect them to miscategorize exceptions to the general case that count nouns denote discrete objects and mass nouns denote substances. If they do not make such errors, but rather follow an adult-like pattern, then it is plausible to conclude that words are classified in their grammars in a way that cannot be reduced to semantic, non-syntactic properties. In one of Gordon's experiments, children aged two to five responded to questions concerning shops and shopping – for example:

(58)   Do you know what you get in the $\begin{Bmatrix} \text{vegetable} \\ \text{fruit} \end{Bmatrix}$ section?

The correct (adult) answer is a plural form for the count noun ('vegetables') and a singular form for the mass noun ('fruit' not '*fruits'), despite the fact that the mass noun has the perceptual properties associated with count nouns. For children who knew the words involved, there were very few errors in which children treated the mass nouns as count nouns, incorrectly pluralizing, and there were no errors of this type for two-year-olds. No support was found, therefore, for the claim that children's early word classes are semantically rather than syntactically based.

Not only do children appear to use syntactic categories in their grammars at an early age, but syntactic environment appears to be at least as much a driving force in the acquisition of new words as semantic and perceptual properties. In experiments with children aged three and older Gordon (1985a) was able to show that syntactic clues to the mass–count distinction have a stronger effect on children's categorization of nonsense words than perceptual properties of the items denoted by the nonsense word. Recent work by Gleitman and others argues that syntactic frames (such as the presence or absence of an object NP) guide responses to nonsense words for children as young as two years (see, for example, Gleitman 1989).

There is thus a growing body of evidence that at an early stage children do have syntactic categories. That still leaves open the second question above (is there a special relation between syntactic and semantic categories in early speech?) and part of the third question (children may have some, but not all, of the adult categories).

Even though studies such as Gordon's demonstrate that the child early on has a sense of grammatical category that cuts across semantic (perceptual) categories, the evidence from such studies does not preclude a very brief, initial stage in which syntactic and semantic categories are related in a non-adult way. Such a special relationship is at the heart of 'semantic bootstrapping' discussions of the beginnings of syntax.

Advocates of 'semantic bootstrapping' reason that a close, perhaps isomorphic, relation between syntactic categories and semantic categories provides the basis for knowledge of the particulars of phrase structure syntax for the language the child is learning. For example, Pinker (1982) suggests that if a child hypothesizes correspondences between the semantically definable class 'concrete object' and nouns, and the semantically definable class 'action' and verbs, she will be able to use this identification to sort out the basic rules of her syntactic component. Given the child's guess as to the correspondence between semantic categories and word classes, a sentence such as 'dogs run' would give the child a handle on the fact that word order (phrase structure) rules of English specify that the subject precedes the verb. The hypothesized syntax–semantics isomorphy thus 'bootstraps' the child into syntactic rules. Once the NP–VP order is established, the syntax–semantics match can be relaxed to accommodate counter-examples to the 'noun = concrete object' and 'verb = action' generalization. Similar ideas are found in Grimshaw (1981). Although studies such as that of Gordon (1985a) argue that such a stage of isomorphy between syntactic and semantic categories cannot last very long, a brief stage of this kind might provide an effective way into the establishment of a syntactic (phrase structure) system.

Despite its intuitive appeal, there is no positive evidence in favour of the isomorphy and bootstrapping approach to the development of phrase structure syntax. Moreover, isomorphy and bootstrapping are not necessary conditions for successful learning if it is granted (as Pinker would grant; see Pinker 1987) that the child has innate access to the constraints that govern phrase structure schemata in human languages. For example, if the child exposed to English is able to work out from context the meaning of one or two verbs and registers the fact that they are followed by their direct objects, then knowledge of the principles governing phrase structure grammars may take her to the conclusion that the language to which she is exposed is a right-branching language, with head–modifier order. Verb–object is one exemplar of that order and can in principle set the child rules to the basic order subject–verb–object, since

that is the only basic order permitted where the verb immediately precedes
the object (right-branching languages are generally S–V–O or V–S–O and
left-branching languages are S–O–V in their basic order).

The third question posed above – do children have all of the syntactic
category types used in the adult grammar? – has been researched with
some intensity recently, following new ideas in the theory of phrase structure and lexical categories. The basic hypothesis being explored in fact
straddles the line between the broad notions of 'semantics first' and 'syntax
is late', proposing that a certain type of syntactic category, corresponding
to certain kinds of semantic entities and notions, has priority in
acquisition.

Chomsky (1986b) makes a distinction between *lexical* categories (noun,
verb, adjective, preposition) and *non-lexical* (or *functional*) categories,
which include complementizer, determiner and inflection. Intuitively, the
functional categories are 'small word' categories that fill in details of
meaning, such as tense of the sentence and definiteness of nouns. Both
types of category head phrases and the functional categories serve to
provide a kind of superstructure over the structure provided by the lexical
categories. Structures of the sort we have worked with so far in this
chapter, with S and S′ as the topmost node in the trees, I (inflection) as a
node under S, and DP (determiner phrase) as a node under NP, are
replaced in the new type of system with structures in which complementizer phrase (CP) is the topmost node in the tree (replacing S′), inflectional
phrase (IP) is the next highest node (replacing S) and in which determiner
phrase (DP) dominates NP. For example, we can 'translate' a structure
such as (58) into the new notation as follows:

(58)

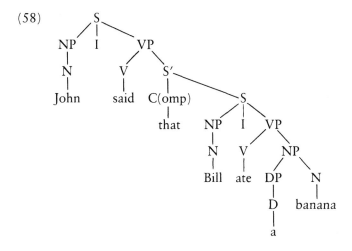

(59)   corresponds to:

```
                    IP
                 /  |  \
              NP    I    VP
              |          |  \
              N          V    CP
              |          |   /  \
            John       said C    IP
                        |   / \
                     that NP  I    VP
                          |      /  \
                          N     V    DP
                          |     |   /  \
                        Bill   ate D    NP
                                   |    |
                                   a    N
                                        |
                                     banana
```

The basic proposal made by several different researchers is that at an early stage in development, children lack functional categories (see Guilfoyle and Noonan 1988; Lebeaux 1989; Platzack 1989; Radford 1988b, 1990). These researchers observe that the words children tend to leave out in telegraphic speech (see section 4.3 above) correspond very often to functional categories. The general hypothesis is that there is a stage in which children have some syntactic categories, but not others, and in which categories that do exist can be described in terms of the lexical–functional category distinction of recent syntactic theory.

Strong evidence for or against the primacy of lexical categories in development is hard to come by, because of the young age of the children involved. However, it is an interesting idea that generates many predictions and claims concerning early speech. For example, as we have seen above, question formation in the adult grammar involves movement of the questioned phrase into a presentential slot, under S' (or CP in the new type of phrase structure system just sketched). If children at or around the period of telegraphic speech do not have a CP node, since complementizer is a functional category, then at a minimum it must be claimed that the child's syntactic structure for a question such as 'Where doggie?' differs in a basic way from the adult structure for questions (see Radford 1990 for discussion of this and similar points).

To sum up this section, children clearly do have some syntactic categories from an early age. The evidence of research such as that of Gordon (1985a) argues that the categories children use are at least partially independent of perceptual/semantic categories at a young age. Whether at the very earliest stages there is an isomorphic or near-isomorphic relation between syntactic categories and semantic categories (as proposed under the semantic bootstrapping hypothesis) or whether there is a stage in which the child has some but not all syntactic categories (as proposed under the lexical category hypothesis) are unsolved problems at present. Possibly more progress will be made with these questions when better technology is available for getting at the nature of early grammars. An important recent development in the study of very early child speech has been the use of ingenious experimental techniques (frequently similar to those used to study infant speech perception) to tap syntactic distinctions. For example, Hirsh-Pasek et al. (1987) have demonstrated that infants as young as seven months (well before the onset of one-word speech) are sensitive to clause boundaries in the speech stream. In their study, infants oriented (turned to face) for a longer time towards speech samples that were segmented by pauses at the adult clause boundary than to speech samples that were segmented by pauses inserted inside clauses. Such sensitivity to syntactic units on the part of pre-linguistic infants makes claims that very early speech is syntactically structured less surprising than might otherwise be the case (and also raises important questions concerning the perceptual mechanisms by which the child analyses the speech stream – for example, the role of intonation in helping the child to recognize clause boundaries).

4.6.2 'Syntax is Late'

Another idea that occurs frequently in the literature on child language is the contention that 'syntax is late'. This idea is a natural complement to 'semantics first' hypotheses. Since we have seen both that 'semantics first' has little support and that there is good evidence that children have a more-or-less developed syntactic system in place by the third year, any very general form of a 'syntax is late' hypothesis cannot be correct. Why, then, has this idea been popular?

One reason is simply that much of the evidence for very early syntactically based grammars has only recently been published. A second reason is that studies of the acquisition of syntax in the 1970s were frequently influenced by Carol Chomsky's 1969 book, *The Acquisition of Syntax in Children from 5 to 10*. Chomsky's thesis was that there may be important areas of grammar where development goes on into the school years – an idea that, as we saw in section 4.5, has a certain amount of evidence to support it. A brief look at the phenomena studied by Chomsky will show that her results do not present a barrier to claiming that pre-school children have a complex syntactic system.

All but one of Chomsky's tests involved lexically restricted phenomena, such as the rule for interpreting the missing (PRO) subject of a complement clause ('promise' vs. 'tell') and the distribution of missing object constructions ('easy'/'eager'). The relatively late acquisition of matches between rules and individual lexical items in no way precludes a complex syntactic system on the part of younger children.

The one non-lexically-restricted phenomenon dealt with by Chomsky was restrictions on definite pronoun interpretation, in particular the block on co-reference between a definite pronoun and a following NP in sentences such as 'He said that Pluto was sick'. As we saw above, co-reference in such sentences is currently analysed as involving a violation of principle C of the binding theory. Chomsky noted that some errors of co-reference were made by children; she observed a breaking-point for success in her study at around five and a half years (the youngest children she tested were five). In section 4.4.4 I summarized the results of studies that argue that children as young as three are sensitive to the restrictions imposed by principle C of the binding theory. How can Chomsky's findings be reconciled with these later studies? Can it be argued that the errors that Chomsky recorded were slip-ups that did not reflect the true extent of children's knowledge? Two points support this view. First, Chomsky used for her test of pronoun interpretation a task (picture verification) that may perform relatively poorly as a test of grammatical knowledge (see Gough 1966; Forster and Olbrei 1973). Second, the more recent studies rely on contrasts in children's performance with different sentence types (e.g. the contrast in performance with sentence types (36) and (37) above). What is taken to be more important than the fact that some errors are made in interpreting pronouns is the fact that children distinguish between sentence types containing pronouns in a way that can only be accounted for by attributing to them knowledge of principles of grammar that govern the adult system.

To summarize, on the basis of studies reviewed in this chapter we can say with confidence that by three or four years children have acquired the basics of complex syntax (phrase structure configurations appropriate to their language) and interpret sentences using structurally-based principles. Thus a 'syntax is late' hypothesis cannot be maintained in any very strong form (i.e. that children for an extended period in a fundamental way lack syntax). Chomsky's 1969 study (which inspired many of the studies on syntax acquisition reviewed above) does not present any substantial problems for the claim that pre-school children use a complex syntactic system. Chomsky's original idea that syntax acquisition may go on into the school years may well be correct, however, as we saw in section 4.5.

4.7 Summary and Conclusions

Recent studies of syntactic development have argued that from an early age (two to three years) children have a syntactic system that is tuned to the syntax of the language around them and reflects principles governing adult grammars, such as the principles of the binding theory. Two ideas frequently occur in one form or another in the literature: 'semantics first' and 'syntax is late'. It is quite clear that 'syntax is late' is an untenable idea, if it is taken to mean that the child's syntactic system is fundamentally impoverished or non-existent for any extended period, although it may well be that the child's system of rules is not identical to the adult's until well into the school years. Various versions of 'semantics first' continue to be debated. Within syntactic theory, there has been an explosion in detailed and sophisticated studies of language variation; language acquisition studies are only beginning to address the questions that such studies raise with respect to language development. Comparative studies of, for example, children learning English and Italian, and English and Japanese, have helped resolve some questions about the nature of early grammars, but many important syntactic phenomena for which variation in adult grammars is well documented are only beginning to be studied from the perspective of language acquisition. For example, languages vary with respect to the definitions of 'domain' used for the application of principles A and B of the binding theory and this variation has only recently been the focus of child language studies.

Notes

1 The reader may wonder if the position of determiner phrase before the noun in the structures above is also an exception; on a somewhat different analysis of phrase structure sketched below (section 4.6.1) it is not.
2 The structure given is still not accurate, by the lights of the theory. The main clause subject in such sentences is not moved from object position of the embedded clause, but is linked to an abstract element (O, for operator) that moves from the embedded object position to the front of the embedded clause:

Children$_i$ are nice [O$_i$ PRO to understand t$_i$]

3   Here and below, details of structures are omitted where not essential, and lexical material dominated by a single node is indicated by a triangle.

4   In addition, some types of re-ordering rules may apply to S-structure to produce a linear surface order not relevant to the computation of logical form; the output of such 'stylistic' rules, together with phonological rules, is phonetic form (see chapter 2). The term surface structure is properly used for the output of stylistic rules, although it is also used interchangeably with S-structure.

5   The reader may ask what the 'government' of the title *Government and Binding* is and what role it plays. Suffice it to say here that *government* is a local relationship between elements (for example, a verb governs its object NP) that, like the concept of height (c-command) already mentioned, plays a role in several of the subtheories of grammar.

6   One central concept that has been used partially to unify the various constraints listed in the text is that of *subjacency*, which is briefly described in chapter 6.

Further Reading

De Villiers and de Villiers (1986) give an overview of syntactic development in English, covering some structures not dealt with in this chapter. Papers in Roeper and Williams (1987) contain a number of up-to-date analyses of some aspects of the development of syntax; the linguistic analysis in those papers is more technical than the analysis given here, and the papers are suitable for readers with a background in syntactic theory.

Questions and Exercises

1.   If 'pivots' are head-words and 'open' words are complements, which order would you expect a child learning Japanese to favour, 'pivot–open' or 'open–pivot'? Why?

2.   Consider the following utterances from a two-year-old child; word-by-word glosses are given in quotation marks and the approximate meaning is given in brackets:

ottaa hampa 'takes teeth' [takes teeth]	*ei susi* 'no wolf'	*havua pois* 'doggie (take) away' [takes doggie]
pestään käsi 'wash hand' [wash hand]	*ei saa* 'no get'	*piirtää tätä* 'draws this' [draws this]
tää hevonen 'this horse' [this is horse]	*ei tässä* 'no here'	*ajaa brrä* 'drives "car"' [drives car]
äiti, tää bussi 'mother, this bus' [mother, this is bus]		*auto, tässä auto* 'car, here car' [car, here is car]
tässä bussi 'here bus' [here is bus]	*täti tulee* 'aunt comes' [aunt comes]	*Rina anna* 'Rina give' [give to Rina]
tässä kirja 'here book' [here is book]	*Rina syö* 'Rina eats' [Rina eats]	*nalle . . . katsoo* 'teddy bear watches' [teddy-bear watches]
anna Rina 'give Rina' [give to Rina]	*vauva avaa* 'baby opens' [baby opens]	*tässä lehti* 'here magazine' [here is magazine]
ei Pluto 'no Pluto'	*brrä tässä* '"car" here' [car is here]	*tätä pois* 'this take away' [take away this]

What generalizations can you draw from these data concerning the child's word-order rules? What is your best guess for the language type the child is learning (left-branching, right-branching)? Discuss any problems with the analysis you propose. (Data taken from Bowerman 1973, Appendix M.)

3. Solan (1978, 1983) tested the following four sentence types:

(A) He told the pig that the dog would run around   17%
(B) The pig told him that the dog would run around   17%
(C) He hit the pig when the dog ran around   11%
(D) The pig hit him when the dog ran around   39%

The percentages to the right of the example sentences are the percentages in which five-year-old children interpreted the pronoun 'he'/'him' as co-referential with the NP in the subordinate clause ('the dog' in the example). The highest percentage is for sentence type (D). Sentence types (A) and (B) contain a complement sentence embedded in the VP; sentence types (C) and (D) contain a temporal phrase, which is attached to the main clause S node. The structures for (A), (B) and (C), (D) are thus as follows:

Structure for (A), (B)

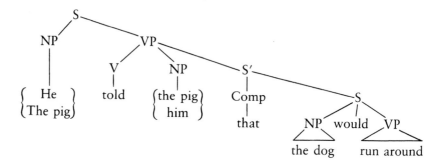

Structure for (C), (D)

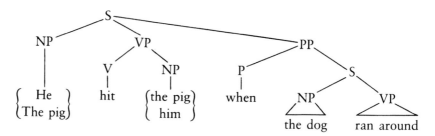

Principle C of the binding theory prevents a referring expression (an NP such as 'the dog' in the examples) from being bound — that is, from being coindexed to another NP that c-commands it.

a. In which of the structures above is there a main clause NP which does not c-command the NP 'the dog'?
b. How does the presence of a non-c-commanding NP relate to the number of co-referential interpretations five-year-olds gave between the subordinate NP ('the dog') and the pronoun in the higher clause?
c. Consider the following rule for co-reference: 'an NP may not refer to a pronoun unless the pronoun is dominated by an S node that does not dominate the NP.' That rule is adequate to account for the co-reference facts in sentences discussed in the text, such as (28) 'When he closed the box, Cookie-Monster lay down' (co-reference permitted) and (27) 'He turned around when Snuffles found a penny' (co-reference blocked). Is it adequate to account for the co-reference facts with respect to sentence types (A)–(D)?

4. Many adult speakers do not find co-reference between the subordinate clause pronoun ('the dog') and the preceding pronoun completely

grammatical in sentence type (D) in the previous exercise, although most agree that co-reference is better in that sentence type than any of the sentence types (A)–(C). What do you think about results from child language studies involving constructions for which adult judgements are not completely clear-cut? Do the adult judgements cast doubt on the child language results? Or do the child language results offer an additional kind of evidence for or against theories that are not unequivocally supported by adult judgements?

5. In Carol Chomsky's 1969 study, she proposed that children's error in interpreting the missing (PRO) subject of the complement to 'promise' was the result of a 'minimum distance principle', whereby the missing subject is made to refer to the NP that is nearest to it in the linear order of words (Chomsky does not commit herself on whether the proposed principle is a structually based rule of grammar or a perceptual strategy). Such a minimum distance principle would account for the facts that children incorrectly interpret the subject of 'leave' as 'Fred', not 'Jane', in

(54)   Fred promised Jane to leave

and correctly interpret the subject of 'tell' as 'Jane' in

(53a)   Fred told Jane to leave

Evaluate the minimum distance principle in the light of the following results (based on Goodluck 1981; similar results are found in Maratsos 1974a). The percentages to the right are the percentages in which the correct main clause NP was chosen as subject of a subordinate clause. When the main clause is active, the correct response is to choose the main clause object ('Jane') in the example as subject of the subordinate clause; when the main clause is passive, the correct answer is to choose the main clause surface subject ('Fred') as the subject of the subordinate clause. The percentages given are based on sentences where the children correctly interpreted the active or passive main clause.

	Percentage correct
Complement to 'tell': active main clause	
Example: Fred told Jane to leave	95%
Complement to 'tell': passive main clause	
Example: Fred was told by Jane to leave	87%

6. Find an example in the text concerning pronoun interpretation where the experimental results cannot be accounted for by reference to linear order relations.

7. It has been proposed that the apparently exceptional behaviour of 'promise' with respect to control of a PRO subject can be explained if 'promise' is subject to a semantically based rule for control of the PRO subject of its complement. (Jackendoff 1972 is an early example of an account of this type). For example, 'promise' might be said to be subject to a rule along the lines: 'The controller is the NP put under obligation to perform some action.' The main clause subject NP is put under such obligation, and it is the subject NP that is controller of PRO:

Sue promised Ted [PRO to leave]

Discuss this proposal with reference to the acquisition facts summarized in the text. (What kind of mistake could it be said the child is making with 'promise' on this account?)

5 Further Aspects of Syntactic and Semantic Development

This chapter takes up a number of topics at the interface of syntactic and semantic knowledge and structures: tense, aspect, modality, negation and quantification. Theories of the development of word meanings are also dealt with, in the context of theories of the meaning of temporal terms.

5.1 The Auxiliary System of English

Languages use various morphological and syntactic devices to situate a sentence in time, to express differences in the type of action or state the sentence denotes, and to express the speaker's attitudes and beliefs with respect to the proposition of the sentence. *Tense* encodes time relations (past, present and future). Sentences do not always indicate tense: for example, in English main clauses in declarative sentences are always tensed, but subordinate clauses may or may not be tensed. *Aspect* is the term used to refer to devices for expressing further properties of the action or state denoted by a verb (for example, whether an action is ongoing or completed). *Modality* is the term used to refer to the expression of various attitudes and beliefs on the part of the speaker towards the proposition expressed by the verb (such as probability and volition; these are described in more detail below). In English, these aspects of the meaning of a sentence are represented by inflection of the verb (morphological suffixes) and auxiliary verbs.

5.1.1 Auxiliary Verbs and Morphological Endings

The gross facts concerning the expression of temporal relations and modality in English are as follows. Modality is expressed via auxiliary verbs: verbs such as 'can', 'should', etc. which occur as the first element after the subject of the sentence (1a,b):

(1a)   Sue can leave
(1b)   Sue should leave

There are two aspects in English, *perfective* and *progressive*, which correspond approximately to whether the action expressed by the main verb is completed or ongoing, as the examples (2) and (3) below respectively illustrate. The auxiliary 'have' expresses perfective aspect – i.e. that the action in question is in some manner completed:

(2)   Sue has died

The auxiliary 'be' expresses progressive aspect – i.e. that the action in question is ongoing:

(3)   The bread is rising

These three types of auxiliary verb (modals, perfective 'have', progressive 'be') are not mutually exclusive, and sentences may occur with all three:

(4)   Sue should have been dancing yesterday

The ordering of the three types of auxiliary is rigid: the modal must precede perfective 'have' and/or progressive 'be', and perfective 'have' must precede progressive 'be'. The last type of auxiliary verb in English is passive 'be', which always follows any other auxiliaries in the sentence:

(5a)   Sue should be arrested
(5b)   Sue has been arrested
(5c)   Sue is being arrested

   Although they are frequently awkward-sounding, combinations of all four types of auxiliary (modal, perfective, progressive and passive) are possible:

(6)   Sue should have been being praised (not vilified)

The presence of perfective 'have' dictates that the perfective suffix '-ed'/'-en' appear on the following verbal element, whether that is a main verb or another auxiliary verb; the presence of progressive 'be' dictates that the progressive suffix '-ing' appears on the following verbal element; the presence of passive 'be' dictates the passive suffix '-ed'/'-en' (homophonous with the perfective suffix) on the following verb:

(6)   Sue should have been being praised

In English, past or present tense is morphologically marked on the first of the verbal elements (auxiliary or main verb) in the sentence, as shown in (7a–j):

(7a)   John can swim [present marked on a modal]
(7b)   John could swim [past marked on a modal]
(7c)   John has cried [present perfective]
(7d)   John had cried [past perfective]
(7e)   John is crying [present progressive]
(7f)   John was crying [past progressive]
(7g)   John is vilified these days [present passive]
(7h)   John was vilified in those days [past passive]
(7i)   John walks [present marked on main verb]
(7j)   John walked [past marked on main verb]

The morphological system of the English verb is rather impoverished: past and present tense are indicated consistently, but (unlike in many languages) with no indication of the type of subject noun phrase, except for the third person singular subject in the present tense of regular verbs ('I/you/we/they walk' vs. 'He/she/it walks'). Futurity in English can be indicated by use of the modal verb 'will'/'would':

(8)   John will leave

As mentioned above, not all subordinate clauses are tensed. Untensed embedded clauses can take three basic forms: those with the infinitive marker 'to', as in (9a); 'bare' infinitives such as those in (9b); and '-ing' forms such as (9c,d). In addition to untensed subordinate clauses, there are subjunctive verb forms used in the complement to some verbs, as, for example, the subjunctive form of the verb 'be' ('were') in (9e).

(9a)   John wants Bill to leave
(9b)   John saw Bill leave
(9c)   John saw Bill leaving
(9d)   John saw Bill after leaving quietly
(9e)   John wished he were dead

5.1.2   Negation and "Do" Support'

If the sentence is negated, the negative morpheme follows the first auxiliary element, if there is one:

(10a)   John may not swim
(10b)   John has not cried
(10c)   John is not crying
(10d)   John was not arrested

If there is no auxiliary, a special auxiliary verb element 'do' is used to 'carry' the negative morpheme:

(11a)   John did not leave
(11b)   *John left not

The same auxiliary verb appears in questions, when there is no other auxiliary in the sentence:

(12a)   Did John leave?
(12b)   *Left John?

When an auxiliary element is present, it is that element that inverts with the subject in questions:

(13a)   Will John leave?
(13b)   Has John left?
(13c)   Is John crying?
(13d)   Was John arrested?

5.1.3 A Syntactic Analysis

The syntax of the auxiliary system in English has been extensively debated in generative grammar. The analysis sketched here is adapted from a recent analysis by Pollock (1989). In this analysis, the auxiliary system of English is characterized by a hierarchically organized series of phrases: tense phrase, (TP); negative phrase (NegP); and agreement phrase (AgrP). The material contained under these nodes covers material contained under the IP (inflectional phrase) node introduced at the end of the last chapter. The tense phrase and the agreement phrase are, respectively, the location of features indicating tense ($\pm$ past) and person (first, second, third) and number ($\pm$ singular). The D-structure position of modal verbs is under tense and the D-structure position of the negative element 'not' is in the negative phrase. A sentence such as (14):

(14)   John may not go

would thus have a D-structure approximately like that in (15):

(15)

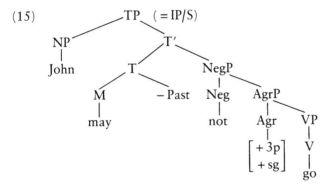

Morphological features are 'spelled out' as inflections on the verbs to which they are adjacent, and for this operation to take place, elements must in some cases move around from their D-structure position. Two sorts of movement may take place: an affix may move lower down to meet up with the verbal element on which it is realized or a verb may move upwards to meet up with its affix. In Pollock's analysis of English, a combination of these two types of operation is necessary. In a simple sentence with no auxiliary verbs or negation, the tense and agreement features move downwards to meet the main verb; thus (simplifying considerably Pollock's analysis) the sentence 'John left' will have a derivation along the lines in (16):

(16)
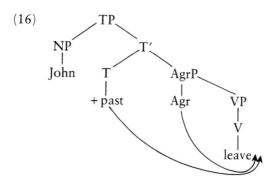

The auxiliary verb 'do', which occurs when the sentence is negative, is gen-
erated under Agr in deep structure and raised (together with Agr features) to
the tense phrase; thus 'John didn't leave' will have a derivation along the lines
in (17):

(17)
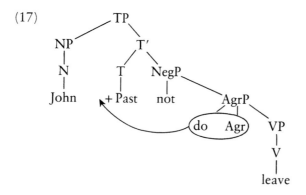

Similarly, the auxiliaries 'have' and 'be' which we will assume (extending
Pollock's analysis) originate as the head of perfective, progressive and passive
phrases, will be raised up to T, stopping at AgrP on the way to pick up
agreement features. Thus, for example, the derivation of 'John has died' will
be along the lines in (18):

(18)
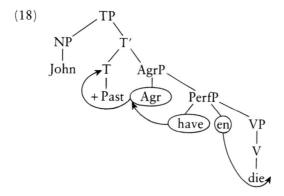

The movement exemplified by verb movement in (17) and (18) is different from the movement operations considered in the last chapter: the formation of wh-questions, passive sentences and other sentence types involves moving a complete phrasal node (NP, PP, AP, etc.), whereas the movement in (17) and (18) involves movement of a word-level unit ('do' and 'have' in the examples). This latter type of movement is constrained in particular ways: most notably, in that the word must move into a 'head' position, becoming the item that fleshes out the syntactic category that determines the phrasal type with a lexical item.

As we saw above, the perfective, progressive and passive auxiliaries determine the suffix on the following verb and this is expressed by placing the suffix in the determining phrase in D-structure and then lowering it to the next verb, as shown for the perfective '-en' suffix in (18).[1]

This summary of Pollock's analysis is quite a bit simplified and does not reflect the manner in which Pollock argues that the operations used to derive the surface structures (particularly verb movement) are motivated and limited by principles of grammar. The English system is also a relatively complex one: structurally similar languages such as French have a somewhat more straight-forward system, which uses verb-raising but not affix-lowering, a difference that Pollock (following Emonds 1978) shows is reflected, among other things, in differences in the positioning of adverbs in the two languages. The difference between English and French illustrated in (19a–d) can be accounted for if French has a rule that raises main verbs (not just auxiliaries, as in English) to a position (TP) outside the VP, as shown schematically in (20):

(19a) *John kisses often Mary
(19b) *Jean embrasse souvent Marie*
(19c) John often kisses Mary
(19d) **Jean souvent embrasse Marie*
(20)   [NP   [[Adv   V ...]]

      John   often   kisses

      Jean   *souvent*   *embrasse*

5.2 The Acquisition of Auxiliary Systems: Syntax

A simple approach to the acquisition of the syntax of auxiliary systems would be to hypothesize that the structural configurations given in the last section for

English represent syntactic specifications that are common to these grammatical phenomena in languages of the general type exemplified by English. The primary task of the language learner would then be to determine the details of the operations that apply to those structures: does his language have movement of main verbs to tense phrase? If there is no movement of a verb to tense phrase, how does tense become realized? Is there affix-lowering? And so on. For the purposes of this chapter I will adopt this approach, although some research suggests in fact that it is too simplistic, and that languages can vary not only in the operations that apply to tense, aspect and negation structures, but in the basic configuration of the structures themselves (see, for example, Rivero 1990). However, to the extent that we can assume that there is a stage at which a basic configuration for the auxiliary system has been fixed without the acquisition of all operations that apply to it, the simplification is a harmless one.

One of the notable facts arising from studies of the acquisition of English is that the auxiliary system is mastered without many of the logically possible errors. Children do overgeneralize regular verbal endings (saying 'goed' for 'went', etc. as we saw in chapter 3) and auxiliaries may be omitted where the adult language requires them. However, children do not appear to make errors in the order of auxiliary elements and the errors of overgeneralization they make with inflection are limited. It is striking that the third person singular inflection is not overextended to modal verbs; children learning English do not produce forms such as 'He mays go'. The absence of this error will follow directly from the structure given above for the English auxiliary system: because modal verbs are placed in D-structure under the tense phrase, above the agreement phrase, they will never come into contact with agreement features and so will never be inflected for person and number.

There are several other logically possible errors that the structure of English auxiliaries would allow, but which are not made. There is nothing in the base structure of the English auxiliary system that would prevent a child from forming questions by inverting a main verb with the subject (producing 'Goes he?', etc); but children do not appear to make this error. English-speaking children do omit inversion where it is needed, but they do not appear to overapply it.

A similar relatively error-free pattern of learning has been observed in the acquisition of German, a language that has verb movement. German is a language with a basic verb-final word order. This order is apparent in the surface order of subordinate clauses but not main clauses. In the surface order of main clauses in German the verb is in second position, following after the subject or a sentence-initial adverbial element. The generally agreed account of these facts is that the verb moves from sentence-final position in main clauses to its surface position. Omitting details of the structures involved, and simplifying, German sentences will involve underlying and derived structures along the lines in (21):

(21a) *Anton im Garten arbeitet*
      A.   in garden works   underlying order

(21b) *Anton arbeitet   im Garten*
      'A.   is working in the garden'   surface order

(21c) *Ich mit meinen Hund spiele, sobald ich nach Hause komme*
      I   with my   dog   play as soon as I to house   come
                                                         underlying order

(21d) *Ich spiele mit meinen Hund, sobald   ich nach Hause komme*
      'I   play with my   dog   as soon as I arrive home'
                                                          surface order

As (21c,d) show, the movement of the verb from its basic position takes place only in the main clause. Where a sentence contains an auxiliary as well as a main verb, it is the auxiliary (which bears the tense) that moves:

(22a) *Er uns gestern besucht hat*
      He us   yesterday visited has   underlying order

(22b) *Er hat uns gestern besucht*
      'He (has) visited us yesterday'   surface order

Clahsen (1985) reports data from the acquisition of German, revealing a series of stages with respect to placement of the verb. First there is vacillation between placing the verb in second or final position, with a preference for final position. At a somewhat later stage, more complex forms with an auxiliary are used; the tensed form (the main verb if there is no auxiliary, otherwise the auxiliary) is placed in second position and the non-tensed form in final position. Finally, as soon as the child begins to use embedded clauses, the finite verb correctly appears at the end of the embedded clause. Examples of utterances from these stages are given in (23). (Deviations from standard German spelling are those used by Clahsen to represent child speech.)

(23) *Stage A*
     boden bürs
     floor brush
     [child is brushing the floor]

hol hund
fetch dog
[child is fetching the dog]

hier autos fahr
here cars drive
[child is putting a car into the service station]

Stage B
das ist theo
that is T.
[looking at a picture book]

jetzt hast du sechs
now have you six
[telling mother she has six crescents]

ich hab ihn aufsetzt
I have it on-put
[child has put on a hat]

Stage C
ich will mal sehen ob das schwarz is
I want just see whether that black is
[child wants to look through video camera]

weiß nich der hingeflogen is
know not he flown is
[child does not know where his father has flown]

The examples in (23) are from different stages in the development of the same child. The examples in Stage A were produced when the child was approximately two and a half years old, those in Stage B when the child was approximately three years old and those in Stage C when the child was approximately three and a half. (This summary omits a stage between A and B above where verb forms incorporating particles (such as '*aufsetzt*' in the last example under B above) come to be favoured for final-placement). From this example, it appears that although there may be a brief period in which the rule for placement of the verb in second position in the main clause in German is not known, once the rule has been introduced into the child's grammar, its application is not overgeneralized to subordinate clauses.

A study by Lundin and Platzack (1988) on the acquisition of Swedish is useful in bringing to light a sequence of stages that clearly suggests the introduction of verb movement. Swedish, like German, has a rule of 'verb in second position'; unlike German, its basic order is subject–verb–object, and so Swedish does not exhibit verb-final order in subordinate (or main) clauses. The effect of the verb-second rule is seen, for example, where there is an adverb in sentence-initial position:

(24a)   *I dag har jag mycket för Fru Svensson*
       today have I a lot for Mrs S.
(24b)   **I dag jag har mycket för Fru Svensson*

Although we have not so far made any mention of the verb's destination in languages with a verb-second rule, a widely-accepted view is that it is placed in the position of the complementizer, as shown schematically in (25):

(25)

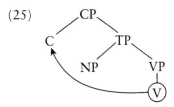

A simple sentence will in fact involve a double movement: of the verb to the head position of the complementizer phrase and of the subject noun phrase to the left of that, as in (26):

(26)

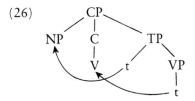

Good evidence for this approach to word order is that when there is a word filling the head position of the complementizer phrase (i.e. an overt complementizer, such as Swedish '*att*', the equivalent of English 'that'), the verb does not occur in second position. This is well illustrated by the contrast between the placement of verbs in main and subordinate clauses that are negative. In main clauses, the verb precedes the negative; in subordinate clauses, the negative precedes the verb:

(27a)   *Han köpte inte boken*
        he bought not book-the
(27b)   *. . . att han inte köpte boken*
        that he not bought book-the

As illustrated in (28), (27a) can be formed by the double movement sketched above; in (27b), however, the complementizer '*att*' will block movement into the C position, resulting in the negative–verb word order:

(28a)   main clause

(28b)   subordinate clause

Lundin and Platzack studied the data from three children's acquisition of Swedish. They observed that each child made errors in placement of the verb, initially failing in some instances to place the verb second in main clauses. Examples of the children's errors are given in (29):

(29a)   *mamma inte spilla i med saften*
        mommy not spill in with juice   (Embla, 27 months)
(29b)   *nu han sitta på, sen dom åka. Nu han kör*
        now he sit on, then they go. Now he drive   (Tor, 30 months)

(29c)   *Du inte bo därinne*
      you not live therein   (Freja, 32 months)

These errors disappear rapidly for children in the course of the third year, a fact that Lundin and Platzack argue is related to the development of finite (tensed) verb forms.

To summarize this section, the errors observed in the acquisition of the syntax of the auxiliary system of English appear to be errors of omission rather than of commission. Children do fail to use the correct, inverted word order in questions (with the auxiliary verb before the subject NP) and they fail to use the auxiliary 'do' when it is needed. But they do not overgeneralize inversion of the auxiliary and the subject to main verbs. Nor do they commit the many other logically possible errors, such as the over-use of regular inflection to modal verbs. To a certain extent such an error-free pattern of learning can be accounted for by hypothesizing that children arrive early on at the correct underlying structural configuration for the auxiliary system of their language and subsequently acquire the operations that apply to those structures. In the case of Swedish, a language that has a rule of main verb movement, we saw this quite dramatically: a period in which the adult underlying word order is used by children precedes the acquisition of the correct, verb-second order.

5.3   The Acquisition of Negation

In the previous sections, we saw an analysis in which negation of the sentence is expressed by a phrasal node (NegP) above the VP. In the case of the acquisition of verb movement in Swedish, the placement of the verb relative to the negative element was used as a test (in both adult and child grammars) for whether verb movement had taken place. This section briefly summarizes some findings concerning the development of negation. The observations are largely based on Klima and Bellugi (1973); Wode (1977); Weissenborn et al. 1989.

Although there are differences in detail, studies of various languages show a broad pattern of development along the lines of the following three-stage process. First, there is a very early stage where the negative form used in negative responses to questions occurs in either initial or final position in the utterance. In English, this negative form is 'no' ('Do you want salt?' 'No, sugar') and this stage in negation includes negative 'pivot–open' type utterances such as 'No milk' and 'No bed' as well as more complex examples such as 'No I see truck'. While the details of interpretation are not clear in all cases, at least for some children such forms appear to be used to express denial of a proposition, as well as negative responses to questions. For denial of a proposition the negative 'not' is required in English (in the case of the third example above, the gloss might be something along the lines 'I can't/don't see the truck'). Second the correct negative form for denial is introduced, but the placement of the negative may be faulty. In English, non-adult types of utterances may result simply from the omission of 'do' and/or modal verbs: 'Kathryn no like celery'; 'Kathryn not quite through'. In other languages, errors may arise from the failure to apply rules that affect surface word order, as in the case of Swedish above. Finally, the correct forms and orders are acquired, including subtle details such as the fact that in German, the negative element follows a definite noun phrase object, as shown in (30):

(30a) *Unser Hund hat den   Mann nicht gebissen*
        Our   dog   has the   man   not   bitten
(30b) *Unser Hund hat nicht den Mann   gebissen*

Wode reports that until the last stage of development, German-speaking children he studied allowed the negative to precede a definite noun phrase.

5.4   An Aside on Developmental Orders and Individual Development

The reader who goes off to consult the sources cited in the previous sections will find quite considerable differences in the developmental patterns reported. For example, while Wode (1977) reports the early stage of sentence-external marking of negation as a cross-linguistic trend, Weissenborn et al. (1989) do not find substantial evidence of such a stage for the development of negation in any of the three languages for which they collected data (French, German and Hebrew). Some of the variation in observed patterns may reflect genuine differences in the development of individuals (some children may skip stages); some of the variation may also be the result of sampling error (a failure of the research to catch all the stages of development). What is clear is that some types of error do occur, and these may provide a window on the type of system that characterizes children's grammar. Early sentence-initial negative placement can be construed as an example of a primitive right-branching structure, along the lines discussed with respect to 'pivot–open' grammars in the last chapter. The verb placement facts from Swedish provide us with an excellent example of grammar formation in action – the acquisition of V-movement changes the grammar to conform with the superficial structures of the adult language.

5.5   The Acquisition of Modality, Tense and Aspect

This section summarizes findings concerning children's knowledge of the semantics of modals, tense and aspect.

5.5.1   Modality

Modality is a cover term for a range of meanings related to the beliefs and attitudes of the speaker. In English, this range of meanings is expressed primarily by means of modal auxiliaries: 'can', 'will', 'shall', 'may', 'must', etc. We have already seen that modal auxiliaries in English have special syntactic properties – the absence of third person agreement ('*He mays go'), for example, distinguishes the modals from both main verbs and the auxiliaries 'have' and 'be'. The meanings of the modal verbs are complex and overlapping. A basic distinction is drawn in the literature between what are termed the *root* and *epistemic* meanings of the modals. (The terminology varies, however; see Palmer 1979; Lyons 1977; Coates 1983 for discussion and definitions.) Broadly, the root meanings convey the speaker's beliefs and attitudes, indicating *inter alia* permission, probability, obligation, intention and ability. The epistemic meanings, frequently related to the root meanings, convey some sense of a process of reasoning – the drawing of a conclusion based on evidence. The two kinds of modal meaning can be expressed by the same auxiliary, resulting in ambiguity. Thus

(31)   John must be honest

is ambiguous between a root meaning of obligation ('It is required of John/I require of John that he be honest') and an epistemic meaning of inference ('Taking the evidence into account, I conclude that John is honest'). In the root paraphrase given for (31) above, I used 'be' (a subjunctive form) rather than the indicative present tense 'is' ('It is required of John that he is honest').

Although the use of the subjunctive is felt by many speakers of English to be archaic, such use of a particular inflectional form or forms to express modal meanings is common in the world's languages.

Stephany (1986) surveys the literature on the development of modality. She reports that for all the languages for which she has examined child language data, root meanings emerge before epistemic meanings, a finding that is perhaps not surprising given that root meanings involve statements about the speaker's knowledge and beliefs about the world rather than inference based on such knowledge and beliefs. For English, several studies surveyed by Stephany, as well as additional studies such as Fletcher 1985, yield the following general picture. Modal meanings are not expressed exclusively by modal auxiliaries in the adult language, and there is an early period (before three years) when certain modal meanings are expressed by the verbal forms 'wanna' (desire, 'want to'), 'gonna' (intention, 'be going to') and 'hafta' (obligation, 'must'). The first modal auxiliary verbs to emerge are the negated forms 'can't' and 'won't', followed by (in order) 'can', 'will' 'shall', 'could', 'would', 'should', 'may' and 'must'. There are minor differences in this order for individual children; but the general pattern of emergence is quite plain. Only one child in the studies surveyed by Stephany was using 'must' in the first half of his third year. The development of knowledge and use of the full range of modal verbs is a process that may extend into middle childhood and later (Major 1974). However, it is plausible that the basic nature of the modal auxiliary system for English is in place in pre-school age children, with problems arising from degrees of syntactic and semantic complexity of particular sentences in which the modal verb is embedded and the relative frequency of the various modals in the adult language.

5.5.2   Tense and Aspect

In the study by Major just mentioned, children had difficulty repeating and performing sentence-transformation tasks with the sentence in (32), containing the modal 'will' used in its futurative sense, plus the perfective auxiliary 'have':

(32)   John will have talked to his teacher

As Major observes, the difficulty of this sentence was probably rooted in its semantic (and conceptual) complexity. To understand the time relations in the sentence, the event of talking must be conceived of as a completed action (because of the use of the perfective auxiliary) that is to take place at some point in the future. We understand the notions 'past', 'present' and 'future' in relation to a particular point, which may or may not correspond to the time of the utterance. The system of time in relation to an abstract 'anchoring point' has been conceptualized in the work of Reichenbach (1947); Reichenbach's system and subsequent studies (in particular, Smith 1978) have proved a fruitful framework for the study of children's knowledge of tense and aspect.

The central concepts in Reichenbach's analysis are those of speech time (ST), event time (ET) and reference time (RT). ST refers to the temporal point at which the utterance takes place; ET to the point at which the event described in utterance takes place; and RT to a point established in relation to ST and ET, by which pastness and futurity are measured. The three points may coincide. In (33),

(33)   Sue is singing (now)

the event of singing is ongoing at the point of utterance. Where ST and ET coincide, as they do in (33), the RT is equal to the ST and ET. This contrasts with the situation in

(34)   Sue was singing (then)

where the use of the past tense signals an ET and RT prior to the ST, and (35)

(35)   Sue will sing (tomorrow)

where the futurative modal 'will' indicates an ET and RT posterior to the ST. A sentence such as (32) illustrates one way in which ET and RT may not be identical: in (32), the use of the perfective aspect requires an RT at some point posterior to the ST, with the ET located between ST and RT (terminating either at RT or before RT).

Smith (1980) puts forward a strong hypothesis concerning the development of temporal relations. She proposes that there is an initial stage in which children command the concept of non-present time (pastness and futurity, although Smith does not discuss the latter), but that their point of orientation is limited to the present. To put it in the terms of Reichenbach's system, at this early stage, RT will always be equivalent to ST. This stage will, Smith suggests, be over for most children by the fourth year.

Smith presents convincing evidence from the spontaneous speech of young children that they are able to use past tense inflections on verbs in a manner similar to adults – that is, that their use of past tense inflections genuinely reflects a grasp of the concept of pastness. For example, Smith describes an experiment by diPaolo and Smith (1978), where it was shown that English-speaking children aged four and older almost exclusively used the past tense to describe events acted out by the experimenter with toys; both the simple past (e.g. 'He walked') and the past progressive ('He was walking') were used. This evidence refutes the suggestion of some researchers that adult tense inflections were used by children to convey aspectual distinctions, such as whether the action was completed or not. Weist (1986) reviews literature on the early acquisition of tense and aspect in a variety of languages, confirming that the two are distinct components of the child's system from a very early stage.

Smith's theory that there is an early stage in which ST and RT are not distinguished is an interesting one, and its predictions have not yet been tested; the lack of complex time expressions (where the reference time differs from the speech time) in the early speech of children may simply reflect limitations in the things and situations about which children converse, rather than a limitation in their cognitive or linguistic abilities. And complexity may lead to error, without the implication that basics of the system are missing; for example, did the difficulty experienced by children in Major's study with sentence (32) arise from the relative complexity of the sentence or from some true deficit at the level of manipulating reference time points? This area of the development of grammatical knowledge remains relatively unexplored.

5.6 The Development of Word Meanings

Smith's study illustrates the usefulness of Reichenbach's system for describing time relations expressed by verbal inflection and auxiliaries. The system has also been used recently in discussions of the development of word meanings. In this section we will look at an influential theory of the development of word meanings (the semantic feature hypothesis), with particular reference to temporal terms. Reichenbach's system has a role to play in providing an explanation of some facts previously used to support this theory.

5.6.1 Word Meanings

A long-standing theory with respect to the representation of word meanings is the *componential* or *feature* analysis of words. The basic idea is that the human mind (linguistic capacity) has a vocabulary of primitives that are used to 'decompose' the meaning of words. So, for example, the meanings of 'dog' and 'puppy' might be partially represented along the lines:

$$
\text{dog} \begin{bmatrix} +\text{ANIMAL} \\ +\text{CANINE} \\ -\text{JUVENILE} \end{bmatrix} \quad \text{puppy} \begin{bmatrix} +\text{ANIMAL} \\ +\text{CANINE} \\ +\text{JUVENILE} \end{bmatrix}
$$

The capitalized words (ANIMAL etc.) represent components of meaning. They may be assigned different ($\pm$) values (though the utility of such $\pm$ values is at best severly limited; Kempson, 1977). Feature representations have various advantages. For example, they provide a way of expressing intuitions about shared properties of non-synonymous words ('dog' and 'puppy' are identical in their representations, with the exception of the feature specification for JUVENILE). However, the use of such features does not resolve a central question: what is the relation between our mental coding of the meanings of words and the 'world outside' (the data of our sense perceptions)? Nor are such feature representations as currently developed adequate to the task of representing everything we may feel to be part of the meaning of a word. Often, discussions of word meaning allow for a word to be tagged with particulars that are wholly or partly culture-dependent. To give a classic example, the word 'bachelor' in one of its meanings will share many of the feature specifications of the word 'man', plus additional statements to the effect 'unmarried'. Thus, while some of the features proposed as part of the meaning of a word might be assumed to be part of the general cognitive/ perceptual capacities of human beings, other specifications may represent culture-specific aspects of our use of words and so are less plausibly part of a universal human capacity for concept representation.

5.6.2 *The Semantic Feature Hypothesis*

A componential analysis of word meanings was a key part of a developmental theory set out in the 1970s, in Clark (1971) and other studies. Clark's analysis focused on two properties of feature analysis of word meanings:

1. Some semantic features can be organized in a hierarchy. For example, the temporal prepositions 'before', 'after' and 'while' can be represented as

governed by a hierarchical organization of features as follows:

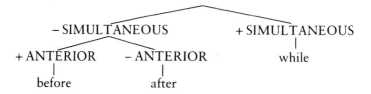

The feature [±ANTERIOR] comes into play only for words specified as [−SIMULTANEOUS].
  2.   Semantic features are given plus and minus values.

Clark's hypothesis was that superordinate features in feature hierarchies would be filled in first in the child's representation of word meanings and that positive feature specifications would be acquired first. In the case of the temporal terms above, a specification for simultaneity would be part of a word's meaning before a specification for anteriority was added, predicting that the difference between 'before' and 'after' would be mastered later than the general distinction between 'before'/'after' and 'while'. In addition, the priority of positive feature specifications in Clark's theory predicted that 'while' (and 'when') would be mastered by children earlier than 'before'/'after' and that 'before' would be mastered by children earlier than 'after'.

  Some early experimental work on children's production and comprehension of temporal terms appeared to support these predictions with respect to children's understanding of 'when', 'before' and 'after' (Clark 1971). In addition, the phenomenon of 'overextension' of word use (partially entailed by the hypothesis that superordinate features have priority) was also shown to be a real and common one in children's use of certain types of words. Clark (1973) examined many cases in which children (typically aged one to two and a half years) overextended the use of words in a way which could be described in terms of a focus on perceptual/semantic features common to sets of lexical items. For example, the word 'moon' might be used to refer not only to the moon, but to all kinds of round objects. Such overextension is compatible with a theory of the development of word meanings in which words are initially underspecified, the details distinguishing their meaning from related items still to be filled in.

5.6.3   Challenges to the Semantic Feature Hypothesis

Despite its simplicity and the early supporting evidence, the semantic feature hypothesis for the development of word meanings has not fared well in recent years. The evidence in favour of the priority of superordinate features has been mixed and is open to alternative explanation. Also, the pervasiveness of overgeneralization of word meanings has been challenged.

Temporal reference and the meaning of temporal prepositions Many studies on the comprehension of temporal prepositions followed Clark's original study, and produced results that were not always consistent with Clark's findings. For example, superior performance with 'before' (as opposed to 'after') was not found in all the studies subsequent to Clark's. Coker (1978) provides a clear review of the literature as well as evidence that children's success in interpreting such prepositions may be dependent on the complexity of the syntactic structures in which the prepositions are embedded, an indication that errors with the prepositions may not be the result of lack of knowledge of the meaning of the prepositions themselves.

Stevenson and Pollitt (1987) have provided a new theoretical perspective, linking findings on children's understanding of temporal prepositions to a linguistic analysis of those temporal terms that uses Reichenbach's model. Stevenson and Pollitt follow Partee's (1984) analysis of 'before' and 'after'. Partee assumes that each new event in a narrative moves the reference time forward. In sentences with subordinate clauses introduced by 'before' or 'after', it is the subordinate clause that sets the time point with respect to which the action of the main clause is evaluated, i.e. the subordinate clause sets the reference time, and the main clause sets the event time.

In one part of their study, Stevenson and Pollitt (like Clark and others) required children to act out both clauses of two-clause sentences with 'before' or 'after', with the subordinate clause in either initial or final position, as illustrated in (36a–d):

(36a)   Before the boy picked up the balloon, he rang the bell
(36b)   The girl picked up the balloon before she rang the bell
(36c)   After the girl rang the bell, she picked up the balloon
(36d)   The boy rang the bell after he picked up the balloon

The subjects were aged between two years eleven months and four years five months. Like Clark and others, Stevenson and Pollitt found some tendency to perform the action of the two clauses in the order in which they are mentioned (correct for (36b,c) and incorrect for (36a,d)). There were also quite a large number of errors in which the action of one or other clause in the sentence was omitted from the child's acting-out. An analysis of these errors of omission showed that for 'before', but not for 'after', there were more subordinate clause omissions than there were main clause omissions. Stevenson and Pollitt point out that this pattern of omission errors fits with Partee's analysis of the role of 'before' and 'after'. While both 'before' and 'after' set the reference time for the main clause, the reference time for 'before', as Partee noted, does not form part of the final event sequence. To put it another way, the action of the reference time (subordinate clause) has to have taken place before the action of the event time (main clause) in the case of 'after', but not in the case of 'before', making it natural that the subordinate clause should be omitted more often in the case of sentences with 'before'.

Overextension and underextension   The role of overextension in supporting the semantic feature hypothesis has also been challenged. It is critical to a theory that says words develop by the gradual addition of more and more detailed feature specifications that overextension (focus on a feature or features of meaning that is/are common to a group of words) should occur more commonly than underextension. Underextension is the use of a particular word with too restricted a range of reference (for example, the use of the word 'shoes' to refer to a particular pair of shoes, and not to shoes in general). However, underextension of word meanings is much more difficult to observe than overextension, since usage in the former but not the latter case is a correct usage in the adult system. Griffiths (1986) argues that underextension, though difficult to spot, may be a quite normal and frequent stage in learning the meanings of words. Griffiths argues for a developmental theory along the following lines: a word (phonetic form) is associated with a mental image (deriving in more or less detail from the perceptual event, the experience, from which the child has learned the word). This association results naturally in underextension. Subsequently the child frees the word from specific associations, assigning it whatever the correct representation is in the adult or near-adult meaning of the word. On this approach to the development of word meanings, the child can be seen as applying an innate vocabulary of semantic primitives (features) gradually to assign an internal representation to the word. This does not mean that the initial proposals of Clark concerning the priority of superordinate features and plus-value features are completely invalidated. But such generalizations appear not to represent a necessary first step in vocabulary acquisition and not to govern in a completely regular way the learning paths for related lexical items.

5.7   Quantification and Logical Form

The reader with a minimal acquaintance with semantic theory will read the heading of this section and think 'Ah, now we're getting to it: a discussion of children's knowledge of quantifier scope relations, the role of that knowledge in restricting pronominal reference, etc.' That reader will certainly be disappointed.

In the model of grammar sketched in the last chapter, movement operations link not only D-structure to S-structure, but also S-structure to logical form. One function of this application of movement was to express the ambiguity of sentences containing quantifiers such as 'all' and 'every' ('Every leprechaun kissed a unicorn') in terms of the ordering of the quantifiers in the hierarchical structure of logical form; this ordering is achieved by the application of movements to S-structure. Quantifiers such as 'all' and 'every' share with question words such as 'what' and 'who' the requirement that they bind a variable in the semantic representation – thus there is a fundamental similarity in the semantic representation of, for example, sentences such as (37a) and (38a), as shown in the schematic semantic representations in (37b) and (38b):

(37a) Every unicorn kissed Sue
(37b) For all x (x a unicorn), x kissed Sue
(38a) Which unicorn kissed Sue?
(38b) For which x (x a unicorn), x kissed Sue

As mentioned in the last chapter, languages are hypothesized to differ in whether they use movement (the creation of an operator–variable representation) as an operation between both D-structure and S-structure and S-structure and logical form or only as an operation between S-structure and logical form. English is a language of the former type, Chinese a language of the latter.

If an operator–variable structure is essential to the interpretation of questions and other sentence types in all languages (as represented by the presence of movement as an operation between S-structure and logical form in all languages), then it would make sense to suppose that this type of abstract (logical form) representation would be present very early on in children's language. If an operator–variable structure is the key to the meaning of a question, then it follows that adult-like use of questions entails a level or levels of representation with operator–variable relations.

We saw in the last chapter that by three years there is evidence from sensitivity to island constraints that children learning English have movement 'in the syntax' (as an operation between D-structure and S-structure). Despite the fact that it appeals to the logic of things that children learning, for example, Chinese, have logical forms of the requisite type if they correctly comprehend questions (involving movement between S-structure and logical form), substantial evidence for such movement is not at present available. Some recent work on English does indicate that adult-like interpretation of quantifiers ('all', 'every') which may depend on the correct application of movement between S-structure and logical form, may take a number of years to develop.

Experiments by J. Piaget and by M. Donaldson and colleagues have tested children's understanding of the meaning of 'all' and 'every' (see Donaldson 1978, ch. 6 for a summary). First, it is important to note that by age three (the youngest age of children in the experiments) children have some understanding of the meaning of quantifiers. For example, faced with an array of toy garages with doors that open, three-year-olds are generally accurate in their ability to inspect the array and verify whether a statement such as 'All the garage doors are open' is correct or not. (In Donaldson's experiments, children were asked to 'correct' the statements of a teddy bear by saying whether what the bear said was right, given the situation.) Where children frequently go wrong is in verifying the accuracy of statements in sentences that involve a quantifier and more than a single set of entities – for example, a set of garages and a set of cars. A basic finding is the following: children appear to focus on one of the sets of entities and evaluate the truth of a statement with a quantifier with respect to whether a particular quantifier relationship holds for that set. For example, a child may be asked to evaluate the correctness of the following two sentences:

(39)   All the cars are in the garages
(40)   All the garages have cars in them

when faced with one of either of two situations: a row of four garages, three of which contain cars; or a row of four garages, each of which contains a car, plus an additional car (not in a garage) at the end of the row. For adults (39) is true in the first of the two situations and false in the second of the two situations and (40) is false in the first situation and true in the second situation. The responses of many children, however, reveal a different understanding of the match between sentences and situations. Children will say that both sentences are false in the situation where there is a row of four garages, three of which contain cars, and they will say that both sentences are true in the situation where there are four garages and five cars. Thus the children respond consistently as if they were responding to the question 'Does every garage have a car in it?'

The basic pattern of results just described has been found in a number of studies and appears to be grounded partly in perceptual and partly in linguistic factors. In the example just described, perceptual properties of the stimuli (the greater salience of the garages than of the cars) may account for the fact that children consistently respond as if they were answering the question 'Does every garage have a car in it?' rather than as if they were answering the question 'Is every car in a garage?', which would produce the opposite of the responses observed. Reporting on a recent series of studies using a picture-cued question response task, Philip and Takahashi (1990) suggest that the existence of errors with the quantifier 'every' (which they use in their experiments in preference to 'all') may follow from the child's analysis of the quantifier as a sentential adverb. In their studies, a question such as (41)

(41)   Is every pig eating an apple?

when asked with reference to a picture of three pigs and two alligators, each of which is eating an apple, produces a relatively high number of incorrect ('no') responses. A question such as (42)

(42)   Is a pig eating every apple?

when asked with reference to the same picture produces a relatively high number of correct (also 'no') responses. Philip and Takahashi suggest that this pattern of responses is due to the child's preference for an interpretation of both questions along the lines:

(43)   Is it always the case that a pig is eating an apple?

They propose that the quantifier 'every' corresponds in the child's logical form of the sentence to an operator equivalent to the operator for adult adverb 'always', on an interpretation of 'always' where 'always' requires that the events described by the sentence correspond exhaustively to a set of 'relevant events'. What is a relevant event may be determined by pragmatic and perceptual factors. Thus it is assumed that each of the five eating events in the picture used for questions (41) and (42) is taken by the child to be a relevant event, leading, in combination with the child's non-adult interpretation of 'every', to 'no' answers to both questions. (Other conditions in the experiment rule out non-linguistic accounts, such as a general tendency to answer 'no'.)

5.8   Summary and Conclusions

This chapter has ranged over a number of topics connected more or less loosely to one another and to the interface between syntactic and semantic representations and knowledge. Children in their third year command some notions of time and aspectual distinctions and are beginning to develop a repertoire of modal meanings. After a very early stage of incorrect use of negative forms (by some if not all children), negative usage begins to approximate to adult usage. Negative sentences can provide a key to observation of the development of some types of syntactic movement (particularly verb movement), which itself may be linked to the acquisition of temporal relations. In recent theories of verb movement (Pollock 1989 and others), finite tense requires an operator–variable structure, which the movement of the verb helps create. The development of word meanings has been the subject of considerable research. An early theory of the development of word meanings (the semantic feature hypothesis) runs up against problems in accounting for the full range of children's errors. Reichenbach's theory of time relations has provided a way of understanding some of the errors that children make in comprehending temporal terms ('before' and 'after') as well as their use and understanding of tense.

Whether children construct logical forms of the kind hypothesized for the adult grammar is not at present well understood, although there is some evidence that by age three children do have some grasp of the meaning of quantifiers and do construct some type of operator–variable structures. One major difficulty with establishing the semantic representations children have at a linguistic level is the cognitive complexity of the concepts involved. The relation between cognitive development and linguistic development is taken up in the next chapter, which deals with theories of language development.

Note

1   The formation of words by lowering affixes can be interpreted as an example of a different type of operation to movement of phrases (as in wh-movement and NP movement) or words (as in V-movement) to positions not internal to a word, and so does not present a problem for the general claim that movement may not lower elements (chapter 4, section 4.1.3).

Further Reading

Chapters by P. Griffiths and U. Stephany in Fletcher and Garman's (1986) collection are particularly clearly written and cover a good deal of material on the development of word meanings and modality. Chien and Wexler (1989) contains further data on children's comprehension of quantifiers, in the context of recent studies of quantification and logical form.

Questions and Exercises

1. Compare and contrast the first stage of negative development described in the text (section 5.3) with the errors Philip and Takahashi (1990) found that children make in interpreting the quantifier 'every' (section 5.7).

2. Linguists have drawn and studied a distinction between aspect and *aktionsart* (see Platzack 1979). Broadly speaking, the former term is used to refer to morphologically and syntactically represented properties of the situation described, such as whether the action is ongoing or completed, as described briefly in the text with respect to English perfective and progressive aspects. The latter term, *aktionsart*, is used to refer to properties of the situation described by a sentence that are inherent to the conceptual basis of the situation, most particularly whether a change in situation or a stable state is involved or not. Although aspect and *aktionsart* are distinct concepts, they go hand in hand to the extent that certain verbs, by virtue of their meaning, will naturally lend themselves to use in certain aspects – thus, for example, verbs denoting an activity leading to actual or potential change in state are readily used in the progressive aspect in English, while those denoting states are not:

(a)   John is running
(b)   John is writing a book
(c)   John is pouring drinks
(d)   John is weighing the flour
(e)   *John is owning a house
(f)   *John is looking like Tom
(g)   *John is knowing the answer
(h)   *John is weighing 150 pounds

Devise an experiment to test whether children's use of progressive aspect is sensitive to different types of verbs (activity vs. state).

6 Cognition, Environment and Language Learning

This chapter takes up some general issues concerning how linguistic knowledge develops. The first section reviews facts that argue that linguistic development is guided by a biologically given set of abilities. The following sections deal with questions concerning the acquisition in real time of linguistic knowledge, particularly the relative contributions of principles of universal grammar and of principles and mechanisms that lie outside grammar *per se*. The final sections of the chapter deal with the role of special speaking styles used to children and the relationship between language development and other aspects of cognitive development

6.1 Innateness

It is a standard assumption among linguists and many psychologists that much fundamental linguistic knowledge is innately given. That is, the child is assumed to be biologically equipped with knowledge of universal grammar – the basics of language structure. The child has, as it were, blueprints for all the possible types of language in her head (although not necessarily from the outset, as we will see below). In the course of language development she settles on the particular grammar of the language surrounding her.

Many facts about language development support in a general way the idea that there is a strong innate component of language structure. Language development exhibits many of the properties of biologically given behaviours (see Lenneberg 1967): three such properties in particular are worth noting here.

1. There is an *orderly progression of stages*. In different areas of grammar, we have seen that there is a distinct sequence in which children develop their linguistic abilities. For example, babbling emerges before first words; a one-word stage generally precedes the emergence of multi-word utterances; and specific morphemes and rules emerge in approximately the

same order across different children learning the same language (as, for example, in the order of emergence of English morphemes in Roger Brown's 1973 study). Although the age at which a particular stage is reached may vary considerably, there are rough guidelines (for example, the babbling period is generally placed between six months and the turn of the first year). A pattern of ordered stages in development is one of the hallmarks of biologically programmed behaviours (Lenneberg 1967). The existence of regular stages in language development is analogous to other biologically triggered phenomena in both humans and other species (such as walking in humans and flight in birds).

2. There is a *critical period*. Related to the fact that there are distinct stages in development is the fact that there is a critical age beyond which our ability to learn a language is significantly impaired. There is substantial debate about what exactly the critical age is, and what physiological changes it may reflect (see Lenneberg 1967; Krashen 1973; Curtiss 1977). None the less, from the early teens onwards most people exhibit a decreasing ability to learn a second language. And in those fortunately rare cases where an individual has been deprived of exposure to a first language in early and middle childhood, certain language skills may be unattainable (Curtiss 1977). Such observations support the view that early and middle childhood is a period in which we are biologically equipped to learn language in a way that we are not able to in later life. Again, there are analogies with other biologically programmed abilities. For example, kittens who are exposed to only restricted visual stimuli at an early period have long-term deficits in vision (see Kolb and Whishaw 1985, pp. 605–6 for a summary of pertinent research on vision).

3. Development is to a degree *independent of external stimuli*. Clear evidence of this is the fact that deaf children babble (see Locke 1983, ch. 1); such activity must be the result of a biologically timed programme that is not dependent on exposure to speech. Another case where a speech stimulus is either unnecessary or only minimally needed is categorical perception of speech sounds by infants who have had little exposure to speech (in chapter 2 we saw that six-week-old infants discriminate between speech sounds that adults categorize as distinct in a similarly categorical manner, and on a similarly fine-grained phonetic basis).

The existence of a biological programme for language learning does not preclude an important role for external stimuli. A child has to be exposed to language for normal development to take place. It is generally agreed that the child is an active learner, who 'works on' the speech she hears, using some form of grammar-forming mechanism. Current views of the nature of that mechanism have been formed in the context of several facts and assumptions about the nature of the learning situation. These are the topic of the next section.

6.2   Input and Errors

Input is usually understood to mean the speech forms to which the child is exposed, which may be augmented by contextual clues as to what an utterance means. The nature of the input itself provides a strong argument for the position that the child is equipped with a highly structured grammar-forming mechanism. The speech to which the child is exposed gives her only limited information concerning the correct rules for the language to be learned. Input can be divided into *positive* and *negative* evidence. The *positive* evidence (or positive input) is evidence that a particular form exists in a language. Hearing a sentence is positive evidence that it exists. One important limitation on positive input is that the sentences children hear do not contain overt information about their structure and meaning. In a sentence such as 'John told Bill to shave himself', the first two words must be analysed as subject noun phrase and verb, the reflexive pronoun 'himself' must refer to 'Bill' (it may not refer to 'John'), and so on. Sentences do not come ready tagged with information about what the component parts of the sentence are or what the sentence can or cannot mean, although the context of utterance may provide clues to possible meanings. Despite this lack of overt information about structure and meaning, children do manage to learn the rules of their language. Another limitation on positive input is that the child may hear only a limited sample of the sentence types that are actually grammatical in her language.

Not only do children get no overt information about structures and meanings, they are also not informed about which strings are ungrammatical. There is a lack of *negative* evidence. A child will generally hear only well-formed sentences and phrases (although the quality of the speech children hear has been a matter of dispute; see the final section of this chapter). Moreover, when children make errors in their own speech, they are not corrected by adults. In a well-known study, Brown and Hanlon (1970) found that parents responded to the truth value of children's utterances, but did not overtly correct ungrammatical forms produced by the child (see Demetras et al. 1986 for a more recent study making the same point). Despite the lack of negative evidence, the child manages to avoid or eliminate errors and arrive at the correct grammar of the language around her.

The restricted nature of the input (the paucity of positive evidence and the lack of negative evidence) is often referred to as the *poverty of the stimulus* and has frequently been invoked by Chomsky and others as a point in favour of a learning mechanism in which the child's innate knowledge of principles of grammar plays a major role in guiding development (see Chomsky 1959; Chomsky 1965; Hornstein and Lightfoot 1981). Without knowledge of such principles, it is claimed, the input would simply be insufficient for the child to arrive at a system of the complexity of adult grammars. An example will help bring home this point.

Consider the set of sentences in (1):

(1a)   Who did John say that Sue kissed t?
(1b)   Who did John say Ø Sue kissed t?
(1c)   *Who did John say that t kissed Sue?
(1d)   Who did John say Ø t kissed Sue?

In (1a,b) the object of the subordinate clause has been questioned; the question is grammatical regardless of whether the complementizer 'that' is present or not. In (1c,d) the subject of the subordinate clause has been questioned, and the question is only grammatical if the complementizer 'that' is absent. Although the matter is far from settled in linguistic theory, this superficially strange set of facts has been argued to follow from quite basic grammatical principles (and to be related to the phenomenon of null subjects, discussed briefly in chapter 4; see section 6.3 below). It is presumably knowledge of the grammatical principles involved that helps the child towards the knowledge that (1c) is an ungrammatical sentence in her language, since it is highly implausible that if the learner had to rely solely on mechanisms of hypothesis formation and generalization from the input she would arrive at the correct grammar. In fact, she might well be expected to arrive at an incorrect grammar (in which (1c) is grammatical).

In general the presence of 'that' before a complement clause is optional, a fact that the learner would be able to extract from examples such as

(2a)   John said that Sue kissed Bill
(2b)   John said Ø Sue kissed Bill

Moreover, the evidence of simple questions (in addition to (1a,b,d)) will tell her that both the subject and object positions can be questioned:

(3a)   Who will arrest him?
(3b)   Who will he arrest?

The learner working with minimal powers of hypothesis formation based on the sentence types she may actually hear might be expected to form a grammar that includes the specification 'the complementizer "that" is optional' and a question formation rule that questions subjects as well as objects. To put it another way, the learner would be predicted, without access to the constraint that blocks (1c), to form a grammar in which (1c) is grammatical, since that is the simplest grammar consistent with the speech forms she hears. This example is a good illustration of the 'poverty of the stimulus'; the learner will have no overt information as to the ungrammaticality of (1c) and the sentence types she may hear (the positive evidence, such as the remaining sentence types in (1) and the sentence types in (2) and (3)), are fully compatible with an incorrect analysis, in which (1c) is a grammatical sentence. The fact that children are capable of ending up with grammars that preclude questions of the type in (1c) is *prima facie* evidence that the child has access to whatever principles of grammar determine the adult grammaticality facts; it is highly unlikely that the child could deduce the facts from the data only.

Two other observations go hand in hand with the limited nature of the input in arguing for a highly structured learning mechanism. These are that language learning is a relatively error-free process and that language learning is a fairly rapid process. Both of these claims can be challenged to a degree. Errors may go unnoticed, and some learning (as we have seen in chapter 4) may go on well into the school years. But none the less the impression left by observation of child language is that the errors children make are of a limited kind and that by five years and plausibly much younger children have a linguistic system that conforms in essential ways to that of the language they are learning.

6.3   The Role of Universal Grammar in Language Development

We will assume that the child analyses input sentences into strings of words via a sentence processing mechanism. (The exact nature of the processing mechanism – for both children and adults – is a complex and vexed issue, and is the topic of the next chapter). Such strings will then be analysed by existing rules of the language being learned and/or principles of universal grammar. The primary role of universal grammar in language development is to limit the hypotheses that a child can form concerning the rules of his language, thus also limiting errors and helping explain the speed and ease with which language is learned.

An important aspect of the idea that universal grammar guides language development is the fact that use of principles of grammar potentially allows the child to form rules and hypotheses that affect and determine the form of sentence types for which he may have no direct evidence in the input itself. For example, sentences such as (1c) above are not ungrammatical in all languages. In Italian, the equivalent of (1c) is grammatical. This fact has been argued to be linked in a principled way to the existence of null subject sentences (see Rizzi 1982). We will not detail the theory here; the analysis is not uncontroversial, nor is it easily extended to all languages that allow sentences such as (1c). The basic argument runs as follows: sentences such as (1c) in English are ungrammatical because a principle of grammar (the 'empty category principle') is violated by movement from the subject position if the complementizer is present. Italian allows the subject and verb to be inverted in non-interrogative sentences (so one can have sentences equivalent to 'Hit Mary John' meaning 'Mary hit John'); it also has null subject sentences (the equivalent of 'walks' for 'she/he/it walks') and a special type of (unpronounced) pronoun will occupy the subject position in null subject sentences and sentences with inversion of the order of subject and verb. Sentences of the type (1c) will be permitted because movement is possible from post-verbal position in the inverted sentence form. Regardless of the ultimate correctness of this analysis, the basic point concerning the role of universal grammar is plain. Knowledge of the grammar of very simple sentences (whether or not the language permits inversion of the subject and verb, and whether or not the language has null subjects) can allow the child, if he is equipped with the appropriate principles of grammar, to make inferences concerning quite complex sentence types about which he may have no direct evidence. One type of sentence can act as a 'trigger' for the formation of rules that govern other types of sentence. Thus, while we argued in the previous section that general inference mechanisms unconstrained by principles of universal grammar would lead the child on the basis of simple sentence types to conclude that (1c) is grammatical in English, if the mechanism for forming grammatical rules is governed by principles of grammar simple sentence types of the language at hand can promote the formation of grammars with rules that make correct predictions concerning the grammaticality of sentences the child has not heard.

6.4   Learnability and Acquisition Principles

Learnability theory is concerned explicitly with the conditions under which successful learning of a system of rules can take place within a finite amount of time. The terms *learnability* and *learnability theory* were originally associated with work on learning formal languages, which may conform only to a degree with natural language systems (Gold 1967; Wexler and Culicover 1980; Wexler 1981). But they have come to be used in a more general sense, to refer to the study of conditions that will permit successful language learning in a limited time span. In this more general sense, learnability theory takes in questions such as the relative contribution of principles of universal grammar and input (the speech forms the child hears) in rule formation, the prevention of errors in learning and the correction of errors that have been made. We consider here two learnability proposals, the first designed to help explain the speed with which language is acquired, the second designed to prevent the learner from making errors.

6.4.1 *Subjacency and Degree-n Learnability*

In chapter 4 we listed some structural positions from which a question word may not be moved, including relative clauses, temporal clauses and indirect questions:

(4a) *What did John see a horse that kicked?
       (cf. John saw a horse that kicked a box)
(4b) *What did John read Dickens before writing?
       (cf. John read Dickens before writing that memo)
(4c) *What did John wonder who loved?
       (cf. John wondered who loved egg rolls)

We saw that there is evidence that from an early stage children learning English are obedient to the constraint on extraction from a temporal clause, and show some sensitivity to the other constraints at least by age five.

Does the existence of such constraints aid the language learner? It can be argued that such constraints do aid learning, in the following sense. Although (as we saw in chapter 4) there are apparent cases of violation of at least some of the constraints, cases where the constraint is not followed are easy to spot, in that they occur in sentences of limited complexity. For example, one finds languages where the equivalent of (4a) is grammatical, but one does not find languages where (4a) is ungrammatical but (4a') is grammatical:

(4a') What did John see a horse that kicked a box that contained?

That is, if a language is going to allow sentences that allow questioning into a relative clause, it will allow such questioning in the simplest possible structures containing a relative – it will not be the case that such questions are permitted only if a relative is embedded two sentences down, or four sentences down, etc. The same is true of the other constraints mentioned above. (Recall from the discussion in chapter 4 that apparent violations of the constraints on movement are frequently assumed to follow from formation of the offending sentences by a means other than movement.)

The facts will be accounted for if the grammatical principles that determine the ungrammaticality of the sentences in (4) are such that they must show up on the simplest sentences to which a constraint could potentially apply – i.e. on the first level of embedding. The *subjacency* principle is one component of the principles proposed to account for the constraints on movement rules and it has precisely the effect of being formulated so that it will restrict movement from relatively simple structures. The principle, which originates with Chomsky (1973), can be stated roughly as follows:

The subjacency principle: an element can move only over one layer of structure (i.e. it can move only from a layer that is *subordinate and adjacent*)

The correct definition of 'layer of structure' is a vexed question. It will be sufficient here to illustrate the role of subjacency in accounting for the difference between the ungrammatical (4a) and a grammatical sentence such as (5), where movement has taken place from within the complement to the verb 'see', rather than a relative clause:

(5) What did John see a horse kick?

In the framework of Chomsky (1986b), all phrasal nodes can potentially constitute (by various mechanisms) layers of structure pertinent to the computation of subjacency values in movement. A phrase has the potential to move from a position infinitely far down in a structure by crossing no more than one layer at a time (in accord with subjacency). The difference between (4a) and (5) is that (4a) contains a stretch of structure 'the horse that' with two layers that must be crossed, in violation of subjacency:

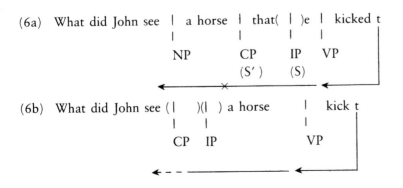

(The IP layer in (6a) and the CP and IP layers in (6b) are parenthesized because other factors void them; in most analyses, the subject position of the relative in (6a) is also derived by movement, not shown in (6a).)

Without spelling out more details, this account may seem arbitrary; however, the abiding virtue of the notion of subjacency in grammatical theory is that it offers a unified or semi-unified account of various constraints. On any version of the formulation of subjacency, it refers to phrasal nodes. In the version of Chomsky (1986b), all phrasal nodes are pertinent, subject to various principles and conditions; in other versions, particular nodes (NP, S/S′) are singled out as pertinent to computing subjacency values. All of these node types are present and embedded one within the other in D-structures with minimal levels of embedding; hence the complexity of sentences needed to see if subjacency is not operative (i.e. to see that the construction is *not* subject to the constraints that characterize movement) is correspondingly limited. The subjacency principle, in combination with the nature of the phrase structure system of the language, ensures this simplicity of necessary input data.

To use terminology deriving from Wexler and Culicover (1980), grammatical constructions are degree-*n* learnable, where *n* corresponds to a numerical measure of complexity of structures needed to deduce the adult grammar from the input data. Following the custom in discussions of learnability, we can take the number of embedded sentences to be the measure and say that, given that the learner works with knowledge of subjacency and that subjacency constrains movement rules, whether or not a particular construction is derived by movement will be degree-1 learnable, that is, whether movement is involved will be deducible on the basis of structures with no more than one embedded sentence.[2]

6.4.2 *The Subset Principle*

In the case of examples such as the one in the previous section, learnability theory does little more than articulate the advantage to the learner of knowledge of universal grammar. If the learner has prior knowledge of the subjacency principle and the fact that the principle constrains a particular type of grammatical operation (movement between D-structure and S-structure), the range of hypotheses he has to entertain with respect to his language is correspondingly limited and language learning should be made easier. The fact that subjacency limits the complexity of sentences that the learner will need to hear ·contributes to an explanation that language is learned in a finite amount of time.

But learnability theory has also thrown up hypotheses that are not in any obvious way a reflection of principles that govern adult grammars. The *subset principle* (Berwick 1985; Wexler and Manzini 1987) is an example. This is a principle designed to prevent the learner falling into error when more than one possible analysis is permitted under principles of grammar. As such, it is a principle of language acquisition, rather than a principle of grammar. Its potential application can be illustrated with respect to the binding of pronominal elements.

We saw in chapter 4 that principles A and B of the binding theory ensure that reflexive pronouns and definite pronouns are in approximately complementary distribution in English. Principle A requires that a reflexive be bound in its local domain; principle B requires that a pronoun be free in its local domain. Taking the local domain to be the first sentence node above the pronominal element, we saw that the principles ensure that 'himself' refers to 'Fred' in (7a), and not to 'Tom'; and, conversely, that 'him' may refer to 'Tom' but not to 'Fred' in (7b):

(7a) Tom said [that Fred had shaved himself]
(7b) Tom said [that Fred has shaved him]

The definition of domain is not invariant across languages, nor is it such that there is complete complementary distribution between reflexives and definite pronouns within a language (see, for example, Wexler and Manzini 1987). Considering just the case of reflexives, there are languages in which a reflexive may refer to the subject of a higher sentence. In Icelandic, for example, a reflexive may refer to a higher subject provided the lower clause is not tensed, and in Korean a reflexive may refer to the subject of a higher clause even if the lower clause is tensed. In Korean, therefore, the equivalent of a sentence such as (7a) will be ambiguous; the reflexive could refer to either the higher or the lower subject. Plainly, since both possibilities (reference to only the subordinate clause subject or reference to either the main or subordinate subject) are allowed in human languages, principles of universal grammar will not give a unique answer as to what the rule is, for any string of words superficially equivalent to (7a). The subset principle (see Berwick and Weinberg 1984; Berwick 1985; Wexler and Manzini 1987) says roughly that in such a situation the language learner opts for the grammatical system that is least permissive – the system that yields the smallest range of grammatical sentences.

The prediction of the subset principle with respect to the example above is that the child learning Korean will start off with an English-type grammar, in which the reflexive can be bound only to the lower subject. Only at a later point will the child revise her grammar to the more permissive, Korean-type system. This should not be a difficult matter, assuming the learner will eventually hear sentences where there is evidence from the context and/or the internal structure of the sentence that the more restrictive rule system is incorrect (for example, the learner might encounter the equivalent of the ungrammatical English sentence 'Tom said that Linda shaved himself').

The appeal of the subset principle in learnability terms is that it promotes error-free learning and so minimizes the need for negative evidence (evidence that a particular form is ungrammatical in the language to be learned). If the child learning English erroneously decided that the reflexive pronoun could refer to the higher subject in sentences such as (7a), how would the error ever be discovered?

There are at least two criteria by which we can evaluate any proposed principle of acquisition, such as the subset principle: (1) Does the principle translate into plausible mental mechanisms? (2) Do the facts of language learning correspond to the predictions of the principle? To the extent that there is evidence available, the performance of the subset principle with respect to these criteria is mixed. With respect to the first point, it is not clear what it might mean to say that the learner selects the most restrictive grammar. Is one to suppose that the learner actively compares the possible analyses, somehow unconsciously reasoning along the lines: 'Heavens, I've no evidence that binding a reflexive to a higher subject is allowed, I'd better stick to lower domain binding for the time being' (see Fodor and Crain 1987 for comments to this effect)? If so, why does similar reasoning not prevent the other overgeneralizations and innovations that the learner does make (for example, the use of innovative causative forms described in chapter 3)?

There is at least some empirical evidence that the predictions of the subset principle are correct, in terms of children's performance. Lee (1987) reports that children learning Korean do indeed prefer the structurally closest possible referent for a reflexive pronoun, in contrast to adult speakers of Korean, who more frequently select a structurally distant referent for a reflexive. (However, not all the recent studies of knowledge of reflexive binding yield a pattern consistent with use of the subset principle; for example, Jakubowicz and Olsen (1988) report data difficult to account for under the subset principle).

The subset principle is an example of a principle that appears in essence to be a principle of learnability – one which provides the learner with an orderly procedure for positing hypotheses about the structure of the language. The principle will prevent errors and so help explain the fact that language is learned in a limited time span.

6.5   Summary: Components of a Learning Model

We can summarize the points made in the previous sections with a diagram (see figure 6.1). The input to the learning mechanism is analysed by a sentence

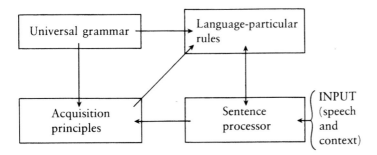

Figure 6.1 Components of a learning model

processor; if the learner's current language-particular grammar contains no rules suitable for the input, the input string may be subjected to analysis by acquisition principles, whose operation is, like language-particular rules, constrained by universal grammar.

6.6 Some Questions and Problems in Acquisition Theory

The roles of universal grammar and of acquisition principles are quite easy to describe in general terms: universal grammar provides the child with analyses of the data; acquisition principles help resolve remaining ambiguities. But there are also many substantial questions and grey areas with respect to the contribution of universal grammar and candidate acquisition principles in real-time learning. Here we briefly consider three related questions: Does learning follow sequences dictated by markedness values? Do children ever violate principles of grammar? And is 'parameter setting' as an account of learning a significant advance over hypothesis testing, within a framework where universal grammar governs children's hypotheses?

6.6.1 Markedness and Orders of Acquisition

In chapter 2 on phonology, we saw that the order in which sounds emerge in child speech is to a degree predictable in terms of the frequency of the sounds cross-linguistically. Sounds that are very common in the world's languages tend to emerge earlier than rarer sounds. In the terminology introduced there, unmarked sounds emerge before marked sounds. We can ask in more general terms whether normal, frequently occurring constructions and rules correspond to the earliest forms and rules in children's grammars. As noted in chapter 2, one goal of linguistic theory is to account for distributional facts (whether a form is frequent or rare cross-linguistically) in terms of principles of grammar. Early emergence of unmarked forms is thus potentially evidence for the guiding force of principles of universal grammar.

As far as the evidence goes, it is probably correct to say that unmarked rules and forms are early acquired. The facts of phonological acquisition are largely consistent with that claim and so are some studies of the development of syntactic constructions. To take one example, in English verbs such as 'give' permit two, more or less equivalent, syntactic means of realizing the semantic roles *theme* (object transferred) and *goal* (recipient) in the verb phrase, as illustrated in (8a,b):

(8a)   John gave the book to the school
(8b)   John gave the school the book

In (8a), the theme ('the book') is direct object and the goal ('the school') is the object of the preposition 'to'. In (8b), there are two NPs in the verb phrase, with the first having the goal role and the second the theme role. It is generally agreed that the NP PP form in (8a) is the unmarked or typical case: that syntactic frame can occur freely with verbs with a suitable basic meaning, whereas the distribution of the NP NP form (8b) is more restricted. (For example, if we substitute the verb 'donate' for 'give' the result is grammatical for (8a), but not for.(8b).) Thus we can consider the NP PP form as normal or unmarked, and the NP NP form as marked, based on distributional facts; moreover, a principled theoretical account of these 'markedness values' is available (Stowell 1981). For these constructions, the facts of language acquisition fit fairly well with the markedness values based on distribution (and linguistic theory). Cook (1976) and Roeper et al. (1981) both find NP NP forms to be harder for children to comprehend than NP PP forms, consistent with the view that the NP PP form is the unmarked construction.

Although the facts of acquisition sequences for syntax as well as phonology can be fitted to observations about marked and unmarked forms, the evidence is perhaps less clear-cut in the case of syntactic development, where the role of markedness values may be obscured by other factors. For example, although the experiments cited above have shown that children do better at comprehending NP PP dative sentences than they do at comprehending NP NP datives, NP NP forms with the verb 'give' do occur in young children's speech quite early on. Brown (1973), for example, provides the following example from a two-year-old:

(9)   Give doggie paper

Plausibly the high frequency of NP NP forms with the verb 'give' in the speech the child hears promotes its early use by the child. (The role of input in learning such structures is returned to below.) Thus, although the experimental studies may reflect some kind of basic asymmetry between the two forms, the child may early on have some mastery of a marked form for reasons external to the structure of the grammatical system.

One interesting question concerning sequences of development is the relationship between markedness and candidate acquisition principles. Cross-linguistic and language-internal frequency is the standard rule of thumb for unmarked situations. The subset principle as currently formulated is not a principle of grammar that is 'active' in grammars of adult languages. But the subset principle does predict that the first-acquired rule should be the most frequent rule cross-linguistically. The logic of the situation is as follows. If there exist languages with only A (where A is some sentence type permitted by rules of grammar – in the example discussed in section 6.4.2, binding of a reflexive to a lower subject) and languages with both A and B (where B is some additional sentence type – in the example, binding to a higher subject), but not languages with B only, it must be the case that A is the most frequent situation in languages of the world, regardless of which language type (languages with A only or languages with A and B) is more common in terms of the distribution of actual human languages. In other words, the logic of the subset principle dictates that the first rules the language learner hypothesizes are the most frequent rules (situations) cross-linguistically. So the predictions of the subset principle are in a manner confounded with markedness predictions. Thus it is possible that the subset principle, at present formulated as a principle of acquisition rather than a principle of grammar, may ultimately reduce to (as yet undiscovered) rules of grammar; or, conversely, that frequent situations in languages of the world do not always follow from principles of grammar, but may reflect in some manner the process of acquisition.

6.6.2   Continuity or Maturation?

The first section of this chapter summarized some general arguments in favour of the view that language development is a biologically guided behaviour. However, a strong component of innate linguistic knowledge does not entail that all constraints and principles of universal grammar are available to the child from the outset. It is logically possible that some grammatical rules and constraints are programmed to emerge (under appropriate conditions of external stimulation) only after a period in which they are not present in the child system. It is not difficult to think of analogies with other aspects of human development – for example, the physiological changes of puberty are biologically programmed changes whose exact timing will depend on conditions in the individual's environment, such as diet.

Although there are many possible ways to frame the problem in detail, we can identify three broad positions about whether some principles of grammar emerge only after a period in which they are absent from children's grammars (this taxonomy is taken from Weissenborn et al. 1992):

1. *Strong continuity*. All principles and constructs of universal grammar are available at the outset and each grammar formed by the child is a correct (partial) grammar for the language to which the child is exposed.

2. *Weak continuity*. All principles and constructs of universal grammar are available at the outset and all child grammars will be 'possible human grammars', in the sense of falling within the patterns of adult grammars (either observed or permitted under the theory). The child's grammar may, however, deviate from that of the language he will ultimately acquire.

3. *Maturation*. Some properties of universal grammar mature. That is, some properties of grammar are biologically programmed to emerge only after a certain period of development. If such a property is an absolute universal (i.e. holds obligatorily for structures and rules to which it is relevant) then child grammars may of necessity fall outside the range of 'possible human languages'.

Since the 1970s, the most popular position in the literature has been some version of weak continuity. That position is appealing, allowing for the child to form rules that are not present in the language he hears, but none the less constrain the acquisition process. However, recent studies have proposed maturational analyses for some grammatical phenomena; see Felix (1987) and Borer and Wexler (1987).

At the present state of evidence, the data in support of maturation do not convincingly challenge the weak continuity position, since the facts attributed to the maturation of grammatical principles are generally amenable to alternative analysis, compatible with strong or weak continuity. For example, Borer and Wexler suggest that the acquisition of the passive construction may follow from maturation of the ability to move an NP into the subject position. As outlined in chapter 4, passives are formed in English by movement of a direct object into an empty subject position:

(10)   [e] were eaten the bananas
       The bananas$_i$ were eaten [t$_i$]

The suggestion that children do not form passives by movement does not mandate a maturational account of the child's development, provided that the theory of grammar gives some alternative way for children who have not undergone the proposed maturational change to form passives without movement. We saw in chapter 4 that there is such an alternative, with the 'passivized' subject NP in subject position from the outset.

Lack of clear counter-evidence does not entail that the continuity hypothesis is right and maturational accounts are wrong. Very early speech (one-word and telegraphic utterances) is a tempting candidate for grammatical systems which are genuinely impoverished by comparison to adult grammar and the first two years of grammatical development at least may involve maturational changes that bring the child's grammar into line with the general shape of adult grammars (see chapter 4, section 4.6). Stevenson (1992) and Clahsen (1992) both discuss the complexities of identifying maturational developments in grammar.

6.6.3 *Parameter Setting vs. Hypothesis Testing*

Another topic that has been at the forefront of recent discussions on the role of universal grammar in language development is whether there is an advantage to 'parameter setting' as a model of development.

An elementary example of parameter setting examined in chapter 4 was the order of heads and modifying material in phrase structure. A language such as English fairly consistently puts heads of phrases to the left; a language such as Japanese fairly consistently puts heads of phrases to the right. So in English a noun precedes a complement sentence or relative clause, a verb precedes its object(s) and complement sentences, etc., whereas in Japanese the general pattern is reversed, with a relative clause preceding its head noun, etc. This division in language types can be accounted for in terms of a general 'head position' parameter for phrase structure, which is set to one value for English and to another value for Japanese. The need for many individual rules (one for each phrase type in the language) is thus in principle obviated and learning made easier: once the child has worked out what the pattern is for one type of phrase, she can then automatically project the correct pattern for other phrase types in the language.

Learning as 'parameter setting' has been opposed to learning as 'hypothesis testing'. On the latter view, the child would have to sort through and decide about a range of hypotheses that she never need entertain under the parameter setting model. To continue the example of basic phrase structure, the child who is equipped with knowledge about what a phrase structure can look like, but not with the knowledge that there is a contingency relationship between the existence of one phrase structure and others, will have to decide for each phrase type separately (NP, VP, PP, etc.) what the shape of the phrase is. So the learner who has knowledge that the head-position parameter imposes regularity across the shape of phrases in the language will only have to make one decision (is her language head-first or head-final?), but the learner who does not have knowledge of the parameter must make several separate decisions (is the noun phrase in her language head-first? is the verb phrase in her language head-first? etc.). Since one decision should be easier than many, it is argued that the parameter setting model helps explain the ease with which children learn language.

Despite the intuitive appeal of this argument, the differences between learning under a parameterized view of grammatical systems and learning as it was conceived under previous models of generative grammar may not be very large. First, although the terms parameter setting and hypothesis testing are often used as if they represented two different styles or methods of learning, they do not in fact represent a difference in the learning process itself. Parameter setting *is* hypothesis testing: the child must, for example, test the hypothesis that her language is either head-first or head-final against the speech forms to which she is exposed. All that differs potentially is the *number* of hypotheses that have to be checked out; parameters that define clear-cut contingency relationships between grammatical phenomena reduce the range of hypotheses to be tested. The potential learning advantage in parameter setting depends, then, on how clear-cut the contingency relationships specified by the parameters are. Very often the contingencies are complex and imperfect, once more than the most elementary examples are considered (see Atkinson 1987; Bach 1988; Roeper and Weissenborn 1990; Valian 1989 for pertinent discussion).

6.7   The Limits of the Linguistic Model: Lexical Learning

In this section we look at the role of mechanisms of learning that lie outside either universal grammar or candidate principles of acquisition. In a restricted range of cases, it seems plausible to assume that acquisition of the details of grammar depends on distributional features of the input, such as the frequency with which particular lexical items are encountered in particular syntactic environments.

The idea that input and frequency constitute an explanation of anything is something of an anathema to many generative grammarians (though not N.

Chomsky; see Chomsky 1981, p. 9). Linguists are right to be dismissive of the possibility of learning fundamental aspects of grammar solely on the basis of the distributional properties of the input. There are many aspects of grammar where we would not expect the child to acquire the right set of rules, unless her rule formation were constrained by knowledge of principles of grammar.

Assume that the role of input and frequency is in some basic way limited. Where might such factors none the less have an effect on learning? Plausibly, in the sorting out of details that are not governed or dictated by principles of grammar: in particular, in sorting out lexical facts that are wholly or partially arbitrary.

Consider the dative sentence discussed above. We saw that there are verbs such as 'give' that permit either an NP PP or an NP NP structure, as shown in (8a,b), repeated here:

(8a)   John gave the book to the school
(8b)   John gave the school the book

As we noted, the possibility of the second frame (NP NP) is more restricted than the possibility of the first frame. Some verbs, such as 'donate', allow only the first frame:

(11a)   John donated the book to the school
(11b)   *John donated the school the book

In most current linguistic analyses, the lexical restrictions on the occurrence of NP NP dative sentences are expressed in the lexicon, in terms of subcategorization frames (or argument structure, in recent discussions) for individual verbs. 'Give' will be entered in the lexicon with two frames and 'donate' will be entered with only one:

Dative subcategorizations
give   [__ NP PP]   donate [__ NP PP]
       [__ NP NP]

(__ indicates the position of the verb and the brackets indicate the boundaries of the verb phrase.) Since 'donate' is not specified for an NP NP frame, it will not be entered into deep structures of that type and sentences such as (11b) will be blocked. As we noted above, the NP PP and NP NP frames are broadly equivalent in meaning; that is, there is a regular relationship between the thematic roles of theme and goal/recipient positions in the syntactic frame.

This regularity will need to be expressed; one way of doing so is to assume that the lexicon contains a statement (sometimes referred to as a lexical redundancy rule) to this effect.

The acquisition of word-to-structure mappings has been quite extensively discussed in the child language literature since the publication of an article by Baker (1979). The basic issue with which Baker was concerned was how the correct adult mappings could be learned.[3] Several different factors have been studied, as they apply to the potential and actual learning paths for lexically restricted phenomena. Three types of generalization are plain.

First, authors such as Mazurkewich and White (1984) and Pinker (1984, 1989) have drawn on linguistic literature to stress the fact that there are generalizations that can be used to predict to some degree whether a word will occur in a particular frame or frames. Thus in the case of the dative, those verbs that occur in the NP NP frame tend to be monosyllabic (such as 'give') and to impose a condition on the first (goal) NP as broadly the possessor of the second NP – compare 'give the doll the box' with the ungrammatical 'open the doll the box'. Randall (in press) discusses other potentially relevant grammatical factors. Gropen et al. (1989) and Pinker (1989) point out that the generalizations found are partially intersecting: for example, while dative verbs that denote 'giving' generally fall under the monosyllabicity condition, those that denote 'future possession' are not subject to the same condition ('She bequeathed him a fortune', etc.). Moreover, there are arguably absolute exceptions. For example, Bowerman (1987) notes that the verb 'choose' is monosyllabic and fits the possessor condition, but does not admit the NP NP frame.

Second, it is clear that learning is not an error-free process. Bowerman (1983) and White (1987) document instances of children producing utterances such as those in (12), which involve use of the NP NP frame with verbs that allow only the NP PP frame:

(12a)   I said her no (from Bowerman, child aged three years one month)
(12b)   Pick me up all those things (from White, child aged five years two months)
(12c)   Mummy, open Hadwen the door (from White, child aged six years)

(12a) is an error with a verb that takes the preposition 'to' in the prepositional form ('I said no to her'); (12b,c) are errors with verbs that take the preposition 'for' ('Pick those things up for me'; 'Open the door for Hadwen'). White also reports experimental evidence that is compatible with the view that children permit the NP NP frame to be used where the adult grammar disallows it.

Third, although children make errors, their performance with lexically restricted constructions is not random. White's experiments show that some children have partial awareness of the correct word-to-structure mappings. More recently, Gropen et al. (1989) have shown that children's propensity to generalize from one syntactic frame to another is constrained by the nature of their learning experience: children taught a nonsense word in an NP PP frame are more likely to produce the verb in that frame than in an NP NP frame and vice versa.

How is this combination of children's partial knowledge of generalizations, children's overgeneralization and children's attention to input (the forms children have heard) to be accounted for? And how is the ultimate adult state of knowledge to be achieved?

Pinker (1989) and Gropen et al. (1989) put forward a view along the following lines: the child has available (plausibly innate) statements of possible and probable relations between syntactic frames, such as the equivalence of the NP NP and NP PP structures in terms of the thematic roles goal and theme; such general equivalences may be quickly built into the child's grammar. More particular restrictions on lexical alternations may be established gradually on the basis of exposure to the speech around the child. Production errors (for both children and adults, who also innovate with utterances similar to those in (12a–c) in their spontaneous speech) can be treated as one-off innovations based on accessing general equivalence statements.

A quantity-sensitive mechanism that allows the learner to register which verbs occur in which frames and to use this record to hypothesize and revise rules relating syntactic and thematic structures is not part of the grammar, in the sense of either the specifications of universal grammar concerning possible and (more or less) likely specifications, or actual language-particular specifications of such relations. Yet a mechanism of that kind would seem necessary if we are to account for children's conservative tendencies (recall that in Gropen et al.'s study children favoured production of the syntactic frame in which they had been taught new words) and our ability to deal with true exceptional cases (such as 'choose', mentioned above). Braine (1971) proposes a model that is potentially adaptable to the learning of lexical facts such as the distribution of dative structures. In a model such as Braine's, knowledge of the exact word-to-frame matches may be effected in terms of a sequence of memory stores. As individual word-and-frame combinations are heard, they are entered in the first of a series of stores. Each individual word–frame combination will pass up through intermediate stores to the final, long-term memory for words, which we can construe as the representation that corresponds to the lexicon in the linguistic model. The learner can presumably work on the organization of stores to form generalizations and subgeneralizations and to innovate. However, the actual lexical items in the stores and their linkage to particular syntactic frames is also continuously updated in terms of input (the child's experience), so explaining the frequency-sensitive aspects of both the learning process and the relatively steady adult state.[4]

6.8   Motherese

In some of Chomsky's early writings, the existence of ungrammatical, fragmentary input was mentioned as enhancing the plausibility of a strong innate component of linguistic knowledge. Adults do not always talk in perfectly well-formed sentences, yet any slip-ups adults make do not seem to hinder language acquisition. The child's apparent ability to filter out such ill-formed input is another prong in the argument for innate knowledge based on the poverty of the stimulus (see section 6.2 above).

In 1972, Snow published a study that challenged the factual basis for the claim that speech to children was rich in potentially misleading errors and disfluencies. Snow found that mothers' speech (more accurately, adults' speech) to children has special features that set it off from the speech of adults to other adults or older children. Specifically, mothers' speech forms are characteristically fluent and intelligible, with fewer hesitancies or mumbled or muffled utterances than speech to adults, grammatical, with very few utterances that are not well formed by the rules of the adult grammar, and short (the average length of utterances of mothers to two-year-old children in Snow's original study was approximately 6.5 words, compared to 9.5 in the speech of adults to ten-year-olds). This special style of speaking to young children, found in numerous studies subsequent to Snow's (see, for example, papers in Snow and Ferguson 1977) earned the name *motherese*. The existence of motherese was widely taken to diminish the force of the innatist position. It was reasoned that there was less need to posit a complex, innate language acquisition device, complete with principles of universal grammar, since mothers' speech was not distorted or misleading. Brown wrote in his introduction to Snow and Ferguson (1977):

> The by-now overwhelming evidence of [motherese] . . . refutes overwhelmingly the rather off-hand assertions of Chomsky and his followers that the preschool child could not learn language from the complex but syntactically degenerate sample his parents provide without the aid of an elaborate innate component. But it has turned out that parental speech is well formed and finely tuned to the child's psycholinguistic capacity. The corollary would seem to be that there is less need for an elaborate

innate component than there at first seemed to be. (Snow and Ferguson 1977, p. 20)

Despite such claims for the efficacy of motherese, it is not at all clear that the special speech forms used to children lessen the need for an innate component.

First, the basic 'poverty of the stimulus' arguments given in section 6.2 are not affected by the existence of motherese. The fact that mothers use short, clear, grammatical forms to children does not in any obvious way answer the point that the input to the child underdetermines the nature of the grammar the child will ultimately acquire. Nothing in the input overtly signals the range of possible meanings for a sentence and nothing in the input directly tells the child which sentences are ungrammatical. For example, how will limiting the forms a child hears help him work out that in noun–noun compounds the first element must be singular if its plural is regular ('rat-catcher', '*rats-catcher'; 'mouse-catcher', 'mice-catcher')? In chapter 3 we saw that children were sensitive to this constraint on compounding, which follows from a principle of the level-ordering model of morphology, and that the input the child receives appears to provide little or no evidence concerning the nature of the constraint. Such facts argue that motherese cannot be seen as seriously limiting or replacing an innate component of linguistic knowledge in language acquisition.

Second, it has been shown that use of motherese is a culturally bounded phenomenon. In settings other than the Western middle classes, there may be less use of the types of speech forms characteristic of motherese (see Snow 1986 for a review). Since children from all classes and cultures normally end up with a complete knowledge of their native language, use of motherese cannot be critical to the learning process.

If motherese does not significantly lessen the need for an innate component, what role does it have in language development? Some studies have tried to look for systematic relationships between the speech forms mothers use and changes over time in children's use of different rules and constructions (Newport et al. 1977; Furrow et al. 1979; Gleitman et al. 1984; Scarborough and Wyckoff 1986). Common sense suggests that motherese might be useful in helping the child to gain exactly that knowledge which is not part of universal grammar – the particulars of rules in the language he is learning. Nothing in universal grammar dictates that the plural ending for nouns in English is '-s', or the particular meanings expressed by individual auxiliary verbs ('will', 'can', etc.). Seemingly meaningful patterns did appear, such as the fact that, in Newport et al.'s 1977 study, the more a mother used imperative sentences (which do not contain an auxiliary verb), the less the child was likely to progress in his use of auxiliaries. But stricter statistical analysis and additional studies have shown that even those relationships that seemed to exist between features of motherese and growth in use of specific grammatical forms may be no more than chance correlation.

Is it the case, then, that the nature and quality of the speech addressed to children is completely irrelevant to language development? Motherese cannot reasonably be supposed to replace a substantial component of linguistic knowledge on the child's part, but the quality and quantity of speech the child hears may affect the speed with which language is learned.

In addition to the properties mentioned above, motherese has special acoustic properties (for example, pitch is characteristically higher in child-directed than in adult-directed speech); these may make motherese a particularly attractive signal to the young infant, leading the pre-linguistic infant to focus on speech input (see Jusczyk and Bertoncini 1988 for a review of pertinent literature and discussion). At later stages, the special, child-directed forms of motherese provide a friendly environment in which to practise language skills. It makes sense to suppose that practising the language being learned will speed acquisition. The mother who uses motherese may be helping the child by presenting him with many chances to put his linguistic knowledge and grammar-forming mechanism to use. In this context, it is relevant to note that research on the effects of the quality of linguistic feedback to children has found that word-for-word repetition of the child's utterance does not appear to promote growth in linguistic abilities, whereas re-casting and/or expanding the child's utterance has been argued to enhance linguistic abilities, for children at the appropriate level of development (see Nelson et al. 1973; Demetras et al. 1986 for pertinent discussion). Re-casts (for example, responding to a child's utterance such as 'book' with 'Yes, it's your book', 'Do you want to read the book?', etc. have the function of exposing the child to new forms and structures. Similarly, at later stages of development (middle childhood) simple exposure to constructions that are generally late acquired has been shown to accelerate development (Cromer 1987). Re-casts and presentation of unfamiliar constructions both plausibly provide the child with more fuel for his language acquisition device than mere repetition, and, by common-sense reasoning, may be expected to help the child learn his language.

Use of motherese, and particular aspects of motherese, may thus have a general effect of enhancement (see Newport et al. 1977; Scarborough and Wyckoff 1986). The mothers in many of the studies cited above were middle-class mothers, prone to using motherese. The effect of motherese may be more exactly understood when the performance of children whose mothers use this style of speaking heavily is compared to the performance of children whose mothers do not (Scarborough and Wyckoff 1986).

6.9 Language Development and Cognitive Development

The claim that the child has tacit knowledge of principles of universal grammar is a claim that the child innately knows something about language *per se*. Is this view correct, or do the rules and structures of language somehow grow out of other aspects of cognitive abilities, innately given, but not unique to language? The most articulate advocates of a task-specific biological programme have been Chomsky and those who work with him; the most widely discussed claims for the non-specific basis of linguistic development have been associated with Piaget and his followers. In this section we look at some typical features of the often polemical dialogue that surrounds this question. The claim that language development involves an innate capacity that is unique to language is labelled *specificity* and the opposing claim, that language development is an outgrowth of other cognitive skills, is labelled *constructivism* (following the terminology of Piaget in various writings; see, for example, Piaget 1980).

Two separate lines of argument favour some version of the specificity position. The first concerns how system-specific properties could be learned if they were not innate; the second concerns the evidence (or lack thereof) for constructivism.

6.9.1 *Specificity and the Logic of Learning*

Fodor (1980) examines the logic of specificity vs. that of constructivism. His position can be summarized roughly as follows. Learning takes place by hypothesis formation and confirmation. The learner can only form hypotheses using the conceptual apparatus that she has in hand at that point. It is therefore impossible for the learner to progress using hypothesis formation and confirmation from a stage in which she works with a certain repertoire of concepts to a subsequent stage in which she works with those concepts plus some additional property or properties not derivable from the concepts available at the first stage. Fodor's example is that it would not be possible to learn quantificational logic – a system using operators and variables – by hypothesis formation and confirmation based on knowledge of non-quantificational logic. The properties of quantification are not completely expressible in terms of the properties of non-quantificational logic. In general, Fodor's argument goes, it will be impossible to learn a 'more powerful' system by hypothesis formation and confirmation, contrary to the spirit of constructivism, which broadly claims that cognitive stages arise one out of the other. Yet the properties of a given system which are unique to that system must be available to the human mind somehow; the only option is to say that they are innately given. A reasonable interpretation of Fodor's position is that those cognitive constructs that are both system-specific and not derivable from some combination of constructs and operations present in other aspects of cognition must be innately available to the learner in their system-specific form – the logic of learning requires them to be.

Do human languages exhibit specificity in the way prescribed by this argument? The obvious way to tackle this is to ask: What kinds of things are found in human language for which there is no evidence in other areas of cognition and which cannot plausibly be derived from other aspects of cognition? If we find such properties then we have candidates for constructs that, by the logic of the argument, must be part of language-specific innate knowledge.

The list of linguistic rules and constructs that are – as far as the evidence goes – unique and non-derivable is a long one. A good example is provided by the facts sketched above concerning questioning and the presence of a complementizer. We saw in (1a–d), repeated here, that there is a constraint in English that blocks questioning from the subject position, but not the object position, of an embedded sentence when the complementizer word 'that' is present:

(1a)   Who did John say that Sue kissed t?
(1b)   Who did John say Ø Sue kissed t?
(1c)   *Who did John say that t kissed Sue?
(1d)   Who did John say Ø t kissed Sue?

The fact that the formulation of the constraint involved in (1c) is a matter of debate in the linguistic literature does not detract from the point here, which is that there is no evidence that this constraint can be derived from constructs that are used in any cognitive domain other than language. Such evidence would presumably require not only that the entities 'subject (position)', 'object (position)' and 'complementizer' all have some analogue in non-linguistic domains (an assumption that might be argued to be plausible for subject and object but already stretches the imagination in the case of complementizer), but that whatever principle determines the ungrammaticality of (1c) also has some non-linguistic analogue. Such evidence lacking, the plausibly language-specific nature of the constraint that blocks (1c) makes it a candidate member of an innate biological programme whose properties cannot be an outgrowth of some other aspect of human mental abilities, according to the structure of Fodor's argument.

6.9.2 Constructivism and Developmental Orders

The preceding section took the tack of looking at properties of human language for which there is no evidence that they generalize beyond language, and using the existence of such properties as support for a task-specific biological programme. We followed Fodor in arguing that to the extent that something is specific to some subsystem of human cognition, and not derivable from a combination of other properties and principles of cognition, it cannot 'grow out' of other properties of cognition in the way suggested by constructivism. Proponents of constructivism have usually gone about things the other way round: they look for properties of human language that have what they consider to be plausible similarities to properties of other mental operations and try to support the constructivist position by looking at how these putatively related linguistic and non-linguistic properties develop over time. This section examines the logic of such studies and the strength of the results.

An essential component of the constructivist position is the notion of a *cognitive precursor*: some mental abilities are held to provide the basis for the development of other abilities. With respect to language development, there is a sense in which this is trivially true. Before a learner can be said to have mastered a language, he must use the words in that language in an adult-like way, and in order to do that he must have the cognitive abilities that allow him to map between concept and word appropriately. So, for example, in order for the learner to use the word 'cow' as it is used in the adult language he must (minimally) have mastered whatever properties are involved in the human concept of cowness.

The contentious part of the constructivist assumption of precursors comes from the linking of specific (non-linguistic) mental operations and the development of specific linguistic structures and rules. The form of the argument is generally along the lines: at stage X, a child has cognitive skill A; at stage X + 1, the child acquires linguistic skill B; therefore, cognitive skill A is a precursor to linguistic skill B. The latter arises out of the former.

There are several studies that follow this line of argument, using Piagetian stages of cognitive development as the exemplar of the precursor cognitive skill. For example, Sinclair de Zwart (1967) and Sinclair et al. (1971) suggest that there is a connection between mastery of the cognitive operations involved in *conservation* and the development of various linguistic skills and structures. Conservation is the term used in Piagetian theory to refer to the ability to recognize that quantity remains stable although it may be differently distributed in space. A conserving child will realize that when a quantity of water is poured from a tall skinny beaker to a short fat beaker the amount of water does not change although the water level (distance from the bottom of the beaker) does. A non-conserving child may, by contrast, judge quantity in terms of height in the beaker, concluding that there is a reduction in quantity when water is poured into a shorter beaker. Sinclair de Zwart (1967, reported in Speidel 1984) observed that children who pass tests of conservation in general use more complex linguistic structures, including the comparative, than non-conserving children, and Sinclair et al. (1971) suggest that conservation may be the key to the child's ability readily to produce the passive construction. The general implication of these studies is that the ability to conserve is a prerequisite for the mastery of some linguistic structures.

The intuitive basis for the suggestion that conservation may be a prerequisite for the development of linguistic structures is plain in many cases. Properties critical to conservation invite use of comparative constructions such as 'more than', 'less than', 'the same as' (try describing what is meant by the term conservation). Conservation entails a level of abstraction from physical form in which some relations are held stable, a fact which Sinclair et al. (1971) use as a rationale for why conservation should be a prerequisite for the use of passive. (In 'Sue hit Fred' and 'Fred was hit by Sue' the NPs 'Sue' and 'Fred' have the same semantic roles, despite the difference in syntactic structure.)

There are two basic problems with constructivist arguments that cognitive skills give rise to linguistic skills. The first is that the data that support the constructivist position are always compatible with an alternative position, in which the cognitive and linguistic skills arise independently (see Fodor et al. 1974; Speidel 1984). That is, even if cognitive stage A consistently precedes or co-occurs with the attainment of linguistic stage B, this does not necessarily entail a causal relationship between the attainment of the cognitive and linguistic skills. The two may arise in the order they do simply through a coincidence of the normal course of development in two separate domains. For instance, children generally start taking their first steps and using their first words at about the same time, but neither development causes the other or is necessary to the other; they are simply two aspects of development that tend to co-occur. Second, the proposed correspondences are not always borne out by the facts. Speidel (1984) studied the hypothesis that conservation is necessary for the ready use of the passive. She found that there was no consistent relation in the order in which conservation and production of passive sentences was mastered, and that at the younger age levels she tested (kindergarten and first grade) the majority of children who had mastered the passive did *not* pass tests of conservation. Further strong empirical evidence for the independence of linguistic and cognitive skills is the existence of severely retarded individuals who possess highly developed grammatical systems (see, for example, Yamada 1984).

Are we to assume, then, that intuitions along the lines of those suggested by Sinclair and her colleagues are simply misleading, and that there are really no connections between cognitive growth and linguistic development? It seems reasonable to suppose, not that cognitive skills form the basis out of which linguistic structures develop, but that they may promote the use of structures and forms already present in the child's linguistic system. To take the example of conservation and comparatives, the ability to conserve may be an important component in mastery of the adult meaning of words used in comparative constructions ('more', 'less', 'as', 'than', etc.). This is simply an extension of the point made above that to use words correctly we must have an adult-like grasp of the concepts expressed by those words. The syntactic scaffolding (phrase structures) that a particular language uses for comparatives may be in place much earlier than the stage at which conservation is achieved. In chapter 4 we saw that pre-school children have formidable syntactic abilities; on standard Piagetian tests conservation may not be achieved until age six or older, although it should be noted that conservation skills may be brought out at earlier stages with some tasks (as demonstrated by, for example, Mehler and Bever 1967; Donaldson 1978). It seems plausible to suppose that cognitive development may enhance linguistic development in the sense of providing the child with the kind of concepts that increase the use of certain constructions; but this is a different matter from the strong constructivist position, with its claim that cognitive structures at the non-linguistic level *are* the linguistic structures, in nascent form.

6.10   Summary and Conclusions

This chapter has dealt with a range of questions concerning the mechanisms by which language is learnt in real time. Language development broadly exhibits the properties of biologically programmed behaviours (stages, a critical age and partial independence from input). The complexity of what is acquired and the limitations on the nature of the input (the speech the child hears) support the view that the child tackles language learning with the aid of innate knowledge of universal grammar. There are many open questions concerning the role of universal grammar in learning, in particular the degree to which unmarked forms are acquired first and whether some grammatical principles mature. Regardless of these uncertainties, it is clear that knowledge of universal grammar reduces the range of hypotheses the child may entertain concerning the structure of the language he is learning; the speed and ease with which language is learned is thus accounted for. In addition to positing knowledge of principles of universal grammar, learnability theory articulates the manner in which principles of grammar (such as the subjacency principle) reduce the complexity of the input the child needs to deduce the particular rules of his language; learnability theory has also projected principles that putatively guide the child's hypothesis formation (such as the subset principle).

Some aspects of real-time learning lie outside the domain of principles of universal grammar or learnability theory. For a restricted range of language-particular facts (lexical idiosyncrasies), quantity-sensitive mechanisms of memory may be important to learning. In addition, within a restricted time framework, quality of input is likely to affect rate of acquisition. 'Motherese' plausibly has the function of helping the child get to grips with language-particular rules (those aspects of his language that cannot be predicted from principles of universal grammar). Simple exposure may be crucial to the timing of the development of rules.

The final section of the chapter looked at the relation between language learning and cognitive development, as exemplified by Piagetian theory. Cognitive growth may indirectly promote linguistic growth, but the two are distinct phenomena. The fact that linguistic constructs cannot be derived from other cognitive constructs or principles is a further argument for the innate nature of linguistic knowledge.

In almost all of the areas touched on in this chapter, there are important and unresolved problems. For example, there are difficult questions concerning the status of principles of acquisition such as the subset principle. What is the status of such a principle when it is translated into mental mechanisms for grammar formation? Is such a principle distinguishable from an arbitrary stipulation that certain grammatical forms (the most frequent rules in languages of the world) have priority in language acquisition? In generative grammar, it is widely (though not universally) assumed that there are 'right' analyses and 'right' grammars and that these are the ones that reflect accurately what is in the mind of the speaker and guide acquisition. The processes involved in real-time acquisition are only now beginning to be explored.

Notes

1   Movement from a position (potentially infinitely) deep in the tree is possible (as in questions such as 'What did Sue see a man see . . . a horse kick?'), because the system permits a phrase to be fronted via a series of limited-distance moves, each consistent with subjacency. Problems occur only when the structure and principles of the system provide no way to avoid a move that violates subjacency.

2   The custom of using S nodes as the basis of computing the degree necessary for learnability derives from Wexler and Culicover (1980), who

presented a proof of 'degree-2' learnability, based on a condition similar to subjacency, where layers of structure were defined in terms of S nodes.

3 Baker discussed the learning problem presented by cases such as the dative alternation in the context of earlier models of grammar, where the two dative sentence frames were related by a transformation. The basic learning problem remains, however, under a non-transformational account such as that sketched here.

4 This section was written without the benefit of Bowerman (1988), who points to some problems with Braine's model in terms of its predictions concerning the limiting of errors. Possibly a mechanism along the lines of that sketched by Braine may be partially implemented in terms of recent connectionist (spreading activation) models of lexical access and processing. The limitations of connectionist models unsupplemented by pre-programmed knowledge are well known, in linguistics and other areas (see, for example, Sutherland, 1987; Pinker and Prince 1988). However, it is interesting in the context of the problems of lexical acquisition discussed in the text that recent work on language production by adults has argued for a distinction between lexical access and the production of syntactic structures, claiming that the former but not the latter are governed by connectionist mechanisms (Lapointe and Dell 1989).

Further Reading

Williams (1987) gives a concise summary of the relation between some recent developments in grammatical theory and language development. Snow (1986) discusses research on speech to children from the perspective of the structure of a language acquisition mechanism. Rice and Kemper (1984) review literature on the relation between cognition and language development.

Questions and Exercises

1. Consider the following passage from M. Donaldson's 1978 book *Children's Minds*:

The primary thing is . . . the grasp of meaning – the ability to 'make sense' of things, and above all to make sense of what people do, which of course includes what people say. On this view it is the child's ability to interpret situations which makes it possible for him, through active processes of hypothesis testing and inference, to arrive at a knowledge of language.

Now there is an important condition which must be satisfied if this account is to hold: the child must be in a general way capable of inference. For it is no longer being claimed that when he learns language he is using skills highly specific to that task. On the contrary, language learning is now presented as being closely bound up with all the other learning that is going on. (Donaldson 1978, pp. 32–3)

Give your own evaluation of this passage, using examples and arguments from this chapter and previous chapters, and/or your own experience.

2.   In section 6.2 the relation between questioning from subject position and the impossibility of omitting the complementizer 'that' was argued to constitute strong grounds for positing a language-specific, innate knowledge of the relevant principles of grammar:

(a)   *Who did John say that kissed Sue? (= (1c) in text)
(b)   Who did John say Ø   kissed Sue? (= (1d) in text)

Consider the following questions:

(c)   What did John say that surprised Sue?
(d)   What did John say Ø   surprised Sue?

(c) is superficially similar to (a), but it has a grammatical reading. (c) differs from (a) in interpretation – it is not paraphrased by its counterpart without 'that' (d). The verb 'say' allows an embedded clause as complement ('John said (that) something surprised Sue') or a direct object, which may be modified by a relative clause ('John said something that surprised Sue'). In (c) 'what' is interpreted as direct object of the main verb ('say'). The 'that' introduces a relative clause which modifies the questioned object, and which can be left behind when the object is questioned; it does not introduce an embedded complement of the type associated with the interpretation of (a), (b) and (d). The relative clause interpretation is precluded as a way to make (a) good because it is anomalous to have an animate object of the verb 'say' ('John said something' is good; 'John said someone' is anomalous). Notice that this is a fact about 'say', not a general constraint on verbs that take the two structures. The questions

(e)   Who did John watch that upset Sue?
(f)   Who did John watch Ø   upset Sue?

have interpretations parallel to (c) and (d), and have an animate question word, the same as the question word in (a).

Do you think these facts weaken or strengthen the argument in the text for an innate knowledge of the constraint that blocks questioning an embedded subject unless 'that' is deleted? Why?

3.   Wexler (1981) considers the following example, concerning the learnability of a hypothetical language. Suppose a language has a transformational rule that takes an element E and moves it to a position in the next highest layer of structure, attaching it at the right edge of the left-hand branch of a constituent (XP) in that layer. The learner could make the error of attaching the moved constituent to the left edge of the right-hand branch of the constituent XP, thus:

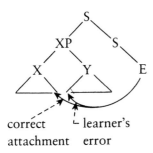

correct   ∟ learner's
attachment   error

The learner could thus formulate a rule that correctly relates the string XYE to the string XEY, without the correct structural analysis for the output string XEY. This error is in principle detectable. If another movement applies to the element X in the structure above, E will be carried along in the correct grammar, but not in the learner's grammar. Faced with output forms such as [...E] ZY, derived by the correct grammar as in the following diagram, the learner could revise his incorrect grammar to ensure that E gets attached in the right place when it is moved.

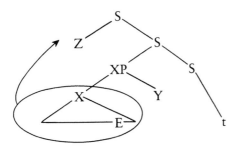

The existence of the second movement rule would be necessary for the error to be detectable and the language to be learnable (where 'learnable' means the learner must arrive at a grammar that generates all the sentences in the language and assigns them their correct structures).

   Chapter 4 mentioned a basic constraint on movement: an element can only move into a position 'higher' in the tree. This constraint can be stated in terms of the relation 'c-command': the moved element must move into a c-commanding position. How does this constraint bear on the situation

Wexler discusses? That is, how does it affect the learnability of human languages?

(The learning situation Wexler outlines has been simplified for the purpose of this problem.)

4.   It is often proposed that children who make errors with lexically restricted phenomena, such as the dative alternation, do so either because they impose non-adult semantic constraints on syntactic frames or because they have adult constraints but the meanings they assign to words to which the constraints potentially apply are slightly non-adult. How plausible do you think this view of errors is? Would such a semantically based account of errors affect the way in which errors are corrected, and how?

7 Performance Development

In chapter 1, the distinction was drawn between grammatical *competence* (knowledge of rules that determine grammaticality) and grammatical *performance* (actual instances of speaking and understanding). The sketch of acquisition procedures given in chapter 6 recognized that a sentence processing mechanism potentially has an important role in acquisition: the processor may mediate between the input (speech the child hears) and the mechanisms for rule formation. This chapter takes up the topic of performance development, primarily in the area of comprehension. The first section looks at ways in which children's grammatical knowledge may be over- or under-estimated on the basis of performance. The next two sections look at some leading ideas concerning the nature of the adult sentence processing mechanism, and the way these have influenced child language studies. The final section of the chapter reviews studies on children's interpretative preferences and the development of procedures for integrating information into a discourse.

7.1 Estimating Competence

Linguists use grammaticality judgements of native speakers as the basis for the theories they propose. Grammars account for the judgements that speakers make. By and large young children are not able to give the types of overt grammaticality judgement that adult native speakers give (see de Villiers and de Villiers 1972; de Villiers and de Villiers 1974; Hakes 1980). Their grammar must be estimated on the basis of their spontaneous speech or experimental tests of their knowledge. Because of the indirect nature of this type of evidence, it is easy either to over-estimate or under-estimate what children actually know – their grammatical competence.

Gruber (1967) gives a good example of how a child's spontaneous speech can give the impression of being more adult-like than it in fact is. A young two-year-old produced questions such as 'Where went the wheel?' meaning 'Where did the wheel go?' Questions of this sort appear to involve inversion of the subject ('the wheel') with the verb ('went'). Inversion is needed in the adult grammar – all that would appear to be lacking in the child's question is the correct auxiliary form ('did'). But Gruber argues that the child's questions do not involve an adult-like inversion rule. Rather, other facts in the child's speech at the period (such as a restriction of subjects to pronouns in utterances other than questions) argue for a child grammar in which the 'subject' in questions such as 'Where went the wheel?' is in fact a sentence-final topic NP. Such questions then have a quite non-adult structure for the child, along the lines:

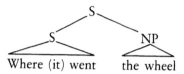

(The phrasal node S is used, rather than IP/TP, following the usage in most of the literature on which this chapter draws.)

But it is probably more usual to under-estimate children's competence than to over-estimate it. Spontaneous production may be a poor guide to competence because the child simply does not produce examples of all the sentence types that are within his grammatical competence (all the sentence types that the child would judge as grammatical, if he were capable of making such judgements). And tests of comprehension may under-estimate children's abilities for a variety of reasons, including the difficulty of the task and the complexity of the sentences confronting the child. An example involving relative clauses will illustrate how experimental tests can produce results that make it look as if children know less than they do.

Relative clauses have been observed in children's spontaneous speech in the third year (Limber 1973), and by the age of three children can be induced to produce relatives in experimental situations (Hamburger and Crain 1982).

However, a number of studies in the 1970s showed that pre-school children did rather poorly in interpreting some types of relative clauses. Using an acting-out task, both Sheldon (1974) and Tavakolian (1977, 1981) found that three- to five-year-old children frequently misconstrue a relative that modifies a direct object as referring to the subject of the sentence. Thus a sentence such as (1) will be interpreted to mean that the horse, not the cow, kicks the dog:

(1)   The horse pushes the cow that kicks the dog

These experiments thus pointed up a discrepancy between children's ability to produce relatives and their ability to interpret them. Tavakolian argued that the characteristic error in understanding relatives of the type in (1) is due to the child's treating the relative as if it were a conjoined clause: (1) would be interpreted as if it were the sentence 'The horse pushes the cow and kicks the dog'. That is, (1) will be analysed as having approximately the structure in (2a), rather than the structure (2b), with the relative embedded within the object NP.

(2a)

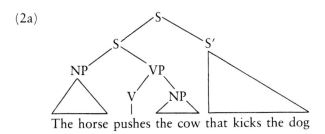

The horse pushes the cow that kicks the dog

(2b)

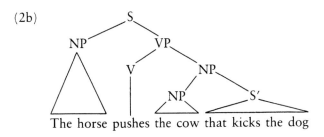

The horse pushes the cow that kicks the dog

Children's performance with sentences such as (1) has been shown to be dependent on the material in the relative. Goodluck and Tavakolian (1982) varied the transitivity of the relative and, for transitive relatives, the animacy of the object in the relative. All of the sentences in Sheldon's and Tavakolian's studies contained animate objects in the relative clause. As shown in table 7.1, Goodluck and Tavakolian found that children aged four to five performed best when the relative was intransitive; and for transitive clauses an inanimate object improved performance. For all sentence types, the commonest error was to make the relative refer to the main clause subject, as in the previous studies where children had done comparatively poorly. Similar results to Goodluck and Tavakolian's are reported by Otsu (1981) and Hamburger and Crain (1982).

These results suggest that children's errors with relatives of the type in (1) do not necessarily indicate lack of knowledge of the grammatical rules for relative clauses, but may rather reflect the difficulty of the test sentences. Linguistic factors, task demands and cognitive complexity at a level other than linguistic rules may all play a role in making a particular sentence type difficult. In the experiment referred to in table 7.1, sentences with complements to 'tell', such as 'The horse tells the cow to knock over the table/sheep'

Table 7.1 Effects of transitivity and animacy on interpretation of relatives

	Percentage correct responses, reference to object
Intransitive relative 'The horse kicks the cow that jumps up and down'	76
Transitive inanimate 'The horse kicks the cow that knocks over the table'	69
Transitive animate 'The horse kicks the cow that knocks over the sheep'	49

Adapted from Goodluck and Tavakolian (1982), Table 1

were also tested; here very few errors involving reference to the main clause subject were made, even when the object was animate (all the 'tell' sentences were transitive). Errors were thus dependent on the particular clause type involved, relative vs. complement to 'tell' (a linguistic effect). Intransitive relatives may be easiest because they involve manipulating fewer objects to act out the sentence (a task effect). And inanimate relatives may be easier than animate relatives because of a general expectation that objects are inanimate (a general cognitive effect).

Support for the conclusion that children's errors with relatives do not reflect a basic lack of relative clause structures in their competence grammar comes from experimental results that argue that the child can construct adult-like structures for relative clauses, in which the relative is embedded under the NP node (Goodluck and Tavakolian 1982; Goodluck 1989).

One important question about studies which show that children can do well if the circumstances are right is whether this kind of result invalidates theories of grammatical development based on the studies in which children do poorly. The answer would seem to be: not necessarily. For example, in the case of relative clause interpretation a conjoined clause analysis remains a plausible source of children's errors. Children who commit conjoined-clause type errors in interpreting relatives sometimes spontaneously repeat relative clauses as conjoined clauses, giving verbal evidence of the basis for their error of interpretation. Moreover, a conjoined-clause type analysis for children's error with relatives is not implausible on general linguistic grounds. Conjoined or adjoined structures have sometimes been posited for certain types of relatives (see, for example, Annear-Thompson 1971; Emonds 1979) and in some languages clauses that receive a relative-clause type interpretation have the same form as adverbial clauses, which, like conjoined clauses, are attached at a relatively high point in the phrase structure tree (see Keenan and Comrie 1977). It is possible that a conjoined or adjoined structure is a very early form of embedding for the child and is reverted to when other factors (such as transitivity or animacy of the object) make the relative clause difficult (Goodluck and Tavakolian, 1982).

To summarize, a child's grammatical competence is usually estimated on the basis of his performance – actual instances of speaking and understanding – rather than on overt grammaticality judgements. Children's linguistic behaviour can mislead by seeming more adult-like than it really is, or by virtue of omissions and errors that obscure the extent of children's grammatical competence. Errors are also potentially revealing, laying bare non-adult rules that may be part of an immature grammar.

7.2   Adult Processing Mechanisms

Performance development involves an increasing ability to use grammatical knowledge in an adult-like way. Models of the adult processing mechanism provide a framework to assess children's successes and failures in the use of language; some proposed processing mechanisms have had an influential effect on the interpretation of children's behaviour.

In the normal case, language comprehension by adults is a rapid, automatic process. An account of language processing must spell out the nature of the mechanism that takes an input string of words and analyses it to produce a representation of the hearer's understanding of the sentence and discourse. Limiting ourselves for the moment to comprehension of isolated sentences, rather than connected discourse, two questions are central to the modelling of adult comprehension: (1) Does the comprehension mechanism use the rules of the competence grammar? (2) What is the 'architecture' of the processor? That is, how does the comprehension device use different types of information (including real-world knowledge as well as grammar) in analysing the input?

7.2.1   A Model

The model of the processing mechanism given in figure 7.1 is adapted from the model in Forster (1979), and takes a particular position on both the question of how the processor uses grammatical rules and the role of different types of knowledge in language understanding. In this model, the arrows

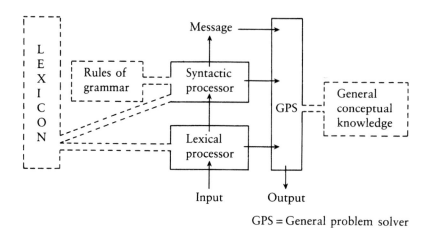

Figure 7.1　The structure of the processor
Source: modified from Forster 1979

indicate the proposed sequence of processing operations on the input (phrase or sentence to be analysed). Information stores that are used in the analysis are enclosed in broken lines; the different parts of the processor (lexical, syntactic, general problem solver) can use those information stores to which they are connected.

The model in figure 7.1 makes some strong claims concerning the operation of the processor and its use of different types of information. The direction of the arrows indicates that the processor constructs a syntactic analysis on the basis of lexical knowledge and rules of grammar, and without the use of general knowledge not encoded in the grammar (general conceptual knowledge), although the latter may affect the final output of the comprehension device. Thus the general answers the model provides for the questions above are that the grammar is used as a first step in processing and that the processor is designed in such a way that heuristics based on general knowledge may not supersede grammar in processing.

7.2.2　Grammar vs. General Knowledge and Strategies

The claims made by Forster's model concerning the use of grammar and the role of general conceptual knowledge in processing are not self-evident claims about the structure of the sentence processing device. It is logically possible that we do not use our rules of grammar in the normal comprehension of a sentence, or do so only when other means of comprehension fail. For example, the only sensible interpretation of the sentence (3):

(3)   The girl watered the flowers

is one where the girl does the watering, since real-world knowledge will tell
us that flowers do not water girls. It is thus conceivable that the rules of the
competence grammar are available for making overt grammaticality judgements on sentences, but that we sidestep grammar and use general inference
mechanisms in normal instances of understanding sentences. The correct
understanding of the sentence above could be reached on the basis of
heuristics for comprehension and without the construction of a syntactic
structure of the form familiar from chapter 4:

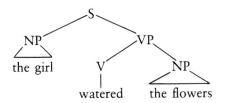

    At the time that Forster proposed the model above, the claim that the pro-
cessor constructs a syntactic analysis of the sentence and does not rely in the
first instance on heuristics of a non-grammatical or semi-grammatical kind
was a relatively controversial one. Two studies were particularly influential
during the 1970s; both argued against a full-blown syntactic analysis as a first
step in sentence comprehension. Slobin (1966) found that the time taken by
adults and school-age children to decide whether active and passive sentences
matched a picture depended on the plausibility of possible interpretations;
syntactic structure had an effect only when the possible interpretations were
equally plausible. Specifically, Slobin found that for active and passive sentences where the nouns in the sentence could sensibly be assigned only to the
role actor or patient, as in (3) above and its passive counterpart (4):

(4)   The flowers were watered by the girl

there was no difference in verification times. But for active and passive pairs
such as (5)–(6), where either of the nouns in the sentence could perform the
action on the other, the passive sentence took longer to verify than its active
counterpart:

(5)   The boy punched the girl
(6)   The girl was punched by the boy

Slobin's result fitted with a picture in which the processor first assigns roles to nouns in the sentence on the basis of lexical and real-world knowledge and resorts to grammatical analysis only where these sources of information do not give a clear indication of the probable meaning. That would mean that no grammatical analysis was necessary for (3)–(4), but that the active and passive syntax would need to be computed for (5)–(6). The fact that no difference in picture verification times was found for actives and passives such as (3)–(4), whereas a difference was found for (5)–(6), would thus be accounted for. This result was therefore compatible with a picture of the sentence processing mechanism in which syntax was computed only as a back-up procedure where real-world and lexical knowledge did not provide a single sensible interpretation.

A somewhat different approach was proposed by Bever (1970). Like Slobin, Bever took the view that the processor did not in the first instance attempt a full syntactic analysis of the input string. Bever proposed that the processor uses a number of strategies that refer to superficial properties of the sentence, particularly the linear order of words. The most often discussed of Bever's strategies was the following:

noun–verb–(noun)
=
actor–action–(object)

The claim is that the processor scans the input string, picks out the major category items (the nouns and the verb), and assigns a functional interpretation to these items on the basis of their linear positions in the string. Since the strategy assigns the first noun the role of actor, the strategy will result in the misanalysis of passive sentences as active sentences – that is, a sentence such as (6) would be misanalysed as meaning 'The girl punched the boy', under use of the N–V–N = subject–actor–object strategy. The greater difficulty of passive sentences in various sentence comprehension studies can be interpreted as a result of the need to overcome the effects of this strategy in the case of passive sentences.

Under both Slobin's and Bever's approaches, therefore, the syntax of a sentence was not computed automatically as a first step in sentence comprehension. The proposals of Slobin and Bever were perhaps particularly appealing because they came at a time when it seemed to many researchers that models of generative grammar (especially Chomsky 1965) did not provide a good basis for understanding the sentence comprehension process. A number of studies in the 1960s and early 1970s tested the hypothesis that the difficulty of understanding a sentence could be predicted on the basis of the number of transformational operations that had been performed in the sentence. This was the derivational theory of complexity (DTC), which proposed that the processor formed a syntactic parse of the sentence and then 'unpicked' the transformations that had applied to arrive at a deep structure for the sentence (for reviews of the literature on the DTC see Fodor et al. 1974, ch. 4; Foss and Hakes 1978, ch. 4). Some initial results appeared to support this theory: for example, wh-questions were harder to comprehend than corresponding actives, consistent with the idea that processing wh-questions involves the additional operation of placing the sentence-initial question word back into its deep structure position. But other findings went against the DTC; for example, sentences such as (8) were no more difficult to understand than sentences such as (7), although they were transformationally derived in the generative models of the period from a deep structure corresponding to (6) by a rule of particle movement (Fodor et al. 1974, ch. 6, pp. 323–4):

(7)   John threw out the garbage
(8)   John threw the garbage out

And while passive sentences such as (6) were more difficult than actives such as (5), consistent with the DTC and a passive transformation that forms passive sentences from a deep structure similar to that for their active equivalents, active–passive pairs such as (5)–(6) did not differ in complexity, in Slobin's experiment. Overall, the literature of the late 1960s and early 1970s seemed to suggest that syntactic analysis might be performed only under certain circumstances and not as an automatic consequence of inputting a sentence, contrary to the role assigned to syntactic analysis in the model in figure 7.1.

Later studies have shown that a model of the processor in which syntactic analysis is immediately and automatically performed, as in figure 7.1, may well turn out to be correct; the problems with the hypothesis that there is immediate computation of syntactic structure may be more apparent than real. First, Slobin's finding that there was no difference in response times for active and passive sentences where the properties of the words in the sentences allowed only one plausible reading, as in (5)–(6), was not replicated when a different experimental task was used. In a series of experiments that required subjects to judge sentences for grammaticality, Forster and Olbrei (1973) found that passives took longer to evaluate than actives, regardless of whether the nouns could be interchanged to form a sensible sentence. That is, passives such as (4) as well as passives such as (6) were more difficult than their active counterparts. Forster and Olbrei argued that there is a stable component of processing time contributed by the passive syntax. They suggested that

Slobin's result may not reflect normal sentence processing procedures, since there is evidence that picture verification (Slobin's task) is a poor indicator of the actual operations involved in understanding a sentence (Gough 1966).

With Slobin's result set aside, there is no strong evidence that argues in favour of use of real-world heuristics as a first step in processing that may substitute for syntactic analysis. The facts explained by comprehension strategies of the type proposed by Bever can also be explained under a processing model where a full syntactic analysis is immediately computed, rather than after a stage of analysis by semi-grammatical heuristics such as word-order strategies, provided that the processor operates under certain guidelines for the use of the rules of the competence grammar. To take one example, we characteristically misunderstand sentences such as (9), interpreting the first verb 'raced' as the main verb in the sentence:

(9)   The horse raced past the barn fell

'Raced' must in fact be analysed as part of a relative modifying 'horse' (the sentence means 'The horse which was raced past the barn fell'). The error we make in analysing sentences such as (9) can be put down to the N–V–(N) = actor–action–(object) strategy:

but it can also be accounted for in terms of a syntactic processing principle. One possibility (Frazier and Rayner 1982) is that the syntactic processor is constrained to build the simplest analysis consistent with the input, in terms of the number of syntactic nodes in the tree. Thus, faced with the first three words of (9), the parser (sentence processing mechanism) will construct an incorrect tree in which 'raced' is analysed as a main verb, because that tree is simpler than the (correct) analysis, in which the verb 'raced' is part of a relative modifying 'horse':

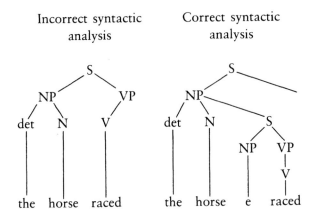

In addition to the lack of positive support for the use of non-grammatical or semi-grammatical strategies in processing, a body of recent experimental evidence supports the view that the sentence processing mechanism does perform a syntactic analysis of a string of words as the string is input to the processor (see, for example, Frazier and Rayner 1982; Crain and Fodor 1985b; Stowe 1986). These studies use techniques that measure sentence processing activity on-line, as the sentence is input, and show in several cases local effects of syntactic structure that are consistent with the processor actively forming a syntactic analysis on a word-by-word basis. For example, it has been demonstrated that the processor locates a position for a question word in the incoming sentence, at times erroneously anticipating the location of the questioned phrase. Thus the processor may place the question word 'what' as the object of 'laugh about' in a sentence such as (10):

(10)   Tom wondered what the team laughed about Greg's hairstyle for

only to discover its error on encountering the true object of 'laugh about': 'Greg's hairstyle' (see Crain and Fodor 1985b; Stowe 1986). Such results support the view that some kind of syntactic analysis is computed as the sentence is input. Moreover, the hypothesis that transformational operations add to processing complexity (the DTC; see above) can be held to be viable, in the light of recent developments in grammatical theory. The lack of any difference in processing time for sentence pairs such as (7)–(8) no longer presents a problem for a model of the processing mechanism in which there is a close relationship between grammatical structure and operations and processing, since many phenomena previously described in terms of transformational rules – including the alternation in position of the particle in (7)–(8) – are no longer analysed as transformationally related (see Berwick and Weinberg 1984 for one discussion of the DTC in the light of recent grammatical theory).

7.2.3 *Words-to-Message Processing*

The thrust of the previous section has been that it is reasonable and consistent with the available evidence to suppose (1) that the adult sentence processor constructs a syntactic analysis of a sentence as it is input; (2) that this syntactic processing is not skipped over, even if the meaning of the words in the sentence points towards a particular interpretation as the only plausible one; and (3) that the processor is not dependent on non-grammatical or semi-grammatical strategies based on superficial properties of the input as a first step in sentence interpretation. These claims are consistent with the model of processing given in figure 7.1.

The model in figure 7.1 gives only a very general picture of the relation between different types of information in processing. More needs to be said about the operation and internal structure of the processor and the way it turns a string of words into a representation at the message level.

First, it seems evident that the processor is engaged in all levels of analysis simultaneously, working on 'higher' message-level analysis of parts of material that has been lexically and syntactically analysed at the same time as it is doing lexical and syntactic analysis of more recently input material. This implies that the input string is segmented into chunks that are passed through the modules of the processor, before being finally integrated into a representation of the meaning of the sentence, at the message level or later (with the aid of the general problem solver). At the level of syntactic analysis, both the length of phrases and their syntactic complexity may affect how the input string is segmented into chunks (see Frazier and Fodor 1978). A variety of different kinds of experimental evidence argues that at some stage (plausibly towards the message end of the analysis process) the sentence or clause is an important unit of analysis, presumably as a consequence of the fact that clauses and sentences frequently express complete propositions (see Foss and Hakes 1978, ch. 4, for one review).

Second, the syntactic processor may operate under principles that determine the use it makes of the rules of the competence grammar. One candidate principle was mentioned above in connection with sentence (9): faced with a potentially ambiguous string, the processor may select the syntactic analysis for the string that is the simplest, in terms of syntactic nodes that are constructed. In some cases, no syntactic processing principle will resolve an ambiguity, and in these cases the processor may make use of strategies that select one reading over another. For example, most adults make use of a strategy to resolve the reference of a pronoun subject in the second conjunct of a con-joined clause. Where the conjoined clauses have the same syntactic structure, the pronoun is made to refer to the subject rather than the object of the first conjunct, although either interpretation is in fact permitted under the rules of the competence grammar. Thus, in (11), although the pronoun 'he' can in principle refer to either 'Fred' or 'Ed', the normal interpretation is to make the pronoun refer to 'Fred', provided the pronoun is read without any special stress:

(11)   Fred punched Ed and then he kicked Tom

(The exact nature of the strategy is taken up in more detail below.) Such examples argue that although there is little to support the use of strategies of the type proposed by Bever (1970), there may be a role for interpretative strategies at the syntactic and message levels in the resolution of ambiguities which remain after the sentence has been analysed in accord with rules of grammar and principles of processing.

We can thus add some details to the picture of words-to-message stages in figure 7.1 to arrive at the picture in figure 7.2.

Even with these details added in, however, many quite basic questions

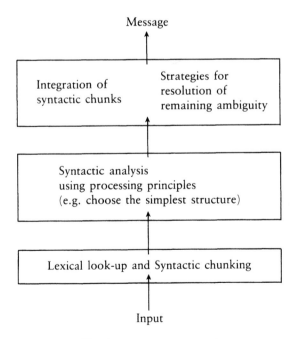

Figure 7.2 Words-to-message processing

remain unanswered: for example, although there is little reason to doubt that some kind of syntactic representation is constructed by the parser, how that representation corresponds to syntactic levels in the competence grammar (surface structure, deep structure and logical form, in terms of the grammatical model sketched in chapter 4) is not at all clear. However, the outline of the adult processing mechanism given above will be useful as a framework for looking at children's developing ability in sentence interpretation.

7.3   Children's Sentence Processing

A reasonable (though not necessary) hypothesis concerning performance development is that the child starts out with a processing mechanism that is qualitatively similar to the adult processing mechanism in terms of the organization of its components. Within the model in figure 7.1, what this means is that the young child will be equipped with a processor that is not deficient in its structure, but is plugged into components of the competence grammar that may be deficient. The child will have access to principles of universal grammar, assuming universal grammar to be innate; but he will lack vocabulary and language-particular syntactic rules. One consequence of this is that the child may rely more heavily than the adult on the general problem solver to work out the meaning of sentences. Lexical items and rules may be added to the competence grammar, based on the child's guesses about what the words and sentences he hears mean, within the bounds of what is permitted by principles of grammar and principles of acquisition.

Is the evidence from children's performance compatible with the model of processing in figure 7.1? The answer is broadly 'yes'. There is evidence that children immediately compute a syntactic analysis for an input sentence; use of strategies can be confined to cases where the processor is under pressure or the grammar does not provide a unique analysis for the input sentence.

7.3.1   *On-Line Computation of Syntactic Structure*

Tyler and Marslen-Wilson (1981) asked children aged five, seven and ten and adults to monitor a pre-designated word in an orally presented prose passage. In the monitoring task, the subject must press a button as soon as he or she hears the word s/he is told to listen for; in Tyler and Marslen-Wilson's experiment, the word was specified before the passage began. There were three types of passage in the experiment:

Normal prose:	A sequence of grammatical sentences with a sensible meaning.
(*Example*:	John had to go back home. He had fallen out of the swing and he had hurt his *hand* on the ground.)
Syntactic prose:	A sequence of syntactically correct sentences, where the choice of vocabulary permits no coherent semantic interpretation.
(*Example*:	John had to sit on the shop. He had lived out of the kitchen and he had enjoyed his *hand* in the mud.)
Random word order:	A sequence of unstructured words, divided into sentence-length chunks corresponding to the normal prose and syntactic prose sentences.
(*Example*:	The on sit shop to had John. He lived had and kitchen the out of his of had enjoyed *hand* mud in the.)

(These examples are Tyler and Marslen-Wilson's translations from the Dutch originals.) The word to be monitored for in the examples is 'hand', italicized in the examples.

The monitoring task, because it requires the subject to respond as soon as she recognizes the word she is searching for, provides a measure of processing as the sentence is input. Figure 7.3 gives the mean reaction times (in milliseconds) in Tyler and Marslen-Wilson's experiment. It is evident that for all age levels normal prose was the easiest type of passage to identify words in, syntactic prose was the next easiest, and random word order was the hardest. Clearly, the difference between syntactic prose and random word order supports the view that a syntactic analysis is constructed very rapidly, as the processor receives the input words.

The difference between syntactic prose and normal (semantically coherent) prose raises the question of when semantics and real-world knowledge affect syntactic analysis. Forster's model (figure 7.1) claims that general conceptual knowledge affects the comprehension process only after some syntactic analysis has been done. This is not incompatible with the results shown in figure 7.3; the longer reaction times at a given point for syntactic prose may reflect difficulty caused by trying to make sense of a syntactic analysis that is already completed. However, the issue of whether semantics and general knowledge intervene in the first stages of syntactic analysis is a highly controversial one, not yet resolved for either children or adults (see, for example, discussion in Forster 1979; Tanenhaus et al. 1985; Altmann 1988).

The results of Tyler and Marslen-Wilson's experiment support in a general way the idea that the child uses a sentence processor with the same structure

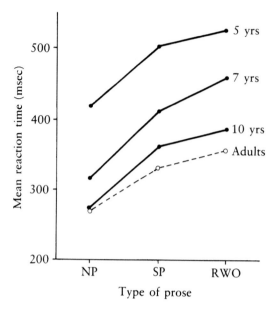

Figure 7.3 Mean reaction times (msecs) in identical monitoring for each prose type and age group
NP = normal prose; SP = syntactic prose; RWO = random word order
Tyler and Marslen-Wilson 1981, figure 1

as the adult's. The overall pattern of results for children is similar to that for adults, although children's reaction times are slower. The effect of syntax is compatible with a model of processing such as that in figure 7.1, where a syntactic analysis is immediately computed, using the rules of the competence grammar. In a recent study, Chafetz and Gordon (1989) have obtained results similar to those of Tyler and Marslen-Wilson with children as young as three years.

7.3.2 Strategies and Children's Comprehension

The idea that the child is equipped with a sentence processing device of the same form as the adult device will be fleshed out in different ways, depending on the conception held of the adult processor. The elaborated model of words-to-message processing given in figure 7.2 allows only one role for comprehension strategies: the resolution of ambiguities that remain after a syntactic analysis has been carried out according to the rules of the competence grammar and processing principles. In that model, adult sentence comprehension is assumed to take place, in the normal case, without the use of comprehension strategies that focus on rather superficial properties of the input, such as the N–V–N = actor–action–object strategy proposed by Bever.

Bever (1970), Slobin and Bever (1982) and others propose strategy-based analyses for children's performance on sentence comprehension tasks. Slobin and Bever's work with children applies their ideas about strategy-based adult sentence processing to the study of children's performance. They show that two- to four-year-old children learning different language types respond best to those word orders which correspond to the 'canonical' order of the language (for English, N–V–N), and conclude: 'children are attuned to canonical sentence forms and . . . early on, they develop schemas embodying the most typical features of such forms; and, further, . . . canonical sentence schemas play a central role in processes of perception of utterances' (Slobin and Bever 1982, p. 257). Where strategies (analysis via canonical schemas, in Slobin and Bever's terminology) are proposed to account for *successes* children have in understanding sentences, an objection can be raised that has also been raised to this approach to adult sentence processing: the strategy will do the job, but so will active use of rules of grammar. The strategy is not necessary to account for children's performance.

Where strategies are proposed to account for errors, however, something more must be said. One possibility compatible with the overall model of processing in figures 7.1 and 7.2 is that the language learner may respond in systematic ways where the task and/or materials are sufficiently difficult to exceed the capacities of the processing device. In addition to resolution strategies, then, the immature processor may use strategies for response as a kind of fall-back solution, when the going is particularly tough. The use of a conjoined-clause type response to relative clauses that are complex for whatever reason (see section 7.1 above) is a candidate for this type of strategy; in addition, it is possible that word-order-based strategies may on occasion be used as a fall-back in experimental situations that fatigue the processing device (see Goodluck 1989 for discussion).

One finding of Bever (1970) is particularly intriguing and was used to support children's reliance on the proposed N–V–N strategy. Bever tested children's comprehension of simple active and passive sentences such as those in (12) and (13), using an acting-out task:

(12) The lion bit the tiger
(13) The lion was bitten by the tiger

At two to three years children did relatively well with simple actives, and less well with passives; by four years, performance on simple actives was generally very good and the gap between actives and passives was closing. Then at around the turn of the fourth year, there was a dip in performance on the passive. Children at this age did less well in interpreting passives than children either slightly younger or older. The characteristic error was to interpret the passive as if it were an active – i.e. to interpret a sentence such as (13) as if it were (12). Maratsos (1974b) found the same temporary regression in performance on the passive. Bever's explanation for this phenomenon was that at around four years children over-apply the proposed N–V–N = actor–action–object strategy, leading to increased errors with the passive, for which the strategy will give an incorrect interpretation.

What kind of alternative explanation can be given, within the framework of grammar and processing outlined in Forster's model? In chapter 4 we saw that it has been proposed that the movement rule for forming passives, which moves the object NP into subject position,

(14)   [e] was bitten the tiger by the lion
        The tiger$_i$ was bitten [t$_i$]   by the lion

may develop relatively late, although we also saw that strong evidence for this hypothesis (late development of movement in the passive) is currently lacking. Prior to acquiring movement in passives, children may perform well on passives by virtue of an analysis of passive structures similar or identical to that for interpreting adjectival constructions, such as 'The lion was angry' (see chapter 4, section 4.4.2). One possible account of the dip in performance with passives at around four years is that at that age children introduce movement as an operation in the formation of the passive; a new rule may be harder to access and apply in processing sentences, accounting for the child's temporary regression with the passive. On this account, children's performance with simple active and passive sentences is compatible with the view of processing proposed by Forster, where syntactic analysis is done actively in processing, and the passive transformation leads to processing complexity and more errors, particularly when it is first introduced into the child's grammar.

To summarize this section so far, it is possible to account for children's successful interpretation of simple sentence types without appealing to the use of the type of word-order strategy proposed by Bever and others to account for children's performance. If the child has a sentence processing mechanism of the kind proposed by Forster, and actively uses the rules of his developing grammar in processing sentences, the same results can be derived. When the sentences the child is dealing with are complex or unfamiliar, he may make errors of a random nature and/or use strategies for interpretation. Such strategies are assumed not to have a place in normal adult sentence comprehension and for children also can be taken as a way of responding to material that is difficult for some reason.

7.3.3 *Resolution Strategies*

Children, like adults, may use strategies to resolve ambiguities that neither rules of the competence grammar nor processing principles (such as minimal attachment) eliminate. Sometimes non-adult rules have been proposed, where a non-adult resolution strategy may in fact be at work.

A good example is backward anaphora in child language. Early work on children's grammar of pronominal reference suggested that children learning English might have a stricter rule on pronoun reference than the adult grammar, blocking all reference between a pronoun and a following NP (see Tavakolian 1978; Lust 1981; Solan 1978, 1983). As we saw in chapter 4, co-reference between a pronoun and following NP is permitted, subject to the structural restrictions imposed by the binding theory. The binding theory permits co-reference between the pronoun 'he' and the following NP 'Bill' in sentences such as (15), although co-reference is not required ('he' and 'Bill' can refer to different persons):

(15)   After he sat down, Bill lit up a cigar

In several studies, children tended to avoid making a pronoun co-referential with a following NP, even where the adult grammar permitted co-reference, and this prompted the proposal that children's rules of grammar actually blocked such reference. But more recent studies have shown that rather young children will allow co-reference between a pronoun and a following NP, where this is permitted in the adult grammar (Goodluck 1980/1987; Lust et al. 1981; Crain and McKee 1985; O'Grady et al. 1986; Hsu and Cairns 1986). Children's avoidance of co-reference between a pronoun and a following NP where the adult grammar allows co-reference is most likely a strategy for resolution of ambiguity, perhaps promoted by particulars of the test (Goodluck 1987).

Children's resolution strategies may also differ in subtle ways from those of adults, and the adult form of the strategy may not be firmly established until well into the school years. Pronoun interpretation provides another example of this type. The example of a resolution strategy given in section 7.1 was the strategy for interpreting the (unstressed) pronoun subject of a conjoined clause. The characteristic adult interpretation is to make the pronoun refer to the subject of the first clause. In (11), repeated here, the pronoun 'he' is made to refer to 'Fred':

(11)   Fred punched Ed and then he kicked Tom

The strategy is one of 'parallel function', where the pronoun is interpreted as referring to the NP in the preceding clause with the same role that the pronoun has in its clause. In the example (11), it is unclear whether parallelism of role is based on grammatical role (subject) or thematic role (agent); either way, the pronoun will be matched to the subject of the first clause. Solan (1983) tested the development of this strategy in children. He found that children, like adults, use parallel function in resolving the reference of pronouns, but that children compute parallelism consistently on the basis of thematic roles, in contrast to adults, who waver somewhat between use of thematic roles and grammatical roles.

Solan tested five- to eight-year-old children's interpretation of sentences such as those in table 7.2, using an acting-out task. In each of these sentence types, there is a pronoun subject in the second of two conjoined sentences. (The pronoun was always 'she'; subjects were taught that all the animals in the experiment were female.) The sentences vary according to whether the two conjuncts have the same syntactic structure or different structures, in terms of active and passive voice. Where the sentences have the same structure (active–active (A) or passive–passive (B)), the subject of both sentences has the same thematic role (agent in (A) and patient in (B)). Where the sentences differ in structure (active–passive (C) and passive–active (D)), the thematic role of the subjects in the two conjuncts differs (agent vs. patient in (C) and patient vs. agent in (D)).

Children tended to interpret the pronoun in terms of whichever NP in the

Table 7.2 Grammatical structure and semantic roles

	Structure of conjoined sentences and thematic roles of the subjects
(A) The dog hit the sheep and then she hit the cow	Like
(B) The dog was hit by the sheep and then she was hit by the cow	Like
(C) The dog hit the sheep and then she was hit by the cow	Unlike
(D) The dog was hit by the sheep and then she hit the cow	Unlike

first sentence shared the semantic role the pronoun bore in the second sentence. In the (A) and (B) examples in table 7.2, the pronoun was made to refer to the subject NP 'the dog', which is agent in both conjuncts in (A) and patient in both conjuncts in (B). In the (C) and (D) examples, by contrast, the pronoun would be made to refer to the object NP 'the sheep', which is patient in both conjuncts in (C) and agent in both conjuncts in (D). Adults were more variable in their responses; they gave parallel responses, but appeared to waver as to whether they matched the pronoun with a referent with the same thematic role, or with the same grammatical role (subject). Thus, where the rules of grammar do not provide a firm directive, children may adopt a strategy for interpreting sentences that is somewhat different from that used by adults (children use thematic roles, adults use either thematic roles or the grammatical role subject). For both children and adults, the basic form of the resolution strategy – parallelism – may, however, be the same.[1] The child's heavier reliance on thematic roles may be part of a general reliance by children on thematic as opposed to grammatical relations (particularly the relation subject) in interpreting constructions for which their grammar does not dictate a unique analysis (Goodluck and Birch 1988), a reliance which may extend into middle childhood.

7.4 Discourse Integration

The study of discourse goes beyond the scope of grammatical rules as we have dealt with them so far and lies at the borderline between the study of grammar and the study of language use. The study of discourse is not purely a matter of performance, since there are rules that govern discourse that are not derivable from the structure and organization of the language production and processing devices; the topic of discourse development is taken up in this chapter largely for convenience.

The formation of a discourse representation can be assumed to take place in the process of comprehension at a level somewhere at or beyond the message level in the model in figure 7.1, using both conventions for the overall coherence of the discourse – the way the sentences 'fit together' best to present and maintain the topic of the discourse – and also knowledge of the world to make judgements about the plausibility of different possible situations represented by a discourse.

Karmiloff-Smith (1986) takes the view that the development of skills in discourse formation may be the most significant of middle-childhood developments. Some evidence that children organize their discourses in ways that depart from the adult conventions comes from studies of guided production of discourses. Karmiloff-Smith (1980, 1985) showed that young children organize their discourse in such a way that the topic of the discourse is consistently made the subject or utterance-initial element of each sentence, and is expressed by a pronoun or an elided (null) NP. Asked to relate the events in a sequence of pictures featuring a small boy and a balloon-seller, one child produced the following discourse (B = boy, referent of the pronoun):

A little boy is walking along. He (B) walks off in the sunshine. He (B) sees a balloon seller. He (B) wants a green balloon. He (B) gets one. He (B) lets go of the balloon and then he (B) starts crying. (Karmiloff-Smith 1980, p. 242)

The boy, established as discourse topic of the first sentence, is thus consistently made pronoun subject of subsequent sentences in the discourse. When asked to relate the events in the same pictures in isolation, children will vary as to choice of 'boy' or 'balloon-seller' as subject of the sentence describing the event, showing that the choice of a single entity as pronoun subject is not merely an artefact of (for example) the pictures used as stimuli. Direct evidence for Karmiloff-Smith's view that the child imposes a 'discourse-topic = subject = pronoun = elided NP structure' on his stories comes from 'repairs' children make in the course of producing a discourse. A subject will sometimes be selected that violates the discourse-topic condition, and this first choice is then corrected to a subject that is the discourse topic:

A little boy is walking along. He (B) sees a balloon-man. The balloon m . . . he (B) asks for a balloon and (B) goes off happily. The balloon . . . he (B) lets go of the balloon and (B) starts to cry. (Karmiloff-Smith 1980, p. 243)

As children get older, they begin to relax the bar on NPs other than discourse topic as subject, using more complex patterns of mapping between thematic and syntactic organization to form a connected discourse (but see also Clibbens 1986 for a study arguing that younger children do have some sophisticated discourse skills).

Comprehension results confirm that children may integrate sentences into a discourse representation in ways somewhat different from adults. Tyler (1983) used a mispronunciation detection task to test children's sensitivity to a variety of factors in discourse organization. In the detection task, the subject is asked to listen and try to spot a word that is not pronounced correctly; previous studies with adults and children had shown that detection times are shortened if the mispronounced word is contextually predictable – for example, the mispronunciation of 'letter' as 'leffer' will be more easily detected if it is preceded in the sentence by the word 'postman' than if it is preceded by some unrelated noun.

In one experiment, Tyler studied the ability to detect mispronunciations of words in different discourse contexts. In discourse (A) in table 7.3 the mispronounced word ('ice' in the example) is related to the subject noun 'skater', in the same sentence; so facilitation in identifying the mispronounced word is expected regardless of the fact that the word 'skater' also occurs in the preceding sentence. In discourse (B), the subject of the sentence containing the word 'ice' is the definite pronoun 'he', which is co-referent with the related word 'skater'; in (C), the subject is 'our nephew', which, like the pronoun in (B), is identical in reference to the noun 'skater' (this identity is established in the preceding sentence). Discourse (D) is the same as (C), except that the related word in the first of the two sentences is replaced by 'the boy', which is unrelated to the mispronounced word 'ice'.

The figures in table 7.4 show that for all age groups the presence of a related word in the discourse context facilitates detection of mispronunciations: detection times were much slower in (D), where there was no related word, than they were in (A), (B) and (C). Reaction times for children were slower than for adults, but the general pattern for (A), (B) and (C) vs. (D) is the same for all age groups.

The youngest children differed from the older children and adults, however,

Table 7.3 Predictability and discourse linking

(A) The skater in the orange suit was our
      nephew.
    The skater fell on the *ice* and broke his
      leg . . .

(B) The skater in the orange suit was our
      nephew.
    He fell on the *ice* and broke his leg . . .

(C) The skater in the orange suit was our
      nephew.
    Our nephew fell on the *ice* and broke his
      leg . . .

(D) The boy in the orange suit was our nephew.
    Our nephew fell on the *ice* and broke his
      leg.

Examples of discourse conditions, Tyler 1983, experiment 3.
(The examples are Tyler's translations of Dutch originals.)

Table 7.4 Mean mispronunciation detection latencies (msecs)

Age group	Discourse			
	(A)	(B)	(C)	(D)
5 years	746	781	770	931
6 years	643	699	669	741
7 years	519	568	548	596
Adults	379	412	373	453

in their handling of (B) and (C). In all cases, detection times were shorter where the anaphoric subject was a full NP (C) than when it was a pronoun (B), but that difference was less for young children (five years) than for older children. Tyler suggested an explanation for this difference, related to the discourse-topic phenomenon observed in Karmiloff-Smith's production experiment. In Tyler's experiment, each of the sentence pairs such as (A)–(D) in table 7.3 was preceded by one or two other sentences, to make a short story. Tyler found that in those cases in her experimental materials where the pronoun was the topic of the discourse, detection times were not appreciably slower for sentences with pronouns (B) than for sentences with full NPs (C): where the pronoun was *not* the topic of the discourse, however, reaction times were slower for (B) than for (C). For older groups, reaction times were slower for (B) than for (C) regardless of whether the (pronoun or full noun phrase) subject was discourse topic. This pattern fits with Karmiloff-Smith's finding that younger children organize their discourse so that the sentence-initial, subject position is filled with a discourse topic, and that topic is expressed by a pronoun. As children get older, they become more adept at coping with exceptions to this restriction.

7.5 Summary and Conclusions

The child's competence grammar must be estimated on the basis of instances of linguistic performance – instances of speaking and understanding. Tests of comprehension can easily under-estimate children's grammatical abilities.

Results from studies of children's sentence comprehension are broadly compatible with a model of processing of the type proposed by Forster, in which rules of grammar are actively used in comprehension. Use of comprehension strategies is plausibly confined to dealing with difficult material or the resolution of ambiguities.

Language development involves development at the level of performance mechanisms as well as of rules of the competence grammar. We saw an example of this in the development of an interpretive (resolution) strategy; the strategy has the same basic form (parallelism), but was applied in slightly different ways by children and adults. The ability to integrate material into a discourse may also undergo significant development. The development of resolution strategies for intra-sentential interpretation and the development of discourse skills are linked, in the sense that both involve the exercise of principles that are not part of sentence grammar *per se*. In this sense, Karmiloff-Smith's (1986) hypothesis that development in discourse skills is a vital change in middle childhood may have a wider scope than she gave it.

The emphasis in this chapter has been on outlining some candidate properties of the sentence processing mechanism. Understanding how this mechanism works is potentially critical in studies that attempt to estimate children's grammar on the basis of their comprehension of sentences; working out what part of the child's behaviour reflects his rules of grammar and what part reflects the structure and capacities of the processing mechanism will no more be possible without a picture of what the processing mechanism is like than it will be possible without a picture of what the grammar itself is like. So for those who want to do experimental studies of grammatical development there is a good practical reason for studying the way the sentence processor works.

There is also another reason for studying the nature of the processing device. The design of the processor may have functional utility, helping to explain the ease and speed with which children learn language. Work in this area is only beginning, but several interesting ideas have been put forward. For example, Berwick and Weinberg (1984, p. 234) argue that there is a learning advantage to a processing mechanism which operates in such a way that one and only one analysis of a potentially ambiguous input sentence is pursued – an analysis which is correct for the input.[2] Using such a processing mechanism, the learner who finds that his processor fails with a given sentence can conclude that there is something wrong with his current grammar (the rules need to be changed so that they will accommodate the input); the learner does not have to consider the possibility that what went wrong was that the processor chose an incorrect analysis of the sentence from among the alternatives made available in the grammar. A processing breakdown thus indicates a problem with the grammar, and pushes the learner along on the road to a grammar with rules that will produce all the sentences in the adult language.

Notes

1 Use of some form of strategy based on parallelism has also been proposed as an explanation of performance on some types of relative clauses; see Sheldon (1974). Tavakolian (1977) argues against this approach to children's relative interpretation.

2 The difficulty of sentences such as 'The horse raced past the barn fell' (section 7.2.2), where adults clearly do make errors, would seem to make the idea that the processor constructs a single *correct* analysis implausible. Marcus (1980) argues that exceptionally difficult sentences such as 'The horse raced past the barn fell' should not fall within the domain of a theory of processing in the normal case. One way to look at such exceptionally difficult sentences is that they are difficult precisely because their analysis contravenes processing principles such as the principle mandating choice of the simplest syntactic structure (section 7.2.2), and correction of the error involves rather large readjustments in the analysis dictated by that principle (Frazier and Rayner 1982). The learner may be seen to be changing his grammar so that processing principles such as the principle of least-structure will do as much work as possible.

Further Reading

Foss and Hakes (1978) contains a clearly written and critical introduction to much of the literature of the 1960s and 1970s on adult sentence processing and production. Dowty et al. (1985) and Carlson and Tanenhaus (1989) are technical collections that contain examples of more current work on adult performance mechanisms. Frazier and de Villiers (1990) is a collection that post-dates this chapter, with several articles pertinent to questions raised in this chapter and chapter 6.

Questions and Exercises

1. Young children by and large are not adept at giving overt grammaticality judgements. Several recent studies have attempted to devise

experimental situations and tasks in which the child gives an indirect type of judgement (e.g. Crain and McKee 1985; Hsu et al. 1985; Pinker et al. 1987; Goodluck 1989). For example, children's knowledge of the world can be used to obtain judgements on sentences. Children know, for example, that pigs oink and cows moo, etc. Find some children and ask them to judge the following sentences as 'good' (G) or 'silly' (S):

		Adult response
(a)	The cow mooed	G
(b)	The pig mooed	S
(c)	The cat meowed	G
(d)	The cow oinked	S
(e)	The pig oinked	G
(f)	The cat mooed	S
(g)	The cow kicked the cat that mooed	S
(h)	The cow chased the pig that oinked	G
(i)	The pig kicked the cat that oinked	S
(j)	The cat looked at the cow that mooed	G
(k)	The pig chased the cat and then oinked	G
(l)	The cat hit the cow and then meowed	G

Check first that the child knows the noises the animals make; children are usually at ease in making judgements of this type if they are told that it is their job to help another person (a doll that the experimenter introduces, for example) to learn how to talk. The adult judgement for sentences (a)–(l) is given to the right of the sentences. If children know that the relative clause in (g)–(j) modifies the object NP, and if they use grammar in making their judgements, they will judge (h) and (j) as 'good', and (g) and (i) as 'silly'. If they use only knowledge of the world, there is no reason why all the sentences (g)–(j) should not be judged 'good', with, for example, (g) having the interpretation that the cow was the one that mooed. The sentences (k, l) have a conjoined clause rather than a relative clause, and a child who judges (g) and (i) as 'silly' but (k) and (l) as 'good' is clearly using grammar to distinguish between the two sentence types, which have the same superficial form (the same sequence of nouns and verb), but differ only in the presence of a relative complementizer ('that') rather than the conjunction ('and then'). Do not expect all children to do well on this test; recall from the text that young children may analyse relative clauses as conjoined clauses. But many children aged four and older will perform in an adult-like way.

2.   As mentioned in chapter 4, several studies have shown that passive sentences are more accurately comprehended when they contain an action verb (such as 'hit', 'kick', etc.) than when they contain a non-action verb (such as 'hate', 'love', etc.) (see Maratsos 1985; Pinker et al. 1987). So passives such as (a, b) will be understood better than passives such as (c, d):

(a)   The lion was hit by the tiger

(b)   The lion was kicked by the tiger
(c)   The lion was hated by the tiger
(d)   The lion was loved by the tiger

Maratsos suggests that this difference in performance with action and non-action passives may reflect a grammar where the passive is restricted to certain verb types in early stages; similarly, Pinker et al. develop a theory in which certain canonical mappings between thematic roles (agent, patient, etc.) and syntactic positions have priority in early child language and render some verbs easier for the child to passivize.

  Another possibility is that the results are not something to do with the passive itself, but with how different verb classes are handled in difficult structures, of which the passive will be just one example. Think of an experiment to test this alternative hypothesis.

3.   Consider the following mind experiment. Children are asked to listen to sentences of the following types and detect a mispronounced word (sentence type (a) has an embedded wh-question and sentence type (b) has an embedded 'if'-clause). The word to be mispronounced is italicized in the examples:

(a)   Tom asked what Sue wrote *letters* to Bill for
(b)   Tom asked if Sue wrote *letters* to Bill often

Suppose that reaction times to detect the mispronounced word were longer in (a) than in (b)? How would you explain this, and what bearing would this finding have for children's grammatical analysis and processing of sentences?

nability along the voicing con-
gs of the Sixth International
demica.

isition of Turkish', in Slobin.

t in Swedish', in Engdahl and

ies and computational models',
7.

inguistic Inquiry 13: 571–612.
ture of relative clauses', in C.
in Linguistics Semantics. New

bdialect of English', Word 17:

Yawelmani Phonology and Mor-
setts Institute of Technology.
e acquisition', First Language 7:

aper presented at the University
age Acquisition and Language

projection problem', Linguistic

The Logical Problem of Language
ss.

acquisition of Warlpiri: compre-
of Child Language 12: 597–610.
English morphology', Word 14:

ntactic Knowledge. Cambridge,

Grammatical Basis of Linguistic
ress.

iguistic structures', in Hayes.

Bloom, L. 1970 *Language Development: Form and Function in Emerging Grammars*. Cambridge, Mass.: MIT Press.

Bloom, L. 1976 *One Word at a Time*. The Hague: Mouton.

Bloom, P. 1989 'Why do children omit subjects?', *Papers and Reports on Child Language Development* 28: 57–64. Department of Linguistics, Stanford University.

Borer, H. and Wexler, K. 1987 'The maturation of syntax', in Roeper and Williams.

Bowerman, M. 1973 *Early Syntactic Development: A Cross-Linguistic Study with Special Reference to Finnish*. Cambridge, UK: Cambridge University Press.

Bowerman, M. 1982 'Reorganization processes in lexical and syntactic development', in Wanner and Gleitman 1982.

Bowerman, M. 1983 'How do children avoid constructing an overly general grammar in the absence of feedback about what is not a sentence?' *Papers and Reports on Child Language Development* 22. Department of Linguistics, Stanford University.

Bowerman, M. 1987 'Commentary', in MacWhinney.

Bowerman, M. 1988 'The "No negative evidence" problem: how do children avoid constructing an overly general grammar?' in J. Hawkins, ed. *Explaining Linguistic Universals*. Oxford: Blackwell.

Bracken, H. 1983 *Mind and Language*. Dordrecht: Foris.

Braine, M. 1963 'The ontogeny of English phrase structure: the first phase', *Language* 39: 1–13.

Braine, M. 1971 'On two types of models of the internalization of grammars', in D. Slobin, ed., *The Ontogenesis of Grammar*. New York: Academic.

Braine, M. 1976 'Review article: Smith, 1973', *Language* 52: 489–98.

Bresnan, J. 1982 'Control and complementation', in Bresnan, ed.

Bresnan, J. ed. 1982 *The Mental Representation of Grammatical Relations*. Cambridge, Mass.: MIT Press.

Brown, R. 1958 *Words and Things*. Glencoe, Ill.: Free Press.

Brown, R. 1973 *A First Language*. Cambridge, Mass.: Harvard University Press.

Brown, R. and Hanlon, C. 1970 'Derivational complexity and order of acquisition in child speech', in Hayes.

Buckley, R. 1982 *Living German*, 4th edn. Sevenoaks, UK: Hodder and Stoughton.

Cairns, C. and Feinstein, M. 1982 'Markedness and the theory of syllable structure', *Linguistic Inquiry* 13: 193–225.

Carey, S. 1978 'The child as word learner', in M. Halle, J. Bresnan and G. Miller, eds, *Linguistic Theory and Psychological Reality*. Cambridge, Mass.: MIT Press.

Carlson, G. and Tanenhaus, M. eds 1989 *Linguistic Structure and Language Processing*. Dordrecht: Kluwer.

Chafetz, J. and Gordon, P. 1989 'Distinctions in vocabulary type in children's processing', MS, University of Pittsburgh.

Chien, Y. C. and Wexler, K. 1989 'Children's knowledge of relative scope in Chinese', *Papers and Reports on Child Language Development* 28: 72–80. Department of Linguistics, Stanford University.

Chomsky, C. 1969 *The Acquisition of Syntax in Children From 5 to 10*. Cambridge, Mass.: MIT Press.

Chomsky, N. 1959 Review of Skinner, *Verbal Behavior*, *Language* 35: 26–58.

Chomsky, N. 1965 *Aspects of the Theory of Syntax*. Cambridge, Mass.: MIT Press.

Chomsky, N. 1973 'Conditions on transformations' in S. Anderson and P. Kiparsky (eds) *A Festschrift for Morris Halle*. New York: Holt, Rinehart and Winston.

Chomsky, N. 1980 *Rules and Representations*. New York: Columbia University Press; Oxford: Blackwell.

Chomsky, N. 1981 *Lectures on Government and Binding*. Dordrecht: Foris.

Chomsky, N. 1982 *Some Concepts and Consequences of the Theory of Government and Binding*. Cambridge, Mass.: MIT Press.

Chomsky, N. 1986a *Knowledge of Language: Its Nature, Origin and Use*. Westport, Conn.: Praeger.

Chomsky, N. 1986b *Barriers*. Cambridge, Mass.: MIT Press.

Clahsen, H. 1985 'Parameterized grammatical theory and language acquisition: a study of the acquisition of verb placement and inflection in children and adults'. Revised version appears in S. Flynn and W. O'Neill, eds, *Linguistic Theory and Second Language Acquisition*. Dordrecht: Kluwer.

Clahsen, H. 1992 'Learnability theory and the problem of development in language acquisition', in Weissenborn et al.

Clahsen, H. and Muysken, P. 1986 'The availability of universal grammar to adult and child learners: a study of the acquisition of German word order', *Second Language Research* 2: 93–119.

Clancy, P. 1986 'The acquisition of Japanese', in Slobin.

Clark, E. 1971 'On the acquisition of the meaning of "before" and "after"', *Journal of Verbal Learning and Verbal Behavior* 10: 266–75.

Clark, E. 1973 'What's in a word? On the child's acquisition of semantics in his first language', in T. Moore, ed., *Cognitive Development and the Acquisition of Language*. New York: Academic Press.

Clark, E. 1982 'The young word maker: a case study of innovation in the child's lexicon', in Wanner and Gleitman.

Clark, E. and Hecht, B. 1982 'Learning to coin agent and instrument nouns', *Cognition* 12: 1–24.

Clark, E., Hecht, B. F. and Mulford, R. 1986 'Coining complex compounds in English: affixes and word order in acquisition', *Linguistics* 24: 1, 7–29.

Clements, G. N. 1988 'The role of the sonority cycle in core syllabification', to appear in *Papers in Laboratory Phonology*. Cambridge, UK: Cambridge University Press. (Cited in Martohardjono 1989.)

Clements, G. N. and Keyser, S. J. 1983 *CV Phonology: A Generative Theory of the Syllable*. Cambridge, Mass.: MIT Press.

Clibbens, J. 1986 'Constraints on the use of full and reduced forms of nominal reference in children's production of connected discourse', in R. Stevenson, R. Crawley and M. Tallerman, eds, *Proceedings of the 1986 Child Language Seminar*, Durham University, UK.

Clumeck, H. 1980 'The acquisition of tone', in Yeni-Komshian, Kavanagh and Ferguson, vol. 1.

Coats, J. 1983 *The Semantics of the Modal Auxiliaries*. London: Longman.

Coker, P. 1978 'Syntactic and semantic factors in the acquisition of *before* and *after*', *Journal of Child Language* 5: 261–77.

Cook, V. 1976 'A note on indirect objects', *Journal of Child Language* 3: 435–73.

Cook, V. 1988 *Chomsky's Universal Grammar: An Introduction*. Oxford: Blackwell.

Crain, S. and Fodor, J. D. 1985a 'On the innateness of subjacency', in G. Alvarez, B. Brodie and D. McCoy, eds, *Proceedings of the East Coast Conference on Linguistics*, Ohio State University.

Crain, S. and Fodor, J. D. 1985b 'How can grammars help parsers?', in Dowty et al.

Crain, S. and McKee, C. 1985 'Acquisition of structural restrictions on anaphora', in S. Berman, J-W. Choe and J. McDonough, eds, *Proceedings of the 16th North Eastern Linguistics Society Meeting*. Amherst, Mass.: Graduate Linguistics Student Association.

Cromer, R. 1970 'Children are nice to understand: surface structure clues for the recovery of a deep structure', *British Journal of Psychology* 61: 367–408.

Cromer, R. 1983 'A longitudinal study of the acquisition of word knowledge: evidence against gradual learning', *British Journal of Developmental Psychology* 1: 307–16.

Cromer, R. 1987 'Language growth with experience without feedback', *Journal of Psycholinguistic Research* 16: 223–32.

Curtiss, S. 1977 *Genie*. Academic Press.

Dale, P. 1976 *Language Development*, 2nd edn. New York: Holt, Rinehart & Winston.

Demetras, M., Nolan Post, K. and Snow, C. 1986 'Feedback to first language learners: the role of repetitions and clarification questions', *Journal of Child Language* 13: 275–92.

Demuth, K. 1989a 'Problems in the acquisition of grammatical tone', *Papers and Reports on Child Language Development* 28: 81–7. Department of Linguistics, Stanford University.

Demuth, K. 1989b 'Maturation and the acquisition of the Sesotho passive', *Language* 65: 56–80.

Deutsch, W. and Koster, J. 1982 'Children's interpretation of sentence internal anaphora', *Papers and Reports on Child Language Development* 21. Department of Linguistics, Stanford University.

Deutsch, W., Koster, C. and Koster, J. 1986 'What can we learn from children's errors in understanding anaphora?', *Linguistics* 24: 203–25.

de Villiers, J. and de Villiers, P. 1974 'Competence and performance in child language: are children really competent to judge?', *Journal of Child Language* 1: 11–22.

de Villiers, J. and de Villiers, P. 1985 'The acquisition of English', in Slobin.

de Villiers, J., Tager-Flusberg, H., Hakuta, K. and Cohen, M. 1979 'Children's comprehension of relative clauses', *Journal of Psycholinguistic Research* 8: 499–518.

de Villiers, J., Roeper, T. and Vainikka, A. 1990 'The acquisition of long distance rules', in Frazier and de Villiers.

de Villiers, P. and de Villiers, J. 1972 'Early judgment of syntactic and semantic acceptability by children', *Journal of Psycholinguistic Research* 1: 299–310.

diPaolo, M. and Smith, C. 1978 'Cognitive and linguistic factors in the acquisition of temporal and aspectual expressions', in P. French, ed., *The Development of Meaning*. Tokyo: Bunka Hyoron. (Cited in Smith 1980.)

Donaldson, M. 1978 *Children's Minds*. New York: Norton.

Dowty, D., Karttunen, L. and Zwicky, A. eds 1985 *Natural Language Parsing: Psychological, Computational and Theoretical Perspectives*. Cambridge, UK: Cambridge University Press.

Dresher, B. E. and Kaye, J. 1986 'A computer-based learning theory for metrical phonology', paper presented at the annual Generative Linguists of the Old World Meeting, Gerona, Spain.

Eilers, R., Gavin, W. and Wilson, W. 1979 'Linguistic experience and phonemic perception in infancy: a cross-linguistic study', *Child Development* 50: 14–18.

Eimas, P. 1975 'Speech perception in early infancy', in L. Cohen and P. Salapatek, eds, *Infant Perception*. New York: Academic Press.

Eimas, P. 1985 'The perception of speech in early infancy', *Scientific American* 252: 46–52.

Eimas, P., Siqueland, E. R., Jusczyk, P. and Vigorito, J. 1971 'Speech perception in infants', *Science* 171: 303–6.

Emonds, J. 1978 'The verbal complex V'–V in French', *Linguistic Inquiry* 9: 151–5.

Emonds, J. 1979 'Appositive relative clauses have no properties', *Linguistic Inquiry* 10: 211–43.

Engdahl, E. and Ejerhed, E., eds 1982 *Readings on Unbound Dependencies in Scandinavian Languages*, Umeå Studies in the Humanities, vol. 41. Stockholm: Almqvist and Wiksell.

Felix, S. 1987 *Cognition and Language Growth*. Dordrecht: Foris.

Ferguson, C. and Slobin, D., eds 1973 *Studies of Child Language Development*. New York: Holt, Rinehart & Winston.

Finer, D. 1987 'Comments on Solan', in Roeper and Williams 1987.

Fischer, S. 1971 *The Acquisition of Verb–Particle and Dative Constructions*, Doctoral dissertation, MIT.

Fletcher, P. 1985 *A Child's Learning of English*. Oxford: Blackwell.

Fletcher, P. and Garman, M., eds 1986 *Language Acquisition*, 2nd edn. Cambridge, UK: Cambridge University Press.

Fodor, J. A. 1980 'On the impossibility of acquiring more powerful structures', in Piattelli-Palmarini.

Fodor, J. A., Bever, T. and Garrett, M. 1974 *The Psychology of Language*. New York: McGraw-Hill.

Fodor, J. D. 1977 *Semantics: Theories of Meaning in Generative Grammar*. Cambridge, Mass.: Harvard University Press.

Fodor, J. D. and Crain, S. 1987 'Simplicity and generality of rules in language acquisition', in MacWhinney.

Forster, K. 1979 'Levels of processing and the structure of the language processor', in W. E. Cooper and W. Walker, eds, *Sentence Processing*. Hillsdale, NJ: Lawrence Erlbaum.

Forster, K. and Olbrei, I. 1973 'Semantic heuristics and syntactic analysis', *Cognition* 2: 319–47.

Fortescue, M. 1984/5 'Learning to speak Greenlandic: a case study of a two-year-old's morphology in a polysynthetic language', *First Language* 5: 101–13.

Foss, D. and Hakes, D. 1978 *Psycholinguistics*. Englewood Cliffs, NJ: Prentice-Hall.

Frazier, L. and de Villiers, J., eds 1990 *Language Acquisition and Language Processing*. Dordrecht: Kluwer.

Frazier, L. and Fodor, J. D. 1978 'The sausage machine: a new two-stage model of the parser', *Cognition* 6: 291–325.

Frazier, L. and Rayner, K. 1982 'Making and correcting errors during sentence comprehension: eye movements and the analysis of structurally ambiguous sentences', *Cognitive Psychology* 14: 178–210.

Furrow, D., Nelson, K. and Benedict, H. 1979 'Mother's speech to children: some simple relationships', *Journal of Child Language* 6: 423–42.

Gandour, J., Holasuit Petty, S., Dardarananada, R., Dechongkit, S. and Mukngoen, S. 1986 'The acquisition of the voicing contrast in Thai: a study of voice onset time in word-initial stop consonants', *Journal of Child Language* 13: 561–72.

Garrett, M. 1980 'Levels of processing in sentence production', in B. Butterworth, ed., *Language Production*, vol. 1: *Speech and Talk*. London: Academic Press.

Gimson, A. 1970 *An Introduction to the Pronunciation of English*, 2nd edn. London: Edward Arnold.

Gleitman, L. 1989 'The structural sources of verb meaning', *Papers and Reports on Child Language Development* 28: 1–48. Department of Linguistics, Stanford University.

Gleitman, L., Newport, E. and Gleitman, H. 1984 'The current status of the motherese hypothesis', *Journal of Child Language* 11: 43–79.

Gleitman, L. and Wanner, E. 1982 'Language acquisition: the state of the art', in Wanner and Gleitman.

Gold, E. 1967 'Language identification in the limit', *Information and Control* 10: 447–74.

Goldsmith, J. 1976 'An overview of autosegmental phonology', *Linguistic Analysis* 2: 23–68.

Goldsmith, J. 1990 *Autosegmental and Metrical Phonology*. Oxford: Blackwell.

Goodluck, H. 1980 'Backwards anaphora in child language', paper presented to the 55th Annual Meeting of the Linguistic Society of America, San Antonio, Texas. (Expanded version appears as Goodluck 1987.)

Goodluck, H. 1981 'Children's grammar of complement subject interpretation', in Tavakolian, ed.

Goodluck, H. 1987 'Children's interpretation of pronouns and null NPs', in B. Lust, ed. *Studies in the Acquisition of Anaphora*, vol. 2. Dordrecht: Reidel.

Goodluck, H. 1989 'When grammar wins over sense: children's interpretations of extraposed relative clauses', *Journal of Psycholinguistic Research* 18: 389–416.

Goodluck, H. 1990 'Knowledge integration in processing and acquisition: comments on Grimshaw and Rosen', in Frazier and de Villiers.

Goodluck, H. and Behne, D. 1992 'Development in control and extraction', in Weissenborn et al.

Goodluck, H. and Birch, B. 1988 'Late-learned rules in first and second language acquisition', in J. Pankhurst, M. Sharwood Smith and P. van Buren, eds, *Learnability and Second Language Acquisition: A Book of Readings*. Dordrecht: Foris.

Goodluck, H. and Rochemont, M., eds forthcoming *Island Constraints: Theory, Acquisition and Processing*. Dordrecht: Kluwer.

Goodluck, H. and Tavakolian, S. 1982 'Competence and processing in children's grammar of relative clauses', *Cognition* 11: 1–27.

Goodluck, H., Foley, M. and Sedivy, J. to appear 'Adjunct islands and acquisition', in Goodluck and Rochemont.

Goodluck, H., Sedivy, J. and Foley, M. 1989 'Wh-questions and extraction from temporal adjuncts: a case for movement', *Papers and Reports on Child Language Development* 29: 123–30. Department of Linguistics, Stanford University.

Gordon, P. 1985a 'Evaluating the semantic categories hypothesis: the case of the count/mass distinction', *Cognition* 20: 209–42.

Gordon, P. 1985b 'Level ordering in lexical development', *Cognition* 21: 73–93.

Gough, P. 1966 'The verification of sentences: effects of delay and sentence length', *Journal of Verbal Learning and Verbal Behavior* 5: 492–6.

Grégoire, A. 1937 *L'apprentissage du langage. Les deux premières années.* Liège/Paris.

Grégoire, A. 1947 *L'apprentissage du langage. La troisième année et les années suivantes.* (No place of publication in edition.)

Griffiths, P. 1986 'Early vocabulary', in Fletcher and Garman.

Grimshaw, J. 1981 'Form, function and the language acquisition device', in Baker and McCarthy.

Grimshaw, J. and Rosen, C. 1990 'Obeying the binding theory', in Frazier and de Villiers 1990.

Groat, A. 1979 'The use of English stress assignment rules by children taught either with traditional orthography or with the initial teaching alphabet', *Journal of Experimental Child Psychology* 27: 395–409.

Gropen, J., Pinker, S., Hollander, M., Goldberg, R. and Wilson, R. 1989 'The learnability and acquisition of the dative alternation in English', *Language* 65: 203–57.

Gruber, J. 1967 'Topicalization in child language', *Foundations of Language* 3: 37–65.

Gruber, J. 1973 'Playing with distinctive features in the babbling of infants', in Ferguson and Slobin. (Originally published 1968.)

Guilfoyle, E. and Noonan, M. 1988 'Functional categories and language acquisition', paper presented at the annual Boston University Conference on Language Development.

Hakes, D. 1980 *The Development of Metalinguistic Abilities in Children*. Berlin: Springer-Verlag.

Hale, K. 1976 'The adjoined relative clause in Australia', in R. Dixon, ed.,

Grammatical Categories in Australian Languages. New Jersey: Humanities Press.

Hale, K. 1983 'Warlpiri and the grammar of non-configurational languages', *Natural Language and Linguistic Theory* 1: 5–47.

Halle, M. and Clements, G. 1983 *Problem Book in Phonology*. Cambridge, Mass.: MIT Press (Bradford Books).

Hamburger, H. and Crain, S. 1982 'Relative acquisition', in Kuczaj.

Hammond, M. 1988 *Constraining Metrical Theory: A Modular Theory of Rhythm and Stressing*. New York: Garland Press.

Harris, M. and Davies, M. 1987 'Learning and triggering in child language: a response to Atkinson', *First Language* 7: 31–9.

Hayes, B. 1982 'Extrametricality and English stress', *Linguistic Inquiry* 13: 227–76.

Hayes, J., ed. 1970 *Cognition and the Development of Language*. New York: Wiley.

Hirsh-Pasek, K., Kemler Nelson, D., Jusczyk, P., Wright, W., Druss, B. and Kennedy, L. 1987 'Clauses are perceptual units for young infants', *Cognition* 26: 269–86.

Hochberg, J. 1988 'Learning Spanish stress', *Language* 64: 683–706.

Hornstein, N. and Lightfoot, D., eds 1981 *Explanation in Linguistics: The Logical Problem of Language Acquisition*. London: Longman.

Hsu, J. and Cairns, H. 1986 'Control and coreference in early child language'. MS, Williams Paterson College and City University of New York.

Hsu, J., Cairns, H. and Fiengo, R. 1985 'The development of grammars underlying children's interpretation of complex sentences', *Cognition* 20: 25–48.

Hyams, N. 1986 *Language Acquisition and the Theory of Parameters*. Dordrecht: Reidel.

Hyams, N. and Sigurjonsdottir, S. 1990 'The development of "long-distance anaphora": a cross-linguistic study with special reference to Icelandic', *Language Acquisition* 1: 57–93.

Ingram, D. 1986 'Phonological development: production', in Fletcher and Garman.

Iverson, G. and Wheeler, D. 1987 'Hierarchical structures in child phonology', *Lingua* 73: 243–57.

Jackendoff, R. 1972 *Semantic Interpretation in Generative Grammar*. Cambridge, Mass.: MIT Press.

Jaeggli, O. and Safir, K., eds 1989 *The Null Subject Parameter*. Dordrecht: Kluwer.

Jakobson, R. 1968 *Child Language, Aphasia, and Phonological Universals*. The Hague: Mouton. (Originally published 1941.)

Jakobson, R., Fant, G. and Halle, M. 1952 *Preliminaries to Speech Analysis*,

Technical Report 13, MIT Acoustics Laboratory. (10th printing, Cambridge, Mass: MIT Press, 1972.)

Jakubowicz, C. 1984 'On markedness and binding principles', in C. Jones and P. Sells, eds, *Proceedings of the 14th North Eastern Linguistics Association Meeting*, University of Massachusetts-Amherst. Amherst, Mass.: Graduate Linguistics Student Association.

Jakubowicz, C. and Olsen, L. 1988 'Reflexive anaphors and pronouns in Danish', paper presented to the annual Boston University Conference on Language Development.

Jensen, J. 1990 *Morphology: Word Structure in Generative Grammar.* Amsterdam/Philadelphia: John Benjamins.

Jusczyk, P. 1981 'Infant speech perception: a critical appraisal', in P. Eimas and J. Miller, eds, *Perspectives on the Study of Speech.* Hillsdale, NJ: Lawrence Erlbaum.

Jusczyk, P. and Bertoncini, J. 1988 'Viewing the development of speech perception as an innately guided learning process', *Language and Speech* 31: 217–38.

Karmiloff-Smith, A. 1980 'Psychological processes underlying pronominalization and non-pronominalization in children's connected discourse', in J. Keimanand and A. Ojeda, eds, *Papers from the Parasession on Pronouns and Anaphora.* Chicago, Ill.: Chicago Linguistic Circle.

Karmiloff-Smith, A. 1985 'Language and cognitive processes from a developmental perspective', *Language and Cognitive Processes* 1/1: 61–85.

Karmiloff-Smith, A. 1986 'Some fundamental aspects of language development after age 5', in Fletcher and Garman.

Kean, M-L. 1976/1980 *The Theory of Markedness in Generative Grammar.* PhD dissertation, Massachusetts Institute of Technology/Indiana University Linguistics Club.

Keenan, E. and Comrie, B. 1977 'NP accessibility and universal grammar', *Linguistic Inquiry* 8: 63–99.

Kempson, R. 1977 *Semantic Theory.* Cambridge, UK: Cambridge University Press.

Kiparsky, P. 1983 'From cyclic phonology to lexical phonology', in H. van der Hulst and N. Smith, eds, *The Structure of Phonological Representations*, part 1. Dordrecht: Foris.

Klein, H. 1984 'Learning to stress: a case study', *Journal of Child Language* 11: 375–90.

Klima, E. and Bellugi, U. 1973 'Syntactic regularities in the speech of children', in Ferguson and Slobin.

Kolb, B. and Whishaw, I. 1985 *Fundamentals of Human Neuropsychology*, 2nd edn. New York: W. H. Freeman.

Krashen, S. 1973 'Lateralization, language learning and the critical period: some new evidence', *Language Learning* 23: 63–74.

Kučera, H. and Francis, W. N. 1967 *Computational Analysis of Present Day American English*. Providence, R.I.: Brown University Press.

Kuczaj, S., ed. 1982 *Language Development*, vol. 1: *Syntax and Semantics*. Hillsdale, NJ: Lawrence Erlbaum.

Kuhl, P. and Miller, J. D. 1975 'Speech perception by the chinchilla: voiced–voiceless distinction in alveolar–plosive consonants', *Science* 190: 69–72.

Kuno, S. 1986 *Functional Syntax: Anaphora, Discourse and Empathy*. Chicago, Ill.: University of Chicago Press.

Labelle, M. 1988 *Prédication et Mouvement: Le Développement de la Relative chez les Enfants Francophones*. Doctoral dissertation, University of Ottawa.

Lapointe, S. and Dell, G. 1989 'A synthesis of some recent results in sentence production', in Carlson and Tanenhaus.

Lasky, R., Syrdal-Lasky, A. and Klein, R. 1975 'VOT discrimination by four to six and a half month infants from Spanish environments', *Journal of Experimental Child Psychology* 20: 215–25.

Lebeaux, D. 1989 'Parameter setting, the acquisition sequence, and the form of grammar: the composition of phrase structure', paper presented at the Generative Linguists of the Old World Conference, Utrecht, 1989 (cited in Platzack 1989).

Lee, H. 1987 'The acquisition of reflexive and pronoun in Korean', paper presented to the Annual Boston University Conference on Language Development.

Lehiste, I. 1970 *Suprasegmentals*. Cambridge, Mass.: MIT Press.

Lenneberg, E. 1967 *Biological Foundations of Language*. New York: Wiley.

Li, C. and Thompson, S. A. 1977 'The acquisition of tone in Mandarin-speaking children', *Journal of Child Language* 4: 185–99.

Li, C. and Thompson, S. A. 1978 'The acquisition of tone', in V. A. Fromkin, ed., *Tone: A Linguistic Survey*. New York: Academic Press.

Liberman, M. and Prince, A. 1977 'On stress and linguistic rhythm', *Linguistic Inquiry* 8: 249–336.

Lieber, R. 1983 'Argument linking and compounds in English', *Linguistic Inquiry* 14: 151–85.

Lillo-Martin, D. 1986 'Parameter setting: evidence from use, acquisition and breakdown in American Sign Language'. Unpublished doctoral dissertation, University of California, San Diego.

Lillo-Martin, D. to appear 'Sentences as islands: on the boundedness of A'-movement in American Sign Language', in Goodluck and Rochemont.

Limber, J. 1973 'The genesis of complex sentences', in T. Moore, ed., *Cognition Development and the Acquisition of Language*. New York: Academic Press.

Lisker, L. and Abrahamson, A. 1964 'A cross-linguistic study of voicing in initial stops: acoustic measurements', *Word* 20: 384–422.

Lisker, L. and Abrahamson, A. 1970 'The voicing dimensions: some experiments in comparative phonetics', in *Proceedings of the Sixth International Congress of Phonetic Sciences*. Prague: Academica.

Locke, J. 1983 *Phonological Acquisition and Change*. New York: Academic Press.

Lundin, B. and Platzack, C. 1988 'The acquisition of verb inflection, verb second and subordinate clauses in Swedish', *Working Papers in Scandinavian Syntax* 42: 43–55.

Lust, B. 1977 'Conjunction reduction in child language', *Journal of Child Language* 4: 257–87.

Lust, B. 1981 'Constraints on anaphora in child language: prediction for a universal', in Tavakolian, ed.

Lust, B. and Chien, Y-C. 1984 'The structure of coordination in first-language acquisition of Mandarin Chinese: evidence for a universal', *Cognition* 17: 49–83.

Lust, B. and Wakayama, T. K. 1979 'The structure of coordination in children's first-language acquisition of Japanese', in F. Eckman and A. Hastings, eds, *Studies in First- and Second-Language Acquisition*. Rowley, Mass.: Newbury House Press.

Lust, B., Loveland, K. and Kornet, R. 1980 'The development of anaphora in first language: syntactic and pragmatic constraints', *Linguistic Analysis* 6/4: 359–92.

Lust, B., Solan, L., Flynn, S., Cross, C. and Schuetz, E. 1986 'A comparison of null and pronominal anaphora in first-language acquisition', in B. Lust, ed., *Studies in the Acquisition of Anaphora*, vol. 1. Dordrecht: Reidel.

Lyons, J. 1977 *Semantics*. Cambridge, UK: Cambridge University Press.

McClean, R. 1969 *Swedish: A Grammar of the Modern Language*, 3rd edn. Sevenoaks: Hodder and Stoughton.

McDaniel, D. and McKee, C. to appear 'Which children did they show know strong cross-over?' in Goodluck and Rochemont.

McKee, C. 1989 'A comparison of pronouns and anaphors in Italian and English acquisition'. MS, University of Arizona.

Macken, M. 1979 'Developmental reorganization of phonology: a hierarchy of basic units in acquisition', *Lingua* 49: 11–49.

Macken, M. 1980 'The child's lexical representation: the "puzzle–puddle–pickle" evidence', *Journal of Linguistics* 16: 1–17.

Macnamara, J. 1982 *Words for Things*. Cambridge, Mass.: MIT Press (Bradford Books).

MacWhinney, B., ed. 1987 *Mechanisms for Language Acquisition*. Hillsdale, NJ: Lawrence Erlbaum.

Major, D. 1974 *The Acquisition of Modal Auxiliaries in the Language of Children*. The Hague: Mouton.

Manzini, M. R. 1983 'On control and control theory', *Linguistic Inquiry* 14: 421–46.

Marantz, A. 1983 *On the Nature of Grammatical Relations*. Cambridge, Mass.: MIT Press.

Maratsos, M. 1974a 'How preschool children understand missing complement subjects', *Child Development* 45: 700–6.

Maratsos, M. 1974b 'Children who get worse at understanding the passive: a replication of Bever', *Journal of Psycholinguistic Research* 3: 65–74.

Maratsos, M. 1985 'Semantic restrictions on children's passives', *Cognition* 19: 167–91.

Marchand, H. 1969 *The Categories and Types of English Word Formation*, 2nd rev. edn. Munich: Beck.

Marcus, M. 1980 *A Theory of Syntactic Recognition for Natural Languages*. Cambridge, Mass.: MIT Press.

Martohardjono, G. 1989 'The sonority cycle in the acquisition of phonology', *Papers and Reports on Child Language Development* 28: 131–9. Department of Linguistics, Stanford University.

Mazurkewich, I. and White, L. 1984 'The acquisition of the dative alternation: unlearning generalizations', *Cognition* 16: 261–83.

Mehler, J. and Bever, T. 1967 'A cognitive capacity of very young children', *Science* 158: 141–2.

Menn, L. 1975 'Counter example to "fronting" as a universal in child language', *Journal of Child Language* 2: 293–6.

Menn, L. 1978 'Phonological units in beginning speech', in A. Bell and J. Hooper, eds, *Syllables and Segments*. Amsterdam: North-Holland.

Mills, A. 1985 'The acquisition of German', in Slobin.

Mohanan, K. 1983 'Functional and anaphoric control', *Linguistic Inquiry* 14: 651–74.

Nelson, K. 1973 *Structure and Strategy in Learning to Talk*. Monographs of the Society for Research in Child Development, 149.

Nelson, K. E., Carskaddon, G. and Bonvillian, J. 1973 'Syntax acquisition: impact of experimental variation in adult verbal interaction with the child', *Child Development* 44: 497–504.

Newmeyer, F. 1980 *Linguistic Theory in America: The First Quarter Century of Transformational-Generative Grammar*. New York: Academic Press.

Newport, E., Gleitman, H. and Gleitman, L. 1977 'Mother, I'd rather do it
    myself: some effects and non-effects of maternal speech style', in Snow and
    Ferguson.
O'Grady, W., Suzuki-Wei, Y. and Cho, S. 1986 'Directionality preferences in
    the interpretation of anaphora: data from Korean and Japanese', *Journal
    of Child Language* 13: 409–20.
Ohio State University, Department of Linguistics 1982 *Language Files*, 2nd
    edn. Renoldsburg, Ohio: Advocate Publishing Company.
Otsu, Y. 1981 'Towards a theory of syntactic development'. Doctoral disser-
    tation, Massachusetts Institute of Technology.
Palmer, F. R. 1979 *Modality and the English Verb*. London: Longman.
Partee, B. 1984 'Temporal and nominal anaphora', *Linguistics and Philos-
    ophy* 7: 243–86.
Peters, A. M. 1977 'Language learning strategies: does the whole equal the
    parts?', *Language* 53: 560–73.
Peters, S. 1972 'The projection problem: how is a grammar to be selected?',
    in S. Peters, ed., *Goals of Linguistic Theory*. Englewood Cliffs, NJ:
    Prentice-Hall.
Philip, W. and Takahashi, M. 1990 'Children's interpretation of sentences
    containing universal quantification', paper presented at a workshop on the
    acquisition of wh-movement, University of Massachusetts-Amherst, May.
Piaget, J. 1980 'The psychogenesis of knowledge and its epistemological
    significance', in Piattelli-Palmarini.
Piattelli-Palmarini, M., ed. 1980 *Language and Learning: The Debate
    Between Jean Piaget and Noam Chomsky*. Cambridge, Mass.: Harvard
    University Press.
Pinker, S. 1982 'A theory of the acquisition of lexical interpretive grammars',
    in Bresnan.
Pinker, S. 1984 *Language Learnability and Language Development*.
    Cambridge, Mass.: Harvard University Press.
Pinker, S. 1987 'The bootstrapping problem in language acquisition', in
    MacWhinney.
Pinker, S. 1989 *Learnability and Cognition*. Cambridge, Mass.: MIT Press.
Pinker, S., Frost, L. and Lebeaux, D. 1987 'Productivity and constraints in
    the acquisition of the passive', *Cognition* 26: 195–267.
Pinker, S. and Prince, A. 1988 'On language and connectionism: analysis of
    a parallel distributed processing model of language acquisition', *Cognition*
    16: 73–193.
Platzack, C. 1979 *The Semantic Interpretation of Aspect and Aktionsarten:
    A Study of Internal Time Reference in Swedish*. Dordrecht: Foris.
Platzack, C. 1989 'A grammar without functional categories: a syntactic study
    of early Swedish child language'. MS, Lund University.

Pollock, J-Y. 1989 'Verb movement, universal grammar and the structure of IP', *Linguistic Inquiry* 20: 365–424.

Pulleyblank, D. 1989 'Non-linear phonology', *Annual Review of Anthropology* 18: 203–26.

Pye, C. and Poz, P. 1988 'Precocious passives (and antipassives) in Quiche Mayan', paper presented at the annual Child Language Research Forum, Stanford University, California.

Radford, A. 1988a *Transformational Grammar: A First Course*. Cambridge, UK: Cambridge University Press.

Radford, A. 1988b 'Small children's small clauses', *Transactions of the Philological Society* 86: 1–46.

Radford, A. 1990 *Syntactic Theory and the Acquisition of English Syntax: The Nature of Early Child Grammars in English*. Oxford: Blackwell.

Randall, J. 1982 'The acquisition of agents: morphological and semantic hypotheses', *Papers and Reports on Child Language Development* 21: 87–94. Department of Linguistics, Stanford University.

Randall, J. 1992 'The catapult hypothesis', in Weissenborn et al.

Reichenbach, H. 1947 *Symbolic Logic*. Berkeley, Cal: University of California Press.

Reinhart, T. 1976 'The syntactic domain of anaphora'. PhD dissertation, Massachusetts Institute of Technology.

Rice, M. and Kemper, S. 1984 *Child Language and Cognition*. Baltimore, Md: University Park Press.

Rivero, M-L. 1990 'The locative non-active voice in Albanian and Modern Greek', *Linguistic Inquiry* 21: 135–46.

Rizzi, L. 1982 *Issues in Italian Syntax*. Dordecht: Foris.

Roeper, T. 1981 'On the deductive model and the acquisition of productive morphology', in Baker and McCarthy.

Roeper, T. and Siegel, M. 1978 'A lexical transformation for verbal compounds', *Linguistic Inquiry* 9: 199–260.

Roeper, T. and Weissenborn, J. 1990 'Making parameters work', in Frazier and de Villiers.

Roeper, T. and Williams, E., eds 1987 *Parameter Setting*. Dordrecht: Reidel.

Roeper, T., Lapointe, S., Bing, J. and Tavakolian, S. 1981 'A lexical approach to language acquisition', in Tavakolian.

Scarborough, H. and Wyckoff, J. 1986 'Mother, I'd still rather do it myself: some further non-effects of "motherese"', *Journal of Child Language* 13: 431–7.

Schein, B. and Steriade, D. 1986 'On geminates', *Linguistic Inquiry* 17: 691–744.

Selkirk, L. 1982 *The Syntax of Words*. Cambridge, Mass.: MIT Press.

Selkirk, L. 1984 *Phonology and Syntax*. Cambridge, Mass.: MIT Press.

Sells, P. 1985 'Lectures on contemporary syntactic theories', Center for the Study of Language and Information, Lecture Notes 2. Stanford University, California.

Sheldon, A. 1974 'The role of parallel function in the acquisition of relative clauses in English', *Journal of Verbal Learning and Verbal Behavior* 13: 274–81.

Sinclair, A., Sinclair, H. and Marcellus, O. 1971 'Young children's comprehension and production of passive sentences', *Archives de Psychologie* 41: 1–22.

Sinclair de Zwart, H. 1967 *Acquisition de langage et développement de la pensée*. Paris: Dunod.

Slobin, D. 1966 'Grammatical transformations and sentence comprehension in childhood and adulthood', *Journal of Verbal Learning and Verbal Behavior* 5: 219–27.

Slobin, D., ed. 1986 *The Crosslinguistic Study of Language Acquisition*, vol. 1: *The Data*. Hillsdale, NJ: Lawrence Erlbaum.

Slobin, D. and Bever, T. 1982 'Children use canonical sentence schemas: a cross-linguistic study of word-order and inflections', *Cognition* 12: 229–65.

Smith, C. 1978 'The syntax and interpretation of temporal expressions in English', *Linguistics and Philosophy* 2: 46–51.

Smith, C. 1980 'The acquisition of time talk: relations between child and adult grammars', *Journal of Child Language* 7: 263–78.

Smith, C. 1981 'Comments', in Baker and McCarthy.

Smith, N. V. 1973 *The Acquisition of Phonology: A Case Study*. Cambridge, UK: Cambridge University Press.

Smith, P. and Baker, R. 1976 'The influence of English spelling patterns on pronunciation', *Journal of Verbal Learning and Verbal Behavior* 15: 267–85.

Smith, P., Baker, G. and Groat, A. 1982 'Spelling as a source of information about children's linguistic knowledge', *British Journal of Psychology* 73: 339–50.

Snow, C. 1972 'Mother's speech to children learning language', *Child Development* 43: 549–65.

Snow, C. 1986 'Conversations with children', in Fletcher and Garman.

Snow, C. and Ferguson, C., eds 1977 *Talking to Children*. Cambridge, UK: Cambridge University Press.

Solan, L. 1978 *Anaphora in Child Language*. Doctoral dissertation, University of Massachusetts-Amherst.

Solan, L. 1983 *Pronominal Reference: Child Language and the Theory of Grammar*. Dordrecht: Reidel.

Solan, L. 1987 'Parameter setting and the development of pronouns and reflexives', in Roeper and Williams.

Speidel, G. 1984 'The acquisition of linguistic structures and cognitive development', in C. L. Thew and C. E. Johnson, eds, *Proceedings of the Second International Congress for the Study of Child Language*, vol. 2. Lanham, Md: University Press of America.

Spencer, A. 1986 'Towards a theory of phonological development', *Lingua* 68: 3–38.

Stampe, D. 1972 *What I did on my Summer Vacation*. Doctoral dissertation, Chicago University.

Stark, R. 1980 'Stages of speech development in the first year of life', in Yeni-Komshian et al., vol. 1.

Stephany, U. 1986 'Modality', in Fletcher and Garman.

Stevenson, R. 1992 'Maturation and learning: a commentary on Clahsen and Felix', in Weissenborn et al.

Stevenson, R. and Pickering, M. 1987 'The effects of linguistic and non-linguistic knowledge on the acquisition of pronouns', in P. Griffiths, J. Local and A. Mills, eds, *Proceedings of the 1987 Child Language Seminar*, University of York.

Stevenson, R. and Pollitt, C. 1987 'The acquisition of temporal terms', *Journal of Child Language* 14: 533–45.

Stowe, L. 1986 'Parsing wh-constructions: evidence for on-line gap location', *Language and Cognitive Processes* 2: 227–46.

Stowell, T. 1981 *The Origins of Phrase Structure*. Unpublished dissertation, MIT.

Streeter, L. A. 1976 'Language perception of two month infants shows effects of both innate mechanisms and experience', *Nature* 259: 39–41.

Sutherland, S. 1987 'Seeing the wood from the trees', review of J. C. McClelland and D. E. Rumelhart and the PDP Research Group, *Parallel Distributed Processing: Explorations in the Microstructure of Cognition*, vols 1 and 2, *Times Higher Education Supplement*, 27 February.

Tager-Flusberg, H., de Villiers, J. and Hakuta, K. 1982 'The development of sentence coordination', in Kuczaj.

Tanenhaus, M., Carlson, G. and Seidenberg, M. 1985 'Do listeners compute linguistic representations?', in Dowty et al.

Tavakolian, S. 1977 *Structural Principles in the Acquisition of Complex Sentences*. Doctoral dissertation, University of Massachusetts-Amherst.

Tavakolian, S. 1978 'Children's comprehension of pronominal and missing subjects in complicated sentences', in H. Goodluck and L. Solan, eds, *Papers in the Structure and Development of Child Language*, University of Massachusetts Occasional Papers, vol. 4.

Tavakolian, S., ed. 1981 *Language Acquisition and Linguistic Theory*. Cambridge, Mass.: MIT Press.

Tavakolian, S. 1981 'The conjoined clause analysis of relative clauses', in Tavakolian, ed.

Treiman, R. 1985 'Onsets and rimes as units of spoken syllables: evidence from children', *Journal of Experimental Child Psychology* 39: 161–81.

Tyler, L. K. 1983 'The development of discourse mapping processes: the on-line interpretation of anaphoric expressions', *Cognition* 13: 309–41.

Tyler, L. and Marslen-Wilson, W. 1981 'Language processing in children', *Journal of Verbal Learning and Verbal Behavior* 20: 401–16.

Valian, V. 1989 'Children's production of subjects: competence, performance and the null subject parameter', *Papers and Reports on Child Language Development* 28: 156–63. Department of Linguistics, Stanford University.

Van Riemsdijk, H. and Williams, E. 1986 *Introduction to the Theory of Grammar*. Cambridge, Mass.: MIT Press.

Velten, H. 1943 'The growth of phonemic and lexical patterns in infant language', *Language* 19: 281–92.

Vihman, M., Macken, M., Miller, R., Simmons, H. and Miller, J. 1985 'From babbling to speech: a reassessment of the continuity issue', *Language* 61: 397–445.

Wanner, E. and Gleitman, L., eds 1982 *Language Acquisition: The State of the Art*. Cambridge, UK: Cambridge University Press.

Wasow, T. 1977 'Transformations and the lexicon', in P. Culicover, T. Wasow and A. Akmajian, eds, *Formal Syntax*. New York: Academic Press.

Waterson, N. 1971 'Child phonology: a prosodic view', *Journal of Linguistics* 7: 179–211.

Weissenborn, J. 1992 'Null subjects in early grammars: implications for parameter-setting theories', in Weissenborn et al.

Weissenborn, J., Goodluck, H. and Roeper, T. 1992 'Old and new problems in the study of language acquisition', in Weissenborn et al., eds.

Weissenborn, J., Goodluck, H. and Roeper, T., eds 1992 *Theoretical Issues in Language Acquisition: Continuity and Change in Development*. Hillsdale, NJ: Lawrence Erlbaum.

Weissenborn, J., Verrips, M. and Berman, R. 1989 'Negation as a window to the structure of early child language'. MS, Max-Planck Institute for Psycholinguistics and Tel Aviv University.

Weist, R. 1986 'Tense and aspect', in Fletcher and Garman.

Wexler, K. 1981 'Some issues in the theory of learnability', in Baker and McCarthy.

Wexler, 1989 'Some issues in the growth of control', paper presented at the MIT conference on control, March.

Wexler, K. and Chien, Y-C. 1985 'The development of lexical anaphors and pronouns', *Papers and Reports on Child Language Development*: 24. Department of Linguistics, Stanford University.

Wexler, K. and Culicover, P. 1980 *Formal Principles of Language Acquisition*. Cambridge, Mass.: MIT Press.

Wexler, K. and Manzini, M. R. 1987 'Parameters and learnability', in Roeper and Williams.

White, L. 1987 'Children's overgeneralizations of the English dative alternation', in K. Nelson and A. van Kleek, eds, *Children's Language*, vol. 6. Hillsdale, NJ: Lawrence Erlbaum.

Williams, E. 1980 'Predication', *Linguistic Inquiry* 11: 203–38.

Williams, E. 1981 'Argument structure and morphology', *Linguistic Review* 1: 81–114.

Williams, E. 1987 'Introduction', in Roeper and Williams.

Wode, H. 1977 'Four early stages in the development of L1 negation', *Journal of Child Language* 4: 87–102.

Yamada, J. 1984 'On the relationship between language and cognition: evidence from a hyperlinguistic retarded adolescent', in C. Thew and C. Johnson, eds, *Proceedings of the Second International Congress for the Study of Child Language*, vol. 2. Lanham, Md: University Press of America.

Yeni-Komshian, G., Kavanagh, J. and Ferguson, C., eds 1980 *Child Phonology*, vol. 1: *Production*; vol. 2: *Perception*. New York: Academic Press.

Index

Note: Page references in *italics* indicate tables and figures.

Index compiled by Meg Davies